A Floating World

Poles Apart

High Life at the foot of Wellesley Island:

The ultimate trophy yacht, Henry Alexander Laughlin's 172-foot *Corona*.

The Simple Life at the head of Grindstone Island:

Virginia Murray Bacon and her guide cook a shore dinner.

A Floating World

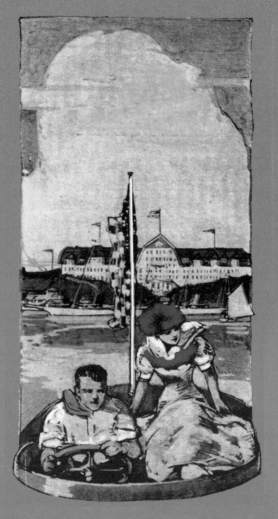

More People, Places, and Pastimes
of the Thousand Islands

Paul Malo

Copyright 2004 by the Laurentian Press

2 Harris Hill Road

Fulton, New York 13069-4723

(315) 598-4387   phmalo@syr.edu

00 01 02 03 04 05   6 5 4 3 2 1

Includes Index

ISBN 0-9669729-2-9

Library of Congress Control Number: 2004093733

PRINTED IN CANADA

The front cover reproduces the painting by Theodore Gegoux, *The Salute*. It depicts the steamer *St. Lawrence* on an evening searchlight excursion.   The author's photograph of Scow Island appears on the rear cover. The Afterword mentions sources of other illustrations.

For my wife, Judy,
the real historian in the family.

Judith Wellman's standards of scholarship surpass mine,
but I hope may have raised them.

The author, about the age he appears in this book, with his sister, Annette, cruising on one of the last Great Lakes steamboats, the 1902 *Western States*, about 1945.

Contents

Embarkation

Occasional freight trains still came to Clayton before World War II. The tracks provided a hot but colorful shortcut to town for a boy, skipping sun baked ties that smelled of creosote. Alternately I balanced on a shiny rail. The village was the terminus of the line, so there was little danger of a fast train taking me by surprise. Before coming into Clayton the engineer would always sound the whistle and come chugging in at a slowing pace.

Dozens of dark passenger cars had once filled five sidings, alongside gleaming white steamboats and yachts tied along the dock. During the Depression years the station site was merely a gritty lot. The terminal building was gone, together with the long covered passenger platform. The yard was vacant, not yet a parking lot, let alone the park that it is today.

Late one Saturday morning my father put us all in the black Packard and drove to that railroad dock in town—which was unusual. After driving up on Friday afternoon, the next day he rarely wanted to get in the car again. I didn't know the mission, but was merely told a treat was in store. My mother wore flapping bell-bottom slacks with her hair tied up under a bandana (in the sporting manner considered chic at the time)--not her normal camp attire so I knew something was up. Rolling down Webb Street, Dad said, "That must be the boat, ahead." I recognized the pilot house and furled canvas awnings of a yacht tied up at the dock.

We had been invited to lunch and a cruise by a visiting yachtsman, a business associate of my father. The boat was not new—there were few new boats on the river in those lean years—but her brass and varnished mahogany glistened in the sun. Even more impressive were the sailor's shining whites. I had been aboard many boats, but never a private vessel with uniformed deckhands. Between the big coal pile of the Consaul-Hall fueling station and the Frink Sno-Plow factory was an apparition from the past, a ghost of the splendid steam yachts that once had lined the pier.

This was no steam yacht, however—they had all disappeared by the thirties. It was a motor cruiser, 1920s vintage. There were still some of those on the river, often moldering in old boathouses. Here was one gleaming as she once did, however--as if proud Gatsby himself were aboard. The boat was fairly large, probably not so grand as she seemed to this impressionable youngster, but likely in the sixty-foot range. She was redolent of luxury and privilege, however. Assisted aboard by a smiling hand, we sank into deep leather cushions on the aft deck, just in time for "elevenses" that appeared: an Art Deco cocktail shaker glistening with beaded condensation. Of course we youngsters were offered libations of some other sort. What I remember more vividly was embarking, waving to tourists ashore as if the grand yacht were my own.

In later years I cruised the Caribbean on a more venerable antique yacht, the *Xebec*—so antique, in fact, that much on board worked only erratically and the heads especially unpredictably. Not knowing the problem to be encountered, one always asked oneself if the trip below were really necessary. The cabins were insufferably hot so some of us slept on the hard deck above. There was no TV, certainly, and nothing much to do on board, really, but the magic was still there. Much of the charm of a boat, in fact, is forced inactivity—compulsory relaxation. One of life's most enchanted moments for me was lying on the *Xebec*'s forward deck in the sun at mid-morning, out of sight of land, feeling totally detached from the world—except for silver flying fish jumping alongside the boat.

You take aboard a boat—or to an island—only as much of the larger world as you need or cherish. The sense of detachment, self-reliance, and awareness of the privileged moment is what boats and islands offer—a world of your choosing, a floating world of your own.

Qui Vive

Length 45'; Beam 9' 6"; Draft 1' 7"; Speed 20 knots

Built in 1916 at Alexandria Bay by Hutchinson Brothers for Houston Barnard of Rochester, N.Y., she was chartered by the U.S. Navy in 1917 and assigned to patrol duty. She served, however, as a hospital boat at Norfolk, Virginia for the duration of World War I. She was decommissioned and returned to her owner in May 1919.

Barnard was one of Hutchinson's best customers. An earlier boat, his 1914 *Voyageur*, burned near St. Lawrence Park the year she was built. Hutchinson was one of many but perhaps the major builder of boats on the river during the early twentieth century. Hutchinson employed as many as sixty craftsmen, but barely survived the Depression—and was the only Alexandria Bay boat builder to do so. Hutchinson provided military craft for the Navy during the First and Second World Wars. The firm no longer builds boats but now sells them and provides marine services at Alexandria Bay.

Days on the river
have their moods.

Julia Bingham McLean Hass

A gallant lady, she was a family friend. "Julie," as
we knew her, lived on welfare year-round in a
Clayton walk-up apartment. As related in the
preceding volume, *Fools' Paradise* (which I dedi-
cated to her) she was without family and legally
blind. Despite her misfortunes, Julie was a joyous
person—an inspiration.

I took the photograph on the facing page in 1948.

I. Julie Recalls Celebrities on the River

Days on the river have their moods. Do they seem more varied than elsewhere—more intense at times, yet more subtle? Maybe it's because the open expanses of water reflect the sky, sometimes merging imperceptibly with it. We have a peculiar mix of water and fragmented land. Our small worlds float ambiguously between water and sky. The magic on an island derives not merely from disengagement with the larger world, but from uncertainty about where one is and what is real.

There are those hazy days of late summer when the sun shines fiercely but can't dispel the vapor. Those are the bright but humid days of August. Then there are the even hazier days when the sky is overcast. We are blanketed with a gray cloud that seems to descend to envelop the distant horizon. The sky is leaden, but the water shines as silver.

It was one of those days on our porch, when the river was very still, like the heavy air. Occasionally glistening swells would roll slowly into shore, gently splashing against the seawall, and we heard the distant whine of a retreating motor and the nudging of boats against the dock. But otherwise these silver afternoons were quiet. Even the terns were still.

Julie's white hair was like a diaphanous cloud, shimmering brightly against the leaden sky as she tilted and nodded her head in lively conversation. Julie never seemed to be assuming a pose or playing a role, but with her loud voice and agitated manner she was ever the actress she had been when younger. She had presence.

There was something about her diction—more than the broad "a" and articulate delivery. Her voice seemed to come from deep within her. She had a throaty laugh and even a charming sort of lisp—very slight (in retrospect I suspect ill-fitting teeth may have been a problem). I can hear her voice still, even after more than fifty years have passed.

"I'm talking about events that happened long ago," she observed. "It's been a half-century since the heyday of the islands—and my heyday as well. We're going to seed together." In retrospect I realize that Julie was speaking during "the Gathering Storm," as Churchill called it, at that grim threshold between the Great Depression and World War II. "And things may get worse," she continued, "before they get better. I wonder how your world, and this floating world of ours, our islands, will look a half-century from now, when you're my age, Paul." I'm her age now, but was a youngster then.

"Isn't it interesting how our lives overlap?" Julie put on a smile, as if to brighten the mood. "My father knew this place before it was much of a resort, before there were any big hotels or even very comfortable cottages. It was more rustic in those days, with more tenting or simple fishing shacks. Just think how I've seen so much come and go, seen so many great houses and grand hotels rise and vanish. I wonder what you'll see, my young friend." I was too innocent to grasp the full meaning of her sigh, for I had little awareness of larger world affairs at the time. I was, however, familiar with mansions around us that were closed. I had never seen them open, except those that were wide open to the weather, intruding varmints or vandals—or curious youngsters like me. I couldn't understand what had happened, at that young age, but was deeply moved by the poignant decline of beautiful things, by the waste and loss—and already by a youthful notion of history as inevitable change that came with mixed blessings. I suppose some of my later interest in history came from Julie, who recalled the Thousand Islands during their brief golden age as "our Fools' Paradise."

Distant islands on a clearer, brighter day often meld together as if a single mass. Hazy days on the river filter out minor incidents and blur details of the distant landscape. The thick atmosphere simplifies larger forms and renders the place more spatial. Separated by gauzy veils of vapor, islands recede as distinct planes of progressively lighter grey. Distant forms become more distant, as they dissolve into the atmosphere. Ultimately there is no distinction between water and sky as islands float in the luminous haze.

Beads of condensation on her tall glass glistened like the shining water beyond. Julie wiped silver rings from the white oilcloth, lest her worn album covers get wet. Her long fingers suddenly struck me as crooked—a surprise because I knew few people older than my parents. Ours wasn't a close, extended family. I was accustomed to the company of adults, but they had generally been my parents' age. The revelation that Julie was old probably came as a surprise because she was so vibrant.

Julie kept fat scrapbooks. Theater people usually collect momentos of their varied engagements. Knowing that I was a good audience, she would bring several volumes when she came to stay for a few days. They lay on the card table between us, waiting to be explored. Julie often came from her Clayton apartment for a stay, although our place at Steele's Point was within easy walking distance of town—easy for me, of course, at age fifteen or so, but not so for Julie with her cane and limited eyesight. She enjoyed our screened porch and the activity of the cottage, after long winters living alone. Some afternoons when others went elsewhere, Julie and I would have the cottage to ourselves, except for Whiskers, the dog who snoozed contentedly.

Beyond the screens, the boats alongside the dock barely moved. Through the haze Round Island seemed farther way—the big houses on the head of the island even more remote and intriguing than usual. Next to the big island, but a bit farther off, lay smaller Hogsback, totally wild and, to me, irresistible. Farther still lay Pine, Bluff, Picton—and then countless others farther off. The boats at the dock were my access to that floating world.

My parents, for some reason, thought I was safer—or perhaps would be less adventurous—if restricted to rowing. The motorboat was off-limits, when I was a youngster, so the range of my exploration was restricted. Probably the limitation, and the stretching of bounds, added to the fascination of all those unseen islands—hundreds upon hundreds of them. It seemed it would take a lifetime to explore them.

It has.

The dock at Steele's Point, place of embarkation on many island adventures. Little Board Island is offshore—there is now a house there. Round Island appears at the right.

Steele's Point

A hazy morning on Spong Island, summer home of my friend Ian Coristine

"This place is so different now," Julie observed. "It used to be . . . well, in a word, 'glamorous.'"

"There were more rich people," I suggested hopefully. Julie laughed.

"Oh, I suppose," she granted, "but money doesn't make people interesting (although interesting people often make a lot of money). What was glamorous was celebrity. There were so many outstanding personalities here, really famous figures of the day. You've never even heard of Arthur Brisbane, I'll bet. He was even better known across America at the time than May Irwin—but a youngster like you wouldn't know her either. Brisbane talked to thirty million Americans every day, by way of his syndicated newspaper column, 'Today.' What a dynamo! He used to type his daily column while speaking to others about something altogether different. Talk about 'ambidextrous!' Arthur seemed to have two heads. And glamorous! The Brisbanes were the fashion plates on the river—they were perennially on the 'best-

Arthur Brisbane

Abraham Abraham

dressed' list down in the City."

"Where was their place on the river?"

"They leased the place at the foot of Cherry Island, from Nathan Straus. That's one of the 'Twin Cottages,' you know. Nathan came less after his dear next-door neighbor who had the matching house, Abraham Abraham, died suddenly while on the river. Actually, the houses weren't exactly identical—and actually Abraham didn't die at the house, but had an attack while fishing out on the lake on his yacht. They took him to the Kingston hospital, where he died. That was 1911, when the heyday of the resort was ending. But I digress."

She shook her head in smiling disparagement. "Yes, we regarded the Brisbanes as being 'ultra smart,' belonging to 'the 150' of Manhattan society. Arthur was so cosmopolitan. A Buffalo boy, he had been a student in France and Germany for many years before returning to New York as a reporter. He

One of the "Twin Cottages," summer home of Abraham Abraham, Cherry Island.

became a star—the 'editorial mouthpiece'—of the Hearst papers and was man-
aging editor of the *New York Journal*, I believe.
They said he was 'Hearst's right hand man' and 'the
highest-paid writing journalist of all time.' Arthur
owned the Ritz Tower Hotel in the City and was
known as a big spender. Oh, he and his wife cut
quite a swath on the river!"

"Did you know them?"

"Only casually, of course. They came to the
yacht club as guests of mutual friends, just as I did.
Arthur was not cut out of the same cloth as most of
the successful businessmen here. He was far more
sophisticated and urbane. I remember him saying,

Nathan Straus

'If you would succeed in journalism, never lose your superficiality.' That's
the way he was. But he was regarded as 'one of the cleverest journalists that
ever lived in America' and 'one of the most popular journalists America has
ever known.'

Cherry Island summer home of Nathan Straus

"But heads didn't turn for Arthur Brisbane the way they did for Christie McDonald. She was at Basswood Island. Do you know that place?"

Christie McDonald

"Sure—on the channel side of Grenell. I row around it often. But I thought that was the Gillespies' island."

"You're right. Christie McDonald, a Broadway beauty noted for her 'pert vivacity,' was a singing star of the musical stage for many years. She became famous in the smash hit of 1907, *The Spring Maid* that ran through the summer of 1908. Christie had a fine voice. Victor Herbert wrote one of his best songs for her, 'Sweethearts.' It has a range of almost two octaves. The classic song was in the show of the same name, from one of her last appearances, back in 1913.

"Christie married Henry Lloyd Gillespie. He was one of the boys at Basswood Island, sons of Thomas Gillespie—such a nice man, so kind and pleasant. Their daughter, Jean, is my age. Like Clover Boldt and Margie Bourne, Jean was daring, piloting her own racing boat. Sorry she's not here anymore. The family came to the river until a few years ago. Then I suppose the

islands seemed depressing, as the Depression set in and so many places remained unopened.

Basswood Island, Woronoco at right

"The Gillespies were from Pittsburgh originally, but they moved to West Orange, New Jersey. Thomas Gillespie was a close friend of George Boldt and served as a pallbearer at his funeral. Tom was one of the mainstays of the community here."

"What was his business?"

"He was a big-time con-tractor, building huge public works projects like the electric power facility down at Massena. He might have built the Panama Canal, as he bid the job, but the government decided to build it without a general contractor. Gillespie also produced munitions for the world war. He served as commodore of the

Jean

Thousand Islands Yacht Club and had one of the Herreshoff boats, the *Jean* (said to be 'the fastest on the river'), and the racers, *Vingt-trois* and *Pawnee*, among others. They had the big houseboat *Amaryllis*, which is still on the river. Gillespie also had a farm on Grindstone Island, like his island neighbors, Emery and Vandergrift.

"Basswood was a lively place, as the Gillespies were sociable. They held an annual cakewalk and ball at their island."

Amaryllis

"A cakewalk?"

"Of course you wouldn't know about such things. There were many Negroes on the river, and they had lively dance contests—often at the Bay, since there were so many hotel employees there. The prize was a cake, you see. These dance exhibitions were a joy to behold. May Irwin was a great fan. Her mainland farm was a stone's throw from the Frontenac Hotel, which also had Negro employees. I suppose May's interest in their music and dancing became shared by others nearby, like the Gillespies. The Negro men

Basswood Island, about 1945

often appeared in local performances, at T.I. Park and other places. They were so musical and danced so naturally.

"Yes, Christie McDonald was pretty, but Geraldine Farrar is beautiful. There's a difference. Jerry was not merely gorgeous when younger, but is lovely still. More important, she has a larger-than-life persona. Geraldine Farrar's probably in the same league with Arthur Brisbane and Jerry's friend May Irwin as a national celebrity. Probably you've heard of Geraldine Farrar?"

Geraldine Farrar as Manon

"I think so. On the radio, maybe?"

"Yes. You may have heard her talk on a Saturday afternoon, during the opera intermissions, if you ever listen to the opera. She was one of the great divas of the Metropolitan Opera before she retired. Now she works hard to save the institution, struggling for survival during these hard times."

"I don't think I heard her there. Wasn't she in the movies?"

"She certainly was. Jerry became a movie star after she became an opera star. Cecil B. DeMille wanted her for a silent film version of *Carmen.* Of course Jerry (that's what we called her) didn't sing a note in the film, but her silent dramatic performance launched her in the movies. It's interesting that going to Hollywood didn't add glory to her reputation, but it was the other way around. As a critic said at the time, ''The entrance into the motion picture field of an artist of the renown and talent of Miss Farrar is bound to raise the prestige of the screen.' That was in 1915.

"Jerry was the highest-paid performer in Hollywood at the time. Previously the largest sum ever paid a legitimate actor or actress for making a picture was paid to the famous French actress Sarah Bernhardt. Jerry earned the same weekly salary—some $5,000 a week for eight weeks, two weeks longer than Bernhardt. Forty thousand dollars was a lot of money in those days, for

The Chalet

two months' employment. And they threw in use of a private railroad car from New York to Los Angeles and back, and gave her a Hollywood house, paying all her expenses while there."

"Did she own an island?"

Jerry and May at "Rainbow's End," July 1936

"No, like Arthur Brisbane, Fay Templeton, and other famous visitors, Jerry sometimes visited friends, like the Reginald Newtons at Cape Vincent or May Irwin at Rainbow's End, May's mainland farm. Jerry liked the Chalet, however—more her style than May's simple bungalow. The Chalet is the big house that George Boldt built on Wellesley Island, near the yacht club and near his own place in later years, Wellesley House. Boldt never lived in the Chalet, but built it to rent, you know, and many prominent people stayed there over the years. It's not that he needed the money, but he wanted to attract celebrities like Jerry to the river—his Waldorf-Astoria crowd.

"Jerry and May were an odd couple. The opera diva was so stunning and elegant; May was . . . well, glamour had never been her strong suit. Personality was, however. What a funny lady!

Fay Templeton

"May and Fay were another curious couple—Fay Templeton, that is. She was also a perennial Broadway star who came to the river. In contrast to Jerry, Fay was more like May in some ways—certainly similar in girth. Both were, frankly, very fat ladies. And Fay had more of May's comic style. Much of Fay's stage career was devoted to light farces. Fay was more feminine in her persona, however—more inclined to parody the charming ingenue, especially funny given her figure, which became increasingly ample as she aged. But when young, Fay really was rather a beauty—and she always was lovely, even when she put on weight—a lifelong problem for her.

"Fay came up doing comic routines with the Weber & Fields company. Joe Weber was on the river often too, as was Charles Frohman, in whose company May Irwin played for a time. Charles Frohman was the most successful theatrical manager of the late nineteenth and early twentieth centuries. Frohman ran half a dozen New York theaters plus more than two hundred elsewhere in America, as well as five in London. He personally managed the careers of twenty-eight leading stars and paid out more than thirty-five million dollars a year in salaries to the ten thousand people on his payroll. His brother, Daniel Frohman, was also a prominent manager. Albert Bial was another New York theatrical producer—Koster & Bial's Music Hall was a major venue. These theater people were all close, as you might imagine. They favored Clayton's old hotels, before they burned.

Charles Frohman

"Fay Templeton was 'the talk of New York' after George M. Cohan wrote *Forty-five Minutes from Broadway* for her as the star of that very successful production."

"You said that she didn't own a place but rented."

"Yes, she rented Florence Island from George Boldt. That's a stone's throw from the Chalet, you know. But for her honeymoon after a purported marriage (which was not made public) she chose Ingleside on Cherry Island, a larger house, taking it for the season. Mrs. Marsh owned that place. Fay also stayed at the Frontenac on Round Island, where as a running joke she (whose ample figure testified to her maturity) and young Blair Frazer pretended to be having an affair. The Frazers later built Nelfred, the big house at the head of Cherry Island, to be closer to their golf game. The gambit between big Fay and little Blair got a lot of laughs. Fay, like me, had three husbands—but she had her own performing company for a while. I never was in that league.

"Fay had several retirements and comebacks. Most recently she sang in Jerome Kern's *Roberta*—a big success. Bob Hope, George Murphy, and Fred MacMurray were in the cast. Fay's big number was "Yesterdays." The slow, bittersweet ballad was especially poignant because Fay had come out of retirement to sing it (and she was so fat they had to wheel her onto the stage). Fay wrote a touching poem while she lived in the actors' retirement home where she died only a couple of years ago.

"The St. Lawrence River and the Thousand Islands have for years been a favorite outing place for theatrical people."

The Hubbard House, Clayton

Favored venue of the
theatrical crowd on the river.

"Famous in the theatrical world since the days of its early prestige.
Every actor or manager who comes to the river always makes it a
point to make headquarters at the Hubbard." The last part of
the hotel, the brick section at left that retained its fine restaurant,
was razed in 1973, replaced by a one-story motel on the site..

"Are you tired of me talking about all these theater people? I'm sure these recollections mean more to me than to you, my young friend. You've never heard of most of these people."

"You're the only actress I've ever known," I replied. "You're talking about another world." Julie smiled, perhaps appreciatively, but possibly because of my self-conscious blush.

"A 'floating world'—that's what the Japanese called the illusion of art. That's what theater is, I suppose—and in a way that's what this place was, an illusory, insubstantial world. The theater people weren't the only actors here. There were a lot of others playing roles in a land of make-believe—these 'enchanted isles.' That's what the king of France called his fantastic parties that lasted for days, 'Pleasures of Enchanted Isles.' But after the brief interval it was over. The stage set was dismantled."

Julia Bingham

"Did you know all these people?"

"I wish I had known some of them better—especially the producers. I dreamed of a real career in the theater, but all I ever had, really, were odd jobs. No one ever sought me out for my special qualities. I was lucky to get some roles, since dozens of others could have done just as well."

"But you were very pretty. I can see that in your photographs."

"You're very kind, sir—except for the past tense. But there are lots of attractive people available, Paul. Star quality is something else. Very few people have it. There's a certain quality that sets them apart. May Irwin was certainly no great beauty, but she was a great star for decades. Did she have a fine voice? No. I could sing better than May—as a vocalist, that is. Not as a performer. There's a difference. May worked an audience with a skill that seemed effortless. She appeared to be having fun herself, at every performance, sometime several times a day, when she was on the vaudeville circuit—day after day, week after week, with the same material. It was an illusion, you can be sure. That's hard work. None of us can have fun all the time. We have our bad days. But May did know how to have fun—especially up here, on the river. What a joy she was to know!"

"You knew her?"

"Not well, but May was so outgoing, so friendly, that everyone thought she knew them and they knew her. George Boldt had that same quality, with a marvelous memory for names. He wasn't funny like May, however. He was more mannered, while May seemed totally natural, totally unconcerned about the approval of others. She was her own woman—a remarkable person.

"Many people think May attracted the rest of the theater crowd to the river. Of course, she was popular with them all, as she was with everyone here. But I think that May really came because she had heard of the river from other Broadway people. Who was first? I don't know for sure, but probably the Hacketts, husband and wife, both nineteenth-century actors, were the earliest theater people here—at least of international prominence.

"The Hacketts weren't Canadian but spent much of their retirement on Wolfe Island." Julie looked through one of her thick theatrical scrapbooks. Since it was so large and heavy, she leaned over the table to inspect the pages at a range of inches.

James H. Hackett

"James H. Hackett," she continued, "was a famous Shakespearean actor. They said he was the 'talk of Drury Lane' when he played Richard II in London during the 1830s. He even wrote a book about Shakespeare. But earlier, like his son after him, he was popular for his 'roaring, swashbuckling' roles, such as the frontiersman in *Lion of the West*. The 1831 play was written expressly for him. The elder Hackett was a great character actor in later years, famous for his Rip Van Winkle. He knew the author, Washington Irving,

James K. Hackett

personally, as well as the novelist James Fenimore Cooper and President John Quincy Adams. James H. Hackett was certainly one of the first celebrities on the river. He died in 1871, before I was born.

"His even more famous son, James K. Hackett, was born over on Wolfe Island in 1869. The elder Hackett was seventy years old when Jimmy was born. The father died when his son was only two years old. Together, the prominent acting careers of father and son spanned a century—most of the nineteenth and much of the twentieth. Although Jimmy never really knew his famous father, he had the acting genes. But he didn't go into the theater initially. He was studying law at Columbia University when the producer Charles Frohman approached him, asking him to try the stage. Frohman was here on the river, too, as I just mentioned. Probably James K. Hackett's famous name had something to do with his early success, but his striking appearance surely had something to do with it."

She turned her scrapbook to show me a faded photo. "I confess I was an ardent admirer of James K. Hackett, which is why I have so much about him and his family here. He made his stage debut in 1892 and became a star very quickly. You might think that his famous father's name helped, but he had died twenty years before. It was more the Hackett presence—that's what I was talking about—that special something. Of course, good looks contribute to it, and James K. Hackett was born to be a matinee idol." She turned to another picture.

"Young Hackett hit the big time in 1895. He was asked to substitute in the title role of the *Prisoner of Zenda* when the star went touring on the road. The stand-in clearly surpassed his predecessor. In that role James K. Hackett, after only three years on the stage, became a great Broadway star. Although known initially for such popular, swash-

James K. Hackett

James K. Hackett

Mary Mannering

buckling roles, like his father, James K. Hackett later became a distinguished Shakespearean actor.

"Hackett married the English actress Mary Mannering, a star in her own right. They kept their marriage secret for years, probably because he seemed more attractive to the public as an eligible bachelor, but also, I think, to allow Mary to be recognized professionally on her own.

"The Hacketts divorced before he bought the Johnson place, Woodland, on Bartlett Point (called 'Prospect Point' in those days) and turned it into a showplace, renaming the mainland estate 'Zenda.' Jimmy Hackett was very athletic, as you might expect, since he excelled at swashbuckling roles. He enjoyed the company of another outdoorsman, the famous painter and sculptor Frederic Remington of Chippewa Bay.

Zenda

Zenda Farms, now a property of the Thousand Islands Land Trust

"Jimmy also was a great ballplayer, joining local teams competing at villages on both sides of the river.

"Hackett was one of the first famous actors of the stage to appear in film. After returning from a 1924 stint in London, Jimmy spent much of his last two years at Zenda. He died in Paris in 1926.

"Merle R. Youngs bought Zenda from the Hackett estate, turning it into a show farm. He built those unusual metal barns and silos."

"What was his business?"

"Something called the Youngs Rubber Company, down in New Jersey, I believe." (Much of the open land, together with the distinctive farm buildings of Zenda, was acquired by the Thousand Islands Land Trust to preserve its scenic and historic quality.)

Joe Weber

"I mentioned Joe Weber as a producer, but he was far more famous as a comedian, half of the famous team of Weber and Fields. Both were born in New York's Bowery of immigrant parents. As boys they were neighbors, first performing together at age ten. They began with the sort of 'Dutch' (German, actually) dialect act that they performed for the rest of their long careers. Joe (whose real

Weber & Fields
"The biggest names in . . . comedy."

name was Morris) was short and stocky while Lew Fields was tall and lanky. Joe always wore heavy padding to appear fatter than he really was.

"As they said, 'By the end of the century they [were] the biggest names in the comedy field.'

"You may never have heard of Weber and Fields, but I'll bet you've heard their most famous lines: 'Who vas dat lady you vas wid las' night?' 'Dat vas no lady, dat vas my vife.' The team became very successful, even opening their own theater. They produced dozens of shows, in which they usually appeared. As I mentioned, Fay Templeton became known for her comic roles in their shows.

"Joe was an avid fisherman who loved the islands, as did his sister, Sadie Friedman. Joe said he wanted to buy one—Dewey's place, Friendly Island, near the Bay. But it never came about. Instead he visited hotels and rented cottages, such as the Martin cottage at Edgewood.

"And speaking of comedians on the river, I haven't mentioned Nat Goodwin. He was more a legitimate actor than a vaudevillian, but he usually played humorous dramatic roles that conveyed his dry Yankee style. He also did Shakespeare—the character roles, that is. Nat often appeared teamed with his third wife, Maxine Elliott. That marriage broke up—Maxine was said to be the mistress of J. P. Morgan.

Maxine Elliott

Nat Goodwin

"Nat was one of the theater crowd that favored Clayton's Hubbard House. May Irwin stayed there, when not on her island or farm—which was generally coming or going in the spring or fall. In later years May went to Clayton's Herald House, when Herold Bertrand owned that hotel as well as the Hubbard House, which housed many other theatrical people, such as Marie Dressler.

"Marie and May were known to get big sums in Hollywood. May received $7,000 from the Famous Players Film Company for one picture, plus a royalty on proceeds."

"You haven't talked much about May Irwin."

"Oh, I suppose it goes without saying that she was probably the major theatrical figure on the river, in large part because she spent the most time here. She had a beautiful island home, you know, and then a mainland farm, which she really loved more.

"But there were many other theater people here. You know, May liked to tell a story about how she found the island she bought. As I recall, according

Marie Dressler

to her tale she simply looked for a place to land in a storm, but she didn't care to relate that the island belonged, not to a local farmer (as she liked to say) but to an actor, Hugo Toland. May bought Club Island from Hugo. I expect May didn't care to explain why she was visiting this actor, when they weren't mar-

May Irwin's Club Island Home

May Irwin

ried." As my mother wasn't around, Julie winked knowingly, making me feel very grown up.

"May had many talents—she was an astute businesswoman who became a millionaire, investing in New York real estate. She was a composer and famous cook, among other things. One of her gifts was a sense of the theatrical, not merely on the stage, but in creating a public persona. She was inventive and daring about publicity, writing articles that were sensational, like the one where she (as a single mother) informed the public about how she told her two teenage boys about sex. She had a series of columns about cooking that were widely read, and her cookbook sold many copies.

"May made history in the movies, you know. But of course, you don't know, since her famous kiss occurred long ago. It was the first time such a

"The Kiss"

Lillian Russell

thing was seen on the big screen, and it was a great sensation—some thought it immoral and were outraged. Well, it surely was shocking, to see a real kiss (not an affectionate peck) as a close-up, blown up to theater scale.

"And there were other actors and actresses who visited the river. One of the most famous, certainly, was Lillian Russell. She liked the Crossmon House, and created a sensation in the Bay or wherever she went. The celebrities were considered prize catches for hostesses, of course. They usually appeared at the yacht club, disembarking from some grand steam yacht.

"There were other theater people of the day—folks don't remember some anymore, like Harold Lockwood and May Ellison. They were well known at the time, however. But May was probably as important theatrically as any of these people, since she was so immensely popular for so long a time—really a superstar of her time."

"And what about yourself?"

Julie laughed "May Irwin is 'a tough act to follow,' as they say in vaudeville. She was the champ. I was never in the same league as May, Jerry, Fay, James K. Hackett, as well as the other theater folks I've mentioned. I was just a supporting actress, one of a 'cast of thousands,' as they might say—although even in *Ben Hur* the cast was not so large as for the later movie versions. We had quite a troop, however, including eight horses. They were the real stars of the stage show, in fact. The big scene, the moment that everyone waited for, was the famous chariot race. Can you image eight live horses racing on a stage?"

"How could they do that without running off?"

"They were on a treadmill. Behind them was a huge painted backdrop of a coliseum crowd on rollers which kept moving behind the horses, giving the illusion that the chariots and riders were actually moving. The scene lasted eight minutes, until one of the chariot wheels would always fall off—planned, of course, according to script. It was really sensational. Compared to that, we supporting actresses hardly were noticed."

"It sounds exciting. I'll bet you had fun."

"Oh, we surely did. There were lots of young people in the companies, and plenty of high jinks. We even had some 'stage-door Johnnys' paying court, even if we weren't the stars." She flipped album pages, looking for a letter. Smiling, peering at it closely through the one transparent lense of her thick glasses, she read, "Just a line to tell you that Reg and I stood and watched your last car pull out. . . . I'm so blue today. . . ." She laughed. "Isn't that touching? That was when the *Ben Hur* company was on the road. We were leaving some city in Maryland. Fred went on, 'I just could not help feeling blue, and am sure you forgive my transgression.' Transgression? I'd forgotten about that—the less said the better!" Julie winked again.

Julia Bingham

"And here's another note: 'It was decided at a meeting of the club tonight that if you sent me a photograph that it would be enlarged and [you] will be proclaimed *Queen* of the Klan Klub.' The letter concluded, 'Lonesome–girlie, that word does not express it.'" Julie laughed. "Isn't that sweet? But the letter was from both Fred and Reg—two of the young men down in Maryland—so I don't know who penned the sentiment." She turned over the yellowed letter on hotel stationery. "I see it was penned at 3:30 a.m.—that figures. There's a P.S.: 'And do not forget the photograph you promised me.' Of course I sent one. Actresses travel with a good stock of them.

Alphonz Ethier and Averell Harris
in *Ben Hur*

"I also traveled with a great crew. We became quite a jolly family. Here's a snapshot of the two *Ben Hur* leads, Alphonz Ethier and Averell Harris, and another photo of the pair in character."

"Did you take the horses with you on the road?"

"There wouldn't be a show without them. We even had a pet camel. Here's a photo of her, 'Nellie,' by name. Oh, it was fun! *Ben Hur* was practically a career, for the show ran for twenty-one years—not that I was in it all that time.

"Nellie"

"I've been talking mostly about actors, but there were other celebrities here on the river. I suppose the most famous, in many ways, was Irving Berlin. Max Winslow introduced him to the river. Max was partner in Irving Berlin, Inc. He and Tillie had a cottage at St. Lawrence Park where Berlin often visited. He equipped one of Captain Bob Fitzsimmons charter boats with a phonograph, to have music on the water.

"The romance and marriage of Irving Berlin and Ellin Mackay were a national sensation. Her father was immensely wealthy. The Mackays had a magnificent chateau out on Long Island. Clarence Mackay was Irish Catholic, however, and could not abide the thought of his daughter marrying a

Jewish tunesmith. The couple wed despite parental objections, however, and came to the river on their honeymoon, staying at the Winslow cottage. Captain Bob tells of the newlyweds cruising on his boat. Irving said he didn't care where they went, only that they escaped the curious public. Asked how far he wanted to

Newlweds Irving and Ellin Macka Berlin

go, for how long, Irving replied again that he didn't care. Bob reminded him that he had to charge fifteen dollars an hour, to which Irving said, 'Who cares? I've just finished a song that will earn more than five thousand.'"

"Did you know Irving Berlin?"

"No, I only saw him on the Winslow dock once. He was a very private person, wanting nothing to do with social life here. Reporters did catch him at St. Lawrence Park, where he met them dressed in white flannels and a white silk shirt. Irving didn't want to talk about his new marriage, however, but only said that he hoped everyone was as happy as he and his wife, and that they only asked for a chance to be left alone.

Honeymooning Berlins

"Geraldine Farrar wasn't our only great opera star—Madam Schumann-Heinck was a diva of the previous generation. As a fledgling singer, I was awed when she performed at the Thousand Island Park Tabernacle. She was world-class.

"Oh, but in all this talk of celebrities, I've left out the most important, perhaps. That depends on what you think is important, of course. The Swami Vivekananda surely was not so well known in his time as these popular stars, but long after they are forgotten, people will still remember and revere the

Madam Ernestine
Schumann-Heinck

swami—mark my words."

"What's a swami?"

"That's a Hindu term for a monk—you know, a man who devotes his life to religion. We think of monks hiding away from the world in monasteries, but this swami was a wandering monk who traveled the world carrying his message. He came to the United States in 1893 to attend a congress of religions at the Chicago World's Fair. He was almost unknown at the time—certainly not well known here. But he made a great impression and became a featured speaker at many religious occasions around the country.

"Elizabeth Dutcher, a maiden lady of T. I. Park who was an artist, studied with him in New York City.

Swami Vivekananda

Although she was a staunch Methodist (and the Park was a Methodist community at the time) she invited the swami to use her cottage there. He accepted the invitation, bringing a clutch of disciples with him. Although Miss Dutcher subsequently had some misgivings about the swami's teachings, her decision was momentous. The Dutcher cottage became an international landmark, and remains so today, since it still is used by adherents of the Swami Vivekananda and has become a destination of pilgrimage of many of his followers.

"The Dutcher cottage was well suited to the swami's needs. It's not right in the built-up area of the Park, where the cottages are so close together. Instead, the frame house crowns a big boulder up on the hill behind the Park.

The steep road and surrounding woods provide a sense of detachment, but there is a view out over the treetops and roofs of the cottage colony—or used to be far more of a panoramic outlook before the surrounding trees grew up around the cottage.

"Swami Vivekananda wrote one of his major works at the Park, the long poem 'Song of the Sannyasin.' His many lectures there were transcribed by followers and have been compiled into a book. Reading it may suggest why Elizabeth Dutcher became somewhat concerned about conflict with the prevailing Methodist theology. The swami preached liberation, freeing the spirit—a rather alarming proposition at a time of

Elizabeth Dutcher

such conformity to religious strictures. Authorities didn't even allow dancing at the Park then—and no boats could land or depart from the place on Sundays. As you may imagine, many residents of the Park were wary of the alien. One girl was cautioned not to go near his place and to avoid the swami, since 'he is a heathen.'

Dutcher Cottage

"Elizabeth Dutcher enlarged her cottage to accommodate the swami and his entourage. Years later the place was modernized. One day an electrician working on the cottage noticed some paper on a pile of rubbish about to be burned. Curious, he glanced at the writing. It was the original handwritten manuscript of the 'Song of the Sannyasin,' which fortunately he retrieved for posterity.

"When Swami Vivekananda finally left the river, he waved his hat from the departing steamboat and shouted, 'I bless these Thousand Islands.'

"Marietta Holley, the very popular writer of the 'Samantha' series of humorous books, described the scene from the swami's cottage, providing an illustration. I doubt that the scene looks like that today. The trees were all younger then, since the island had been lumbered off before the Park developed.

"Marietta Holley, who was famous as a humorous author, was a regular visitor to Thousand Island Park. She didn't have far to come, since she was a native of nearby Adams, New York, where she built a fine house. She described the view from the swami's cottage in one of her Samantha books, where she visits the Thousand Islands. There's also an engraving of the view in the book.

Marietta Holley

"Will Carleton, a popular poet, also frequented the Park. It's hard to realize today how popular a poet could be in the nineteenth century, when life was more slowly paced and folks read those long,

Will Carleton

J. G. Holland

long stories in verse by the evening fire. They seem unreadable today. Carleton attracted huge crowds to his readings at the Tabernacle and elsewhere on the river.

"Even more important on the literary scene was J. G. Holland, who built one of the finest houses on the river, Bonnie-Castle. He came earlier, before my time, but he also wrote those long epic poems and sentimental novels that no one reads anymore. But as editor of *Scribner's* magazine, a national journal, Holland wrote editorials regularly so was widely read. He was also known as a maker of literary reputations, since his important magazine featured many of the most prominent authors of the day.

"More than Holland, maybe history will better remember Inness, the painter. He visited several times, painting local landscapes. The McNallys acquired one, which hangs in the dining room of *La Duchesse.*

"But of course we had our own resident painter. Frederic Remington was certainly one of our most famous islanders. I'd class him with May Irwin as one of our greatest celebrities."

"He was down at Chippewa Bay, wasn't he?"

"Yes, Ingleneuk. He had a studio there as well as

George Inness

a cottage. Although best known for his depictions of the Wild West, many of his paintings portray the Thousand Islands, but he also did some fine bronzes, much sought after by collectors. They're of cowboys on bucking broncos—that sort of thing.

"Fred's not to be confused with Philo Remington—no relation, so far as I know. Philo was the Arms and Typewriter Remington—the one who lived so simply at Thousand Island Park, compared to his super-salesman, William O. Wyckoff, who built the great trophy house on Carleton Island. Philo was more concerned with religion, I suppose—which was why he was involved with the

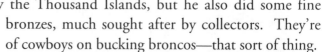

Frederic Remington

Philo Remington

original Methodist camp meeting at Thousand Island Park.

"And as I'm giving you the full cast of celebrities on the river, I must mention Clara Barton. Do you know who she was?"

"The Red Cross," I shot back proudly. I had heard that on the boat tour.

"Yes, she founded it and was one of the most respected people here. She didn't have a cottage, but every summer visited Royal Pullman who tented on Wellesley Island near his brother's island. We always looked for the big Red Cross flag flying there to know if she was here."

Julie wasn't keen about going out on the water anymore. Blind in one eye, with failing sight in the other, she couldn't see much and was uneasy about climbing in and out of boats. She would make an annual trip over to Picton Island, however, to spend a week or so with the Heinemans. They bought that large island in the early thirties. Julie's last husband, Kris Hass, recently deceased, lived there earlier, for many years occupying a fine house provided by the Emery family. The Emerys had a

Clara Barton

farm on Picton, as well as their big yacht house and smaller boathouse. Their summer residence, however, was several miles away, at Calumet Island.

Kris was not a farmer, however, but was a landscape gardener, in charge of all the Emery properties on the river, including the Frontenac Hotel on Round Island, Frontenac Springs on

Kris's House, Picton Island

Wishing you
The Season's Greetings
and
The peace and tranquility
that is found at
"**Picton**"
in the Thousand Islands

The Heinemans

1946　　　　　　　　　1946

the mainland, and another large farm on Grindstone Island. There were big greenhouses that Kris tended on Picton Island.

In one of her scrapbooks Julie had a collection of Heineman's Christmas cards showing Picton Island. I knew the island from rowing around it, as it was only a few miles from Steele's Point and I used to row many miles at a time. I had also taken boat tours where guides pointed out the large Heineman cottage. I mentioned that they said Mr. Heineman was a millionaire who made a fortune from Buster Brown shoes, which we wore as kids.

"Really?" Julie raised her eyebrows. "Well, they don't act like the millionaires down at the Bay. They just enjoy a comfortable old cottage—nothing grand. Of course it's very pleasant. And I wouldn't think of inquiring about Bernard's business, but I believe he's a New York textile broker, not a shoemaker. But he may have several business investments. What Bernard's best known for, however, is being a collector of butterflies. It's a passion with him. You should see his beautiful framed displays—not all them are here on the river, of course. Bernard was coauthor of an important book, *Jamaica and Its Butterflies*, published in London. As I said, he doesn't strike you as a new-rich millionaire. Maybe that's why they prefer being alone on Picton to joining the Alexandria Bay set. They're more like the folks at the head of Grindstone, who don't care for display."

"I caddied for Mr. Morgan," I mentioned proudly (it being my only connection to the Grindstone set). "He was very nice, especially since I couldn't follow the ball." Julie laughed.

"Yes, you told me about that brief venture. You were undone by your poor eyesight, I remember. And I probably told you that the Morgans are one of the old families on the river, like the Clarks from Chicago at Comfort Island. The Morgans built a cottage on Papoose in 1886. They're still there. Here's a snapshot that shows them in their element.

Morgans in the Bush

"Like Teddy Roosevelt (whom they knew) and Fred Remington down at Chippewa Bay, they preferred the 'rugged life.' They were, and still are, real outdoors sports people.

"But we were talking about celebrities. The Morgans, Bacons, and those Grindstone folks weren't celebrities. They avoided the spotlight and enjoyed seclusion. Celebrities are a special breed. Not all distinguished people are celebrities. A celebrity is a person who's famous for being famous.

Oscar Straus

Garret Hobart

"I haven't even mentioned the presidents who came here. They're more than mere celebrities, you see. They're in a different class. Also, I wouldn't classify Oscar Straus as a celebrity. He was Nathan Straus's brother and a frequent visitor at Cherry Island. Oscar was a distinguished public servant, an ambassador and that sort of thing. He was very prominent, often mentioned in the press, but not really a celebrity. I'd say the same for Garret Hobart—he was a vice-president and a friend of Boldt who visited Heart Island. You might say that sort of visitor was famous not

Frank Taylor

Howard Pyle

merely for being famous, but for his distinguished position or contribution.

"I suppose that was true of artists like Inness and Remington. I didn't mention another painter here, Frank Taylor, over at Round Island. He certainly wasn't in the same league as Inness and Remington, but was more of a professional illustrator, I'd say—and something of a journalist, as he wrote publicity pieces that he illustrated. Howard Pyle didn't summer here like Taylor but, in my opinion, was a better artist, producing some of the best depictions of the river and its people. Pyle was certainly better known as an artist, since his work appeared in many national magazines.

"Wealth didn't make one a celebrity. Commodore Bourne of Dark Island was fabulously wealthy, but not widely known to the public. The Haydens, at Fairyland, may have been just as rich, but they kept an even lower profile. Maybe the richest man to ever visit the Thousand Islands—or at least he was said to be the richest man in the world at the time—was the Gaekwar of

Baroda. Now, he *was* a celebrity. Not because of his money, but because the press had made him an international celebrity. What a contrast with our other Indian, Swami Vivekananda. The Swami was a simple monk, concerned with spiritual values, whereas the Gaekwar was a cosmopolitan society figure."

"What's a gaekwar?"

"A maharaja—the ruler, owner practically—of a huge state in India."

"He was at the Frontenac?"

"Yes, I saw him there more than once, as I recall. It created quite a stir whenever he arrived, always with a big and colorful retinue.

The Gaekwar of Baroda

Alva Vanderbilt Belmont

"Alva Vanderbilt Belmont was another Frontenac celebrity. She was very wealthy, too, but her celebrity came from the famous (or infamous) marriage she forced on her daughter, to the duke of Marlborough. It was really the great social coup among that set—the Newport set, that is. Mrs. O. H. P. Belmont (as she was known, after her second marriage) was also a prominent suffragette, marching in Fifth Avenue parades (to the disdain of many in her crowd). When asked incredulously how she could do such a thing, she replied gayly, 'Oh, I have the right outfit, with comfortable shoes.'

William Danforth

Norma Kopp

"Speaking of famous stage personalities, I mustn't leave out William Danforth and his actress wife, Norma Kopp. 'Billy,' as everyone called him, was widely popular as a Gilbert and Sullivan comic actor. He and Norma came to Thousand Island Park initially. They migrated to nearby Gren-ell, where they spent their honeymoon in 1898, then bought a cottage on Murray Island. Their grandsons, Bill Danforth and the Munro boys, Dick and Bill, are about your age.

"Celebrities on the river aren't altogether a thing of the past, of course. You're probably too young to go to the Clayton Casino. It opened a few

Clayton Casino, c. 1945

years ago, in 1934, in spite of the Depression. Folks found money somehow to dance and have a good time. The casino attracted a good clientele. Until she died a couple of years ago, May Irwin used to go there often, always recognized as a great celebrity when she came in. Chuck Emery has been a regular customer, when on the river. The big bands attract large crowds that fill the place—and it's enormous. Paul Whiteman, the Dorsey Brothers, . . . the casino books top entertainment.

"The Clayton Casino was a surprising success, opening as the Great Depression set it, when the river generally was in distress."

"I know. My parents talk about going there. They know Pop Cameron. I think he owns the place."

"Yes."

"And they know 'Tiffy,' we call him. He owns Frontenac Crystal Springs, where they have the trout ponds for fishing. We go there often."

"That's Floyd Tift. He bought the place in 1926. It was quite a rum-runner's joint back then. The run-down, old hotel used to be accessible from the river by a little steamboat that ran up French Creek. It was a popular, lively spot when I was young, with lots of recreational events—climbing greased poles and that sort of thing. I remember my sides splitting watching

Frontenac Crystal Springs

young men trying to wrestle huge sturgeons out of the fish ponds. Charles Emery bought the place in order to bottle its springwater for the grand Frontenac Hotel—and we all bought the water, back in those days. At least we Clayton types. The more pretentious folks down at the Bay favored George Boldt's imported Appolinaris Water. Some also bought his imported wines—that was one of his sidelines. Many people up this way bought my father's."

"I thought your father was a doctor."

"Well, there was more money in the liquor business. We had the biggest store in Watertown, right on Public Square. Although Boldt pushed his favorite German wines on his friends (he imported them—the wines, not the friends) a lot of imported French wines and brandies flowed through our place, much of it coming up here to the river. This place was awash in booze. Naturally I didn't care to be identified with the liquor business, which seemed rather . . . *gauche*, as we might say, putting on the dog." She laughed merrily. "But liquor wasn't so funny as Mayor Comstock's 'Dead Shot Worm Candy'!

Liquor Store, 19 Public Square, Watertown

"I gave up the stage after becoming Mrs. McLean. We had a lovely home in the suburbs, and I only took the train into the city occasionally. I still adored the theater, of course, so often we would go in of an evening, staying overnight in a hotel rather than returning. It was more convenient for Bill to be in town fresh the next morning, rather than returning home late and then rising early. I'd stay in the city for the day, usually, shopping and meeting friends for lunch, returning home with him after he left his office."

"What did your husband do?"

"He did quite well, thank you," Julie laughed. "Bill was in advertising.

"One night when we were in town a distressing incident occurred. Here are some clippings. We were staying at the Hotel Schuyler, this time for several days. I didn't even miss anything until I received an unexpected call, asking me to come down to the police station to identify my stolen jewelry. I didn't even know it was gone until they called. Then I checked the drawer, of course, and was shocked to find it missing. I had put four rings in a cigarette box. When I got to the station, there was the box with the rings inside. I certainly was relieved, since they were valuable. One was a three-carat diamond, another a dinner ring with two-carat stones surrounded by thirty smaller ones. Good Lord, I can't even imagin wearing such things today. Needless to say, I had to dispose of my jewelry long ago, in order to survive."

"They caught the thief?"

"Yes, it was good police work. They were on the lookout after a series of hotel robberies. Suspecting a twenty-seven-year-old porter, they followed him from the hotel to where he met his young wife, who was carrying a baby. The detective suspected something, since the woman seemed distraught and the young man patted her on the back while assuring, 'There, there. Don't worry. Everything will be all right.' When the detective approached the couple, the fellow dropped something down his wife's neck, hoping to conceal it in her dress. The detective asked them both to come with him to the station, but the young man broke into a run. The policeman tackled him, and they wrestled until the detective pulled a loaded revolver out of the young man's hip pocket. Over her scared protests, the policeman patted the back of the woman's dress. Feeling a lump, he told her to accompany her husband to the police station. There they recovered my rings, allowing the woman take her baby home, while locking up her husband."

"That was exciting."

"Oh, but sad. Here's a letter—from the man's wife. It's so sad. She says, 'Dear Madam . . .' Oh, but I don't think I can read this. It's long, and heartbreaking. Maybe you can imagine the situation. She had only been back from having her baby at the hospital twenty-one days. Her husband had only fifty cents when he took my rings. If he were to go to jail now, she would have to 'adopt out,' as she put it, her baby so she could go to work, since they were penniless. She said her husband thought I was 'a person of money' who could spare some—my small rings must have seemed trivial baubles to a young couple with no money and a new baby. The wife hoped I would ask the judge to suspend her husband's sentence. She promised that Ed would never do such a thing again—or at least that she would try to stop him."

"Did you ask to let him off?"

"Of course. How could I not do so? But I knew it was not the first time he had stolen. He had ten thousand dollar's worth of pawn tickets. He had been fencing the loot that way."

Julia Bingham McLean

"What happened to him?"

"I don't know—never wanted to know. But I kept this letter, even though I tried to forget the whole thing. The letter is real, very touching. See how the handwriting changes from beginning to end. It's carefully penned at the beginning, but becomes more agitated. At the bottom of the third page there's this scrawled postscript, 'Call me on phone by 12 o clock and let me know your answer.' I couldn't bear to talk to her. We would have both just broken down. But I did what I could for her. Then I wanted it to be over. Now it's come back. So sad."

"You don't know if he went to jail?"

"No. I never wanted to know. That poor woman. With her child, and penniless." Julie sighed and gazed out over the water. "Well, I'm penniless, too, now—but without a child. I suppose I'm poorer than she."

"But you were rich once."

"Oh? Compared to now, I suppose. Look at the pearls in this photo. But that was a previous life, Paul. Another person, it almost seems. Another role I was playing. Was that real—or is this? Some of us seem to have 'More Lives than One'—that's what Claude Bragdon called his biography. He was a famous stage designer, an architect, too, that I knew. In some ways it's all so dramatic, so unreal. I suppose that's what Swami Vivekananda would call *maya*—our world of fleeting illusion that we only think is real at the moment. You don't have to become aware of some personal experiences before you were born to come to the Hindu notion of reincarnation. When you've lived as long as I you understand it. I've had 'more lives than one.'"

I, of course, was too young to understand, since I was just beginning to know one life. Julie carefully put the old letter back in the envelope. It was addressed to "Complainant Julia McLean, Hotel Schuyler." The return address said, "Police Department, City of New York." Julie looked incredulous. "But here is this letter. I suppose it actually happened—to those people, whoever we were back then."

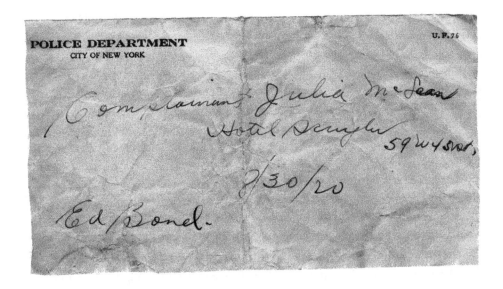

One of the three adjacent cottages at Steele's Point where we stayed.

Interlude: Steele's Point

The main cottage at Steele's Point was not large, but seemed so. Most of the partitions on the main floor had been removed, leaving a single room big enough for parties and dancing. It was, I confess, quite a party house—not that the parties were large, just constant. The small, old-fashioned refrigerator in the tiny kitchen, which had one of those round coils on top, was too small for adequate ice and beer, so there was a huge ice chest out in the garage. It seemed to contain an inexhaustible supply of beer. Apparently the beverage came infrequently in large quantities, for I don't remember many deliveries. They came from town in a truck. There should have been a pipeline.

Actually it wasn't mostly beer, in those days, but Carling's Red Cap Ale. No one was conscious of calories, back then. Oddly, however, fewer people seemed overweight. Perhaps most caloric intake came from the ale. Meals weren't very memorable, as I recall. We had a lot of homemade soup, always simmering on the stove, and good bread, but not much other cooking that I remember—other than fish, of course. I grew to hate fish because we ate (and had to clean) so much of it. In those days, if one simply want something to eat, you could go out and catch a big mess of great northerns by putting out several lines on bobbers, sinking big chubs on leaders down to the bottom where the big fish fed. All you had to do was wait a short time, then haul them in. But then you had to clean them. Night after night we might be served fried pike, sliced into thick slabs like steak. I didn't care for it. Still don't, although smaller pike, four to eight pounds, are still plentiful.

The festive mood of the cottage was enhanced by an old wind-up Victrola—one of those big ones that stood on the floor as a piece of furniture. In a cabinet below the turntable the big, old shellac records were stored. We had lots of original Caruso recordings, but what I enjoyed most were the 1920s vintage foxtrots—those fast, lively tunes, very upbeat. I can still hear "Chloë," with lyrics that began, "Through the dismal swamp I wander. . . ." The lament to a lost love was incongruously sung in a high-pitched male falsetto to the frantically jazzed-up dance tune. Great fun. I gave all those historic records to the Belfer music archive at Syracuse University.

There was a big linoleum "rug" in open space. The slippery surface was great for dancing, especially in socks, since it facilitated lots of sliding. I remember the linoleum usually showing wet footprints as we tracked through from swimming to the dressing room. I also can hear the clatter of Whisker's claws on that surface. Around the walls were many daybeds with lamp tables between. More cots were on the porch, since most of the bedrooms had been removed. There were two other cottages next door that had plenty of rooms. They served as guest houses, or sometimes were rented, as they had kitchens and baths, as well as docks. One room in the main cottage that was retained was used as a big walk-in closet and dressing area, shared by everyone, since in that cottage we slept dormitory-style. This was a pretty informal, casual place. Folks wandered around in robes half the day. But before lunch all the daybeds were made up, properly covered with bedspreads. In the afternoon the dorm room was transformed into a living room—although most living was actually done out on the long porch, as it always is at summer places. If not grand, Steele's Point was heaven to me.

Carrier Bay from Steele's Point

Wau Winet Island

Summer home of Thomas H. Wheeler, an early associate of
John D. Rockefeller. The Thousand Islands Club is seen on
Wellesley Island in the distance, beyond Pullman Island.
Nearby, at the right edge of the picture, appears a bit of the
Thousand Islands Yacht Club on Welcome Island.

II. Wau Winet and Keewaydin
The Wheelers at Wau Winet

Some folks on the river were more pleasant than others," Julie recalled. "Of course, everyone was here to enjoy one another, so generally people were affable—although we have a few who were arrogant at times, or cantankerous. The Wheelers, however, were just wonderful people. You can see that, I suppose, just looking at this photo of them aboard their yacht, the *Empress*. Tom and Celia were a happy couple—or I should say they were a threesome, since Celia would go nowhere without her little Pekinese.

Celia and Tom Wheeler

"There were three Wheeler girls. I knew Mary Louise best, since she was about my age. We called her 'Mamie.' Leita and Stella were younger.

"My friend Mamie was 'an excellent whip,' as we used to say—a proficient horsewoman, like Clover Boldt. Mary Louise was, and still is, I'm sure, a very bright woman. She went to Smith but, like a lot of young women at the time, didn't graduate. Getting married was the objective. Spending much time in Europe, Mamie spoke several languages. She and Clover Boldt occasionally chatted in German. I practiced my German a bit with her, too, but more with Mrs. Wheeler's German maid, Julia. We had something of a bond because of our same first names. Mamie and I had our continental experiences in common, and both of us studied music, but Mary Louise didn't have my theatrical ambitions. She was more clearly destined to make a good marriage and become a socialite. Mary Louise married William Dewart.

Mary Louise Wheeler Dewart and
William Thompson Dewart at a masquerade ball,
Greenwich Country Club, 1912

They stayed on the river, at Keewaydin. Julia, the maid, believe it or not, married Mamie's brother. What a shock to everyone!

"The Wheelers' son, Emmett, was a fat boy. He was older than we girls and seemed exactly what you'd expect a spoiled rich son to be. Emmett's marriage to his mother's German maid didn't enhance his social standing. In truth, however, much island society was new rich, while in fact some prominent people here, like George Boldt, were also German-born. It was the second generation—Mamie's—that became more exacting about social nuances. Emmett became something of an outcast from his sisters and their set, I think—although he was not really alienated from his family. I recall his sons visiting Keewaydin. But his branch seems to have been cut off from the family fortune, or to have run through whatever they got. I believe that his sons are in the navy, are policemen, or something like that. But generally it seems that money passes through the girls."

"Why's that?"

"Well, I suppose parents are more concerned about a daughter's 'marrying well,' as they say. Much attention is devoted to seeking eligible mates for the girls. The sons, more likely, are regarded as capable of fending for themselves. But after being raised as spoiled brats, indulged by rich parents, many sons didn't amount to much. The daughters meanwhile usually were married off to the scion of some other wealthy family, so two fortunes were consolidated—or at least the daughter secured a prospect promising to be 'a good provider,' as we used to say. That was young William Dewart for Mary Louise Wheeler."

"Where were the Wheelers from?" I asked.

"Oh, they had a stone five-story town house on West 72nd Street in New York at the time. It wasn't as pretentious as you might imagine."

"They were rich?"

"Of course. Tom Wheeler, like many of his contemporaries on the river, was a Horatio Alger type who made his way in the world by pluck, as they would say, back then. Pluck and luck, I would say, since Tom happened to be in the right place at the right time, having the good fortune to run into John D. Rockefeller. This was down in Pennsylvania, when Rockefeller was just putting together his oil empire.

"At age ten Tom ran away from his home and went to work in a grocery store. Taken in by a blacksmith's family, he learned that trade. Then he, then moved

Thomas Henry Wheeler, 1844-1926

onto a farm. When sixteen he responded to Lincoln's first call for volunteers. He fought and was wounded in the Civil War. He was in Confederate prisons for seven months, until released in an exchange of Union prisoners for Confederates. After his two-year tour of duty, Tom recognized an opportunity, staying on to conduct a profitable business as a "sutler," selling goods to the troops.

"Tom had a colorful sidekick, a Negro assistant who wore a mixture of Union and Confederate uniforms—probably a slave escaped across the battle lines. I can imagine why affable Tom and his comic partner did very well at the business.

"After the war, Tom sold wooden barrel staves, produced by an uncle in Michigan. This enterprise took him to Pennsylvania, where the oil business was just developing. Oil was shipped in wooden barrels. At booming Pithole City he met young John D. Rockefeller, who needed containers for his oil. That's how they got together. Tom was a born trader, and Rockefeller knew another sharpie when he met one. Wheeler went with Rockefeller to Cleveland and got in on the ground floor of Standard Oil. He was secretary of the corporation when he retired at age seventy.

"Back in the 1880s the officers of the Standard Oil Company had a meeting at the Crossmon House. That visit was Wheeler's introduction to the river. The Wheelers were here for many years before they bought Wau Winet. In early summers they sometimes stayed at the Crossmon, the Edgewood Club and at other times the grand, new Frontenac. They became early members of the Thousand Islands Yacht Club, joining in 1897. Tom also belonged to the Chippewa club and together with Bourne and Boldt was a member of the most exclusive Oak Island hunt club.

The three Wheeler girls about 1896:
Stella stands behind Leita, next to Mary Louise.

"The three Wheeler girls that I knew were about my age then. They were very attractive, and I saw them at the club often, before they built their summer home, Wau Winet Lodge, in 1902.

"The Hills owned Wau Winet previously. C. E. Hill was a Chicago merchant—one of those attracted to the river by the Pullmans. The Hills settled on Wau Winet, building a cottage in 1880. They gave the island its name, said to be that of an Indian village on Narragansett Island. The Hills had a steamboat of the same name. The Watertown architect J. W Griffen designed their large boathouse in 1888, so he may have done other work on the island. The Hills raised and moved the original cottage, adding wings, in 1892. Tom enjoyed Wau Winet for twenty-four years, Celia for twenty-seven."

"I've been there with my parents," I proudly volunteered. "We eat there sometimes, now that it's a restaurant."

"Oh, I'd love to see it again, after all these years. I still imagine it, in my mind's eye. Tell me how it looks now."

"Well, you go from the dock up some wide stone steps to the house, which is built very close to the water but is high up, on top of granite walls.

Wau Winet Island as rebuilt and the Wheeler yacht, *Empress*

"There's a gold-leaf ceiling. They point that out, since it's so unusual."

"I don't remember that. It doesn't sound like Tom and Celia–but they wouldn't have pointed it out, of course. They weren't show-offs—didn't have to be, you know. There was enough prestige being identified with 'Standard Oil', you know—Rockefeller' s huge petroleum monopoly. Before automobiles, their big business was in kerosene for lighting and cooking."

"There's also a dining room on the front of the house," I continued, "which has more big windows. That room's just for show now, like the big living room. They have the old furniture in those rooms. New restaurant tables are out in that huge room at the end of the house—do you remember that? It's sort of a glassed-in porch, but much larger than a porch. It has more big windows on three sides, and the tables are next to them, around the edge of the room, with a big dance floor in the center. I suppose there's a band there sometimes, but mostly the music's from a jukebox."

"Yes, I do remember that well, since it was such a wonderful room for parties. Would you believe that I danced there as a young woman? No jukeboxes back then. Young college men sometimes formed summer orchestras, but the big hotels had professional musicians that played both in the afternoon and evening. We did a lot of dancing. Yes, we had some dandy parties at the Wheelers' since they had four young people in the family. And we cruised on their big boat, which was lovely. She was the *Empress*. They had other boats too, of course.

"Wheeler acquired the Herreshoff yacht in 1902, the same year he built the house. Like Wau Winet Lodge, the *Empress* was not grandiose, compared to other huge trophy yachts on the river. She was a mere 84 feet long. At the time we had many steam yachts exceeding a hundred feet long. The Laughlin's *Corona* was 172 feet long, more than twice the size of the Wheelers' boat.

"But the *Empress* was lovely and well appointed. I remember the white, gold-rimmed Limoges porcelain, dated 1908. The dinner service was not fancy, but decorated merely with the crossed pennants of the New York Yacht Club, of which Wheeler was a member, and his personal standard. The boat had one of those miniature brass cannons on a mahogany naval carriage—they were a fixture on all the big steam yachts."

Empress

"Why did a boat need a cannon?" I wondered.

"They were for salutes," Julie explained, "fired when the ensign was lowered at sundown, or to recognize important visitors.

"We used to call Tom Wheeler 'Commodore,' because he was commodore of the Columbia Yacht Club. That was a prominent New York City organization with a clubhouse on the Hudson at Eighty-sixth Street, not far from the Wheelers' town house. As I said, Tom was also a member of the more prestigious New York Yacht Club, of which Dark Island's Frederick Bourne was commodore. Emery also belonged to that club.

"Wheeler was an avid yachtsman, serving as a governor of the T.I. Yacht Club. He was also a member of the Chippewa Bay Yacht Club. Tom Wheeler loved the river. He died at Wau Winet at eighty-two, late in the season of 1926. His body was carried to Clayton aboard the *Empress*, to be transferred to New York City by private train. Celia continued to come to the river but was diabetic and lost much of her weight in later years. She survived Tom by three years.

"The children were grown up, with families of their own by that time. Only my friend Mamie stayed on the river. While Celia Wheeler was still at Wau Winet, in 1921 Mary Louise and her husband bought nearby Keewaydin as a summer place for their growing family. They didn't keep the *Empress* long, however. Big steam yachts with large crews were already archaic vestiges of the past in the twenties. In 1930 the family sold the *Empress*, which went from the river to be converted from steam to internal combustion.

"Like Tom, in 1929 Celia died at Wau Winet. I think that's where they wanted to be, to the very end."

More about the Wheelers follows in the article, "Tom Wheeler."

Widow Celia Wheeler with her son-in-law William T. Dewart, 1928

Wau Winet before enlargement of the house .

Wau Winet after enclosure of the porches and expansion of the house.

"... Come up to Wau Winet ... where I have a simple shack
and see what we can do with a rod and reel."

1906 invitation from Tom Wheeler to Bob Davis

The *Empress*

The Man Who Found that Happiness Was Contagious

Extract from a rough draft for a column by Robert H. Davis
that appeared in *The Sun*, New York City, September 1926.

My first meeting with "the Commodore" as he was known among his inti-
mates [was on] an evening when [Wheeler's future son-in-law, William T.
Dewart] and I called [at his home] to discuss . . . angling for the small-mouth
black bass.

"Now my idea," said he over the cigars, "is that when a a man passes sixty
that he should spend the winter in California, spring in New York City, and
the summer on the St. Lawrence fishing for the gamy red-eye [using] live
bait. If you are as good as your conversation indicates, I would suggest that
you take a weekend [and] come up to Wau Winet Island . . . where I have a
simple shack and see what we can do with a rod and reel."

The date of June fifteenth which opened the black bass season was set as
satisfactory to the contestants.

"You will probably need companionship going and coming," he con-
tined, "and I will be glad if you will bring four of your friends along; good
eaters and sleepers. That will give us a party of six. I don't care for bridge
fiends, tennis players, or fox-trotters on this trip. I furnish everything
'cludin' fishing tackle and I 'calls for and delivers.' All set for the St. Lawrence. You name the other four. They must be born fishermen."

In due course I received railroad and sleeper accommodations for Clayton, New York, with instructions to arrive on the morning of the fifteenth.
No difficulty had been encountered in selecting four of the best sleepers,
eaters, and anglers in the U.S.A. We arrived at the rendezvous in a solid, ex-
pectant mass. At the Clayton dock lay the *Empress*, an eighty foot yacht
loaded to the Plimsoll line with the sort of provisions that born fishermen
crave.

The Commodore stood at the gang plank and greet us with his cap in his
hand. "Boys, you look good to me," he remarked, surveying the group.
"Mr. Davis, I hand you the headgear. You're the captain of this craft. Make
your friends at home. This trip I'm one of the crew, and at your service."
With that he placed his cap on my head and bowed us aboard.

There is not space enough in *The Sun* to describe all the joys of that excursion. We "struck 'em" at Chippewa Bay and in three days caught one

hundred and fifty black bass running from two to four pounds. Oh, they certainly were there!

[Bob Davis continued to tell how the group returned to fish, mostly at Chippewa Bay, for nearly twenty years. At their table was a sliver pitcher given Tom in 1913 by his guests, engraved with the lines:

> We love the ocean and its tide,
> The babbling brooks that pass our way,
> The rivers we have fished beside—
>   But Oh, you Chippewa Bay!

Davis concluded his column by observing about Tom Wheeler:]

He held to the theory that if unhappiness was contagious, so could happiness be made contagious and that was his mission in this world. He had a divine genius for friendship which marked his career from the cradle to the grave. His children, his children's children, and his neighbors loved him.

I saw him last seated in the bay window of his St. Lawrence home gazing out of the window at the blue river that he knew like a pilot. The soft gurgle of the current sill reached his ears. Lying back on his pillows he reviewed the tide of traffic:

". . . and I wonder if when a man has become a fixture in a chair," said he slowly, "and can't fish any more and can't move among his friends—and is living in the past—whether . . . it isn't just as well . . ."

Four Sports

Keewaydin

The Dewart estate, now Keewaydin State Park, included a working farm. The barns on Route 12, at the bottom of the picture, are now gone, but a farm house (hidden in the trees across the road) remains. The winding driveway and paths, lined with stone walls, are largely und-changed. The large boathouses in the bay were demolished together with the main house. The park now provides a large marina in the bay. Comfort, Jewel, and Wau Winet islands ap-pear, left to right, in the river.

Mary Louise Wheeler   (Mrs. William Dewart)

The Dewarts at Keewaydin

"After their 1908 marriage, Mary Louise Wheeler and her husband, William T. Dewart, leased the Ledges," Julie continued. "That's on the mainland, below Bonnie Castle.

"The Jacksons owned Keewaydin at the time, which was long before the Dewarts bought the place in 1921. James Wesley Jackson purchased Kepler Point and built the big house back in 1893. He enjoyed Keewaydin until he died in 1918. Jackson was a stockbroker and financial advisor from Plainfield (Summit), New Jersey. The Jacksons were close friends of the Pullmans and were early members of the T. I. Yacht Club. I remember their yachts, the *Ella,* which they bought from the Oliphants over at Neh Mahbin, and the *Amabel.* Oliphant, a stone's throw across the way, was another New York stockbroker. Keewaydin was a showplace, much admired, said to be 'a castle-like place that provokes a query from every tourist.'

Mary Dewart gives a hand to her father, William T. Dewart, with Mickey, the wire-haired fox terrier. He is joined by Robert M. Laufer, embarking for a round of golf at the Thousand Islands Club about 1930.

"TheDewarts were starting a young family when they moved in. They had a daughter, Mary, who was six years old during their first summer there. She was a sweet little girl.

Mary Dewart at Keewaydin, 1922

"Then there were two young sons growing up at Keewaydin in the twenties. Mary's younger brothers, William T. Dewart, Jr, and Thomas W. Dewart. It was a wonderful place for a family, with two big boat houses full of boats, a working farm on the estate, horses to ride, those enchanting gazebos along the shore—and close to all the action at the new T.I. Club in the twenties and thirties. And, best of all, there were those fun grandparents, Tom and Celia Wheeler on their little island a short row across the channel—and their wonderful yacht, the *Empress*.

"The Dewarts had an Irish nurse, who we all called 'Nannie,' though her name was really Margaret Cunningham. I suppose I remember Nannie so vividly because she had a thick Irish brogue. She was a font of quaint expressions from the Auld Sod. Exclaiming about last night's sun set, should would say: 'Twar a picture no artist could paint.' (Julie was very good at dialects).

"William T. Dewart—I never knew him well enough to call him 'Bill'—don't know that anyone did. He was not exactly the 'Bill' sort of fellow. As a young man he came to the river to fish with Tom Wheeler, who enjoyed the company of young men on fishing expeditions aboard the *Empress*. I suppose the Wheelers were sizing up suitors for their three daughters, and they did much better with Dewart than the others. He was a smart, hard-working fellow, right-hand man of Munsey, the aging publisher. Actually, Dewart was more taken with Stella initially, but Munsey advised Dewart to choose Mamie. They were all attractive girls, but probably Munsey was astute.

"After Mary Louise Wheeler married William T. Dewart and moved from Wau Winet to Keewayden, I saw less of her. Mamie always was a rather quite woman, seeming to become more so, or at least becoming more preoccupied with her own family. I followed her family with interest, which was not hard to do since they appeared frequently in Dewart's newspapers (as you can see from my clippings). Mamie's husband died a few years ago, in 1944. He was sixty-nine years old. His sons took over the family business".

"He owned newspapers?"

"Yes, the New York *Sun* and *Telegram*. He had other business interests as well—the chain of Mohican grocery stores among them, I believe."

"Did you visit Keewaydin?"

"Yes, but not often. By the twenties many old friends and acquaintances like Mamie Wheeler had married, had families (as I did not), and had new networks. Our old gang of young river rats gradually broke up. But I remember Keewaydin as a beautiful estate. It was a much larger spread than Wau Winet, since it had a whole farm on the property. There was a long, winding driveway through the rolling, rocky terrain leading from the highway to the main house.

Nannie Margaret Cunningham with the Dewart boys.

With lovely gardens and big lawns, the place was more like a Long Island country house than a summer cottage on an island."

"It's such a big house. They must have had many guests."

"I suppose. Since William Dewart was an important newspaper publisher, many prominent people knew him and were delighted to be his guests. I read recently that Irving S. Cobb was there, for instance. You may not know the humorous writer, since much of his work appeared before you were born. But although there were big house parties at Keewaydin, Mamie never was much of a socialite. She didn't aspire to be the grand dame of the Thousand Islands. But she was a gracious hostess, doing things beautifully. I remember that there always were finger bowls with fresh flowers floating in them at every place on the luncheon table. That was not for special occasions, but every day. Some folks here hardly knew what a finger bowl was for—they were likely to try to drink the water!"

"The Dewarts sound very formal," I suggested.

"Oh, they didn't think so, I'm sure. If you're raised with finger bowls on

Thomas W. Dewart and his older brother, William T. Dewart, Jr., flank the prominent artist Howard Chandler Christy on one of the Keewaydin docks in 1922. The boys' mother, Mary Louise Dewart, stands behind.

the table, it hardly seems formal. Like everyone else, the Dewarts were here for a good time—especially at the cocktail hour. And Mamie's father, after all, was Tom Wheeler—hardly a stuffed shirt. I remember little Mary going over to 'Merryland,' as she designated her favorite place on the estate, to sing out to her grandfather on Wau Winet, across the channel, 'Yes, we have no bananas.'"

"What was Merryland?"

"One of several lesser structures along the shore, between the big house and the Ritters' place, Linden Cove. There are two delightful gazebos, quite charming. Tea was often served in one or another of them.

Keewaydin Gazebo, Keewaydin State Park, 2003

"The Dewarts are among the last hereabouts to maintain the grand life-style—or so I suppose, since I don't see them anymore. They did things with a certain flair. Not caring to have broken plates result in incomplete table settings, William ordered from Syracuse China Company a dozen gross of their 'Poppy' dinner plates. That's 144 plates! They had a service for twelve in that pattern. The family would come in a private railroad car, bringing two chauffeurs—his and hers, along with other staff from Green-wich. There was Margaret Cunningham (the 'picture-no-artist-could-paint'

Irish nannie) and Kathleen Smart, I remember, Mamie's personal maid, and others, I suppose. I believe in recent years they've cut back, retaining merely one chauffeur, but so far as I know the Dewarts are still living luxuriously at Keewaydin, still being chauffeured over to the T.I. Club in that twenty-eight-foot Gar Wood."

"Do you see any of the Dewarts nowadays?"

"Oh, heavens no," Julie laughed. "Look at this place. Could I entertain

"Children of Privilege"

Mary Dewart and houseguest Cecilia ("Ceci") Heurtematte returning from the Thousand Islands Club in the *Vagabond King* about 1928. "The Heurtemattes owned about a quarter of Panama." The launch sports the burgee of the Thousand Islands Yacht Club.

the Dewarts here? I don't have any finger bowls. Mamie has a staff of twelve over in Greenwich. Could I dress for her Park Avenue digs, even if I had a way of getting there? I've been out of touch with the people in that league for many years. Here's a clipping showing the Dewarts at the opening of the Met—the parents and young Tom and his sister, Mary, all in white tie and white ermine. The only opera gear I still have are my old opera glasses."

Julie's mother-of-pearl opera glasses lay on the table next to her albums. With her failing eyesight, they connected her to life on the river today, but also connected her to a past. She once was a patron of the same opera.

Mr. and Mrs. William T. Dewart at the opening of the Metropolitan Opera, New York, 1936

Mary Dewart and her bother Thomas W. Dewart at the opening of the Metropolitan Opera, New York, 1936

Keewaydin house party, 1938. William and Kitty Dewart sit at left, Renata Ingraham and Tom Dewart at right. Taylor Woodward clowns at left; Mary Dewart and her future husband, Frederick B. Gleason, Jr., stand at right.

Keewadin kids, 1927: The boys are Freddy and Wardie McNally. Mary Dewart stands next to Freddy at the left.

Riding party picnic, about 1930.
At right are William T. Dewart, Jr., and his sister Mary (looking displeased).

Mary Dewart and relatives waiting for the skipper at a Keewaydin boathouse, 1924.

Hall at Keewaydin about 1895, when the summer home of the Jacksons.

Following twenty-eight years of ownership by the Jacksons (1893–1921, the Dewarts enjoyed Keewaydin twenty-seven years (1921–1948). Then John K. Wallace, a St. Louis manufacturer, acquired the property. After seven years he leased the estate to the Keewaydin Point Club, which had more than two hundred members. Mr. and Mrs. Klaus W. Hauser operated the club. Wallace sold the property to the State of New York in 1961, when it became Keewaydin State Park. Several years later the major structures were demolished, and the state built a new administration building near the site of the main house.

Mary Dewart, Keewaydin, August 1932

More about William T. Dewart and his family follows in another article.

Interlude: Robert M. Gotham
and his Photographs

The *St. Lawrence* approaching the dock at St. Lawrence Park.

The photograph above and those in the following section were taken by Bob Gotham, who is the subject of the following article. Exceptions may be those in which he appears and the landscape vignettes on pages 80-81, which are photographs of Homer Dodge. Some of Robert Gotham's photographs reproduced here appeared in national journals and regional newspapers.

Bob's Case: A Young Man-About-the-River

Eight-year-old Robert Gotham, with his sister Marion and their dog, Curly, 1899.

A small, loose snapshot slipped from Julie's album onto the floor. Picking it up for her, I was surprised to see two small children. Julie had never spoken of children. I supposed she had none of her own, and it occurred to me that her albums were full of pictures of adults. I guessed these might be her sister Clara's children, but hesitated to inquire, since the subject had never come up.

"Aren't they darlings?" Julie didn't need to see the image to recognize the small photo. "Those are the Gotham children—Marion and Bob, with their dog, Curly. They lived in Watertown, which is where I knew them, while I was there. The Gothams weren't summer people on the river—couldn't afford it. Merrit Gotham, the children's father, was killed in a tragic accident, leaving his wife, Kathryn, a widow with three children. Merrit had been a young industrialist with a factory at Brownville and a promising future, but on his death the family was plunged into need. That was the beginning of 'Bob's Case,' if you know that story, but you probably don't."

"What story?"

"It's called 'Paul's Case,' by Willa Cather. It was quite a sensation here on the river, because it was about Boldt's Waldorf-Astoria—and it's not a pleasant tale. But

Robert M. Gotham on graduation from the University of Pennsylvania, 1916

Tenty-four-year-old Bob Gotham,
St. Lawrence Park, 1915

that's another story, not quite the same, but Paul and Bob have something in common. Bob's still alive, however, and that's quite a difference. I see him now and then, but I can't do much for him. I'm as needy as he.

"Bob came to the river to work, I suppose—but he surely had fun! He was one of those dashing college men who worked summers at the hotels. With the perennial shortage of men on the river, we girls idolized those college boys, even if they were mere waiters here. Bob was an Ivy Leaguer, attending the University of Pennsylvania. This gave him all sorts of elite connections, you see. But of course you don't see yet. Remember that Bob's father had been a successful businessman, but when he died the family had to give up their lovely Brownville home, moving into a two-family house in Watertown, to make ends meet. Bob was obsessed all his life with what he considered to be mistreatment. He was always a victim.

"I never knew how they afforded Bob's college education, but I suppose relatives or scholarships helped. There was some money in the family, but they fought over it—which also contributed to Bob's resentment at his plight. He didn't get what he deserved. That was Bob. You see, he always thought that he was 'to the manor born,' but there was no manor house for his mother and sisters. Instead Bob had to go to work at grand manor houses on the river. As a teenager, he worked for the Sharples. They built that big stone house on the summit of Grenell Island, you know. Later the Clarks hired Bob as a boatman at Comfort Island.

Robert M. Gotham, left, twenty-five--year-old First Mate, with "Chub," deckhand on the yacht *Emily*, 1916.

"Because I had known him as a youngster in town, I recognized Bob when visiting various places—and he was conspicuous, quite a man-about-the-river. He hung out at St. Lawrence Park, where a lively gang called themselves the 'St. Lawrence Park Dock Rat Association.' Bob had everything going for him—looks, education, friends, wealthy patrons—everything but money. I suppose that's why I always felt a special rapport for the guy. I was in the same boat, you see—or had been, at his age.

"Bob is something of a braggart, always name-dropping, reminding us of his enviable connections. Sound familiar? As I say, we have something in common. My associations were mostly social, but Bob supposedly knows many prominent men, mostly friends from his university and fraternity days—some of whom actually exist, giving him handouts or even employment, which never lasts long. Bob gets away with this because of his charm, I suppose. He's still an oddly appealing man, despite his failings.

"I might have been attracted to Bob myself, but he's much younger than I—fifteen years or so, I suppose. When he was cutting such a swath on the river I was married and quite comfortable financially. These were the years just before the First World War—the last days of that golden era of steam yachts. With all the eligible heiresses pining for summer company around here, Bob might have made a good marriage—certainly he was handsome and popular (president of his class)—but he never married. My route to success apparently wasn't to be his.

"Bob had been on the Watertown High School football team, but in college he took to the water, favoring the crew team. He was always drawn to the water. He became first mate on a yacht, then enlisted in the navy to serve as an ensign during the world war.

Robert M. Gotham at Ojibway Inn, Grenell Island, 1922
Bob is the tall fellow, left of center, with arms folded in the second row.
The occasion was the wedding in the Grenell Island Chapel of
Bob's sister Merretta Gotham and William Hinds.

"Bob might have been happier if he'd come back to be a river rat the rest of his years. But he had this sense of being born to something finer, you see. Too bad. After the war, he went to work for the Sharples Corporation—he had worked for the Sharples at Grenell Island, you remember—but he was sent to Oklahoma, of all places. Not much water out there." Julie sighed. "From there it was one job after another. Nothing seemed right for him–for

Robert Gotham's *Cara*

long, that is. He never seemed to advance very far. It's wasn't because of lack of ability. Bob was intelligent and well spoken. He read a lot and had a strong interest in history. He just couldn't get his act together and was always 'down on his luck,' as he'd say.

"With his champagne tastes, Bob forever had a beer income. He did manage to acquire a lovely boat of his own—a small yacht, in fact—which must have been a high point of his life. But Bob is perpetually down and out, between jobs, needing help and pleading for it. People avoid him, expecting a pathetic solicitation. Bob–the fellow who had been so very popular as a young man on the river. It's sad.

"And then there's the alcohol. Bob can make an ass of himself—forgive the expression—becoming obnoxious when he's drinking, which is most of the time, it seems. He'll tell anyone–employers included–what they're doing wrong. That's no way to retain your popularity rating.

"But I still have fond memories of that dashing young Bob Gotham. That's why I've kept these photos. It's the way I want to remember him."

Robert M. Gotham, Clayton, 1969
Bob, in his yachting cap and Penn crew blazer, was seventy-seven years old at the time, four years before his death.

Beyond Julie's recollection, I learned more about Bob Gotham from his family and acquaintances. He fell under the romantic spell of the islands during the summer of 1911, between his junior and senior years at Watertown High School. He took a job as a boatman at St. Lawrence Park's Lotus Hotel. Bob also fell in love with boats. He later recalled how "snow white and graceful steam yachts with such intriguing names as *Neieid, Corona, Morning Star, Empress, Winona,* and *Lotus Seeker* moved by in a seemingly endless stream, . . . an unending . . . array of water-borne craft of all kinds, from big Lake freighters, Line steamers, motor cruisers, speed boats, naphtha launches and sailboats to fast, motor-powered St. Lawrence skiffs." Bob's job as boatman required him to take parties out on the river in a motorboat that "glided between islands dotted with 'castles' bearing names that might have come from a story book–St. Elmo, Hopewell Hall, Castle Rest, Fairyland, and Bonnie Castle."

One-Step

The following summer Bob was employed by the Clark family at nearby Comfort Island, which he described as "an immense three-story cottage atop of which a lofty four-story tower reared a tapered peak to the sky." He enjoyed working and playing with the family boats—and socializing with staff, guests, and friends at nearby St. Lawrence Park. Bob was acquainted with many Watertown families there, such as the Skinners, Taylors, C. H. Remingtons, and Kemps. One of his pals, Copley Clark from nearby Chaumont, had a small catboat converted into a miniature cruiser, the *One-Step*. The pair explored the islands and then Bob quit his job so that the two young men could take a cruise around "the Triangle"–down through the rapids to Montreal, up the Ottawa River to Ottawa, then back through the Rideau Canal.

Bob's love for boats led him to become Captain George Comstock's summertime mate aboard the yacht *Emily*. His wintertime education led to a degree in economics from the Wharton School of the University of Pennsylvania. After graduation Bob enlisted in the navy, serving as an ensign on a troop carrier.

Robert M. Gotham died at Watertown, age eighty-one, in 1973. He was buried in the Military Cemetery at Sackets Harbor. Bob was an avid amateur photographer with his own darkroom. He left a visual record of a young man's life on the river in the last heydays of the Thousand Islands.

Comfort Island, where Robert Gotham was employed, remains in the Clark family that built it some 120 years ago. It is remarkably unchanged.

Bob's nephew, Dr. William Hinds (who has contributed many of these illustrations), recalls that when last they visited, "all he wanted to talk about was his life on the river as a youngster. It was always obvious to me that the love of his life was the St. Lawrence River."

The *Winnetka*, yacht of the Alson E. Clark family of Comfort Island.

Captain and Mate

Robert M. Gotham's naval career began on the river. Here, at right, he serves as mate
to Captain George Comstock of Alexandria Bay aboard the steam yacht *Emily*.

Robert M. Gotham
206 Franklin St. Apt. 311 **1912**
Watertown, N. Y. 13601

A real genuine old
time St. Lawrence
Skiff under Lug
sail, without using
rudder + had <u>no keel</u>.

Sailing it is Jared
(Chub) Massey of
Alex. Bay a sailor
aboard steam yacht
Winnetka owned by
the A.E. Clark family of
Comfort Island.

This Skiff is now owned
by Mancel T. Clark, gn. + now
sailed by his son, T.A.D. During
42 years that Comfort Island
was in non-use, Skiff was on
saw horses on front porch of the
cottage. I made inspection +
took inventory of Comfort Island in
June, 1957.

"Taking His Ease," Bob Gotham aboard the *Winnetka*.

The twenty-two-foot *Comfort*, one of the Clarks' boats at Comfo rt Island, 1912. Bob Gotham is at the helm of a "motor-powered St. Lawrence skiff." The Burkes' Jewel Island appears in the distance.

St. Lawrence Park belles, 1911
Alyse M. Tyson, left, and Marion R. Clark on the lawn of the Lotus Hotel.

St. Lawrence Park beaus, 1911
"St. Lawrence Park Dock Rat Association," Bob Gotham at left.

The *One-Step* landed for a picnic.

The "Dock Rat Association" off to see the Gold Cup Races aboard the day cruiser *Sprite II*, owned by H. R. Harris of St. Lawrence Park. Captain was W. H. Gould of Fine View.

The *Newsboy* was something of a joke, considered practically derelict even about 1912, when the heyday of the resort was ending.

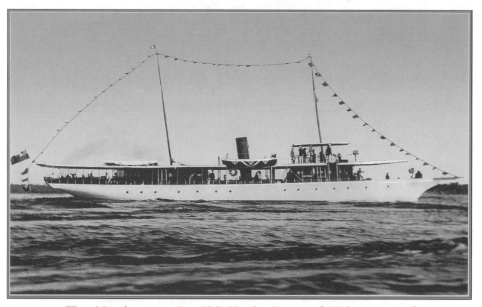

The *Magedoma* carrying H.R.H. the Prince of Wales, guest of Senator Fulford of Brockville, on a cruise of the Thousand Islands.

St Lawrence Park dock

"The Last Windjammer"

Robert Gotham took this remarkable photograph of the three-masted schooner *Bertie Calkins* from the St. Lawrence Park dock in 1911—when, ironically, even the age of steam was almost over. The commerical sailing vessel was a relic of a previous age. The 127-foot vessel was built in 1875 at Manitowoc, Wisconsin.

A Schultz family picnic

Oak Lodge

Carl Schultz

III. Homosassa (Oak Lodge),
Wawbeek (Granny Hill), and Little Watch Island

The Schultzes at Homosassa

Oh, there were so many big, happy families here," Julie recalled. "I suppose this was always something of a family resort, where people settled in—more so than a place like Saratoga, I daresay, which was focused on adult amusements such as gambling, horse racing, and flirting (not that we didn't have some of each here, for sure). Big, happy families were the rule, however, even if some were stressed and strained, given the remarkable personalities of these achievers.

"I think of Tom Wheeler, who we were talking about, and George Boldt. If there was a parallel between these self-made men, who cast off into the competitive world at an early age—then another islander who belonged to this club surely was Carl Schultz."

"I never heard the Schultz name here. Where were they?"

"I don't wonder. They've been gone from Oak Lodge for quite a while, although some of the family is elsewhere on the river still."

"Oak Lodge—that's on Wellesley Island, across from Keewaydin?"

"More or less. The big house with the massive stone pillars running around it. It's one of the Kincaid places now. R. Leland Kincaid (he was 'Robert,' actually) bought it from the Schultzes in 1926. General Kincaid—that's J. Leslie (his first name was 'James')—is across the channel, at Idle

Isle. He's a brigadier general, I believe—in the National Guard, or something like that."

"I've heard of him," I volunteered. "They say on the boat tour that he's president of some hotel corporation. They live not far from us in Syracuse, on Robineau Road, near Mayor Marvin, but we don't know those people."

"Oh? I remember the general having one of those big houses on Onondaga Avenue back when I visited Syracuse. I suppose they moved. Their place was that odd-looking stone house with a pair of stepped gables in the front, as I remember it."

"That's the American Legion now—the place with the big cannon out in front."

"But I was going to tell you about the Schultz family at Oak Lodge—or at 'Homosassa,' as they called the place originally. I can see why *that* name was dropped! They even had a boat named *Homosassa*. Robert Kincaid called the place 'Oak Lodge' after he got it. But to go back to the beginning:

"Carl Schultz was like his friend George Boldt in many ways. Both were German born and German speaking, as both came to the United States when young. No, more correctly, I should say that Boldt was Prussian and Schultz Austrian, but both spoke German.

"The Schultz family was poor. Carl got an education because they had free schools in Austria at the time. Carl was very bright, as his later success suggests—as did his admission to a university. He studied chemistry while teaching mathematics on the side and giving private tutoring in chemistry to pay his way. Carl was smart enough to sense that opportunity was limited in Austria, so he made his way to America, coming in 1853. That was eleven years before Boldt. Schultz was twenty-four years older than Boldt, which is one reason Schultz is not so well remembered on the river. Carl Schultz died in the spring of 1897. He was more George Pullman's contemporary.

"Carl found chemist's employment in New York City. Some objection was raised because he was an employee of a public department but was not a U.S. citizen. He immediately applied and became very proud of his American identity.

"Carl lived in New York City on a modest income. He spent his available time on chemical research, investigating the properties of mineral waters that were highly touted at the time for health-giving properties. His big breakthrough came when it occurred to him that the mineral-spring waters then prized for their natural carbonation could be artificially produced.

Dr. Carl Schultz, second from left, and his wife, Louise,
right, with two daughters and probably sons and guides.

The novel siphon bottle, introduced in France, could keep the water fresh
and sparkling. Carl's association with the medical community proved valuable in introducing the bottled water as healthful. Schultz began his New
York City production of bottled water during the Civil War, in 1862, two
years before thirteen-year-old Boldt would arrive there. Schultz went into the
business with a partner who had brought the siphon bottle from France.
Schultz duplicated the chemical components of some thirty natural mineral
waters and after the Civil War opened a 'spring house' in Central Park.

"This inspired idea proved very successful. City physicians prescribed
drinking of the water together with walks in the park as healthful for patients.
Carl Schultz was a successful business entrepreneur, but, like William H.
Nichols of Nokomis Lodge, Schultz was also a respected chemist. Carl
Schultz was a member of four scientific societies.

"Carl Schultz was characterized as 'an aggressive character, a staunch
friend, a thorough worker, and a firm believer in his method of business and
enterprise.' He was, however, quite a homebody—after all, he and his wife,
Louise, had eleven children—and you can imagine the number of grandchildren! That's why Oak Lodge was such a family place. Schultz differed from
Boldt in this way. Boldt was much more the public figure, always on stage at

the Waldorf-Astoria—as he wanted his own Louise to be (which became part of their problem, but that's another story). Carl Schultz was rarely to be seen at the Waldorf, for sure, since he hated to leave home for social functions."

"Did Schultz know Boldt?"

"I suppose, since they were both upper-class German Americans in New York City. But Boldt was younger, just becoming a millionaire when Schultz died. That was 1897. The Boldts hadn't started the castle project yet.

Homosassa (Oak Lodge) about 1900

"The Schultzes had a big house over in New Jersey—described as 'a magnificent residence' with a model farm. The family came to the river occasionally before Carl died. Then Louise, his widow, decided they needed a place of their own here for all of her grandchildren to get together. Captain Bill Norton rowed Louise over from the Bay to look at a point on Wellesley Island. She bought the property from Sisson and Fox, the Alexandria Bay merchants and landowners. She then built a big house, which she called 'Homosassa.' The family first enjoyed the place during the summer of 1900.

"On the river the Schultz family became active socially, several members belonging to the Thousand Islands and Chippewa Bay Yacht Clubs. Louise's sons Rudy and Walter were well known on the river. One daughter, Orla, built another fine summer home here. Several daughters became linked to other river families through marriages. The youngest child of Carl and Louise, Elsie, became Elsie Vilas after marrying Ward A. Vilas, son of Royal and Carrie Vilas of nearby Oswagatchie Point. Confusingly, Ward's sister also was named Elsie Vilas, at least until she married John Harold Hayden of Fairyland. Another Vilas sister, Eleanor, married Andrew McNally. You probably know McNally-Ravenel places on Wellesley Island and adjoining Island Royal. The great Boldt houseboat has been a landmark there for many decades.

Family fishing at Homosassa. Grandma Louise Schultz is at the left.

"The Schultzes were active outdoors people. Three of the girls were proficient tennis players—Elsie, Marie, and Augusta. Marie Shultz Auferman was regarded as one of the best players in the country, while Augusta became a professional tennis player. She was 1893 runner-up in the National Women's Singles Finals (now the U.S. Open). Augusta and her husband, Clarence Hobart, in 1905 became the only husband and wife team ever to win the U.S. Open Mixed Doubles Championship. Elsie recalled that when Clarence played with them, they made him use his left hand.

"I remember the Schultz family as lively and fun-loving—and certainly colorful. Rudy—that was son Carl Rudolph (all the boys were named

'Carl')– through friendship with the chief of police in New York City, had a police siren on his car. He would roar through Manhattan with the siren blaring. On the river Rudy used the brass eagle atop the flagpole for target practice and riddled it with holes. The boys, after a night of drinking, decided to get rid of the old furniture in the house, dumping it in the river. Rudy's brother Carl Walter was a big-game hunter, bringing home trophies such as a polar bear. Three of the four brothers attended Yale and other graduate schools, the fourth went to Columbia and on to graduate school. All seven sisters attended the elite Miss Porter's School in Connecticut.

"The active and athletic family enjoyed fishing and boating. Among many craft they had the charming old *Lithia,* with its fringed canopy. They liked this one so well they transported it back and forth to Florida. More remarkable was the *Apache,* skippered by Fred Comstock. Built in Boston in 1898, she was 'odd in appearance, being modeled after a German torpedo boat.' Rudy's new *Apache* was 65 feet long with a 250 horse-power engine, going eighteen miles-per-hour. This was in 1903, when internal combustion engines were just beginning to supplant steam engines for yachts. Rudy also bought the notable *So-Long II* from George Hasbrouk of Manhattan Island.

Schultz Picnic

Louise Schultz hollers at the camera, seated in the center. Her son Carl Rudolph Schultz and his wife, a couple particularly well known on the river, are seated at right. A grandson, Carl H. Schultz III, is seated at the left. The elderly woman next to Louise is unidentified, probably one of her friends. Two attending boatmen stand in the back.

"The Schultz family was a close one. Father Carl built ten substantial homes for his children surrounding his own New Jersey establishment. Mother Louise gathered her brood at Homosassa each summer. One who knew her personally characterized her as 'a woman of great beauty (honey blond) and force of character. She was revered by her large family, and she ruled them with inflexible but gentle firmness throughout her long and happy life.' I never know the elder Carl Schultz well, but his wife, Louise, was a wonderful person, not merely pleasant and considerate, but clear headed and responsible—in a word, 'solid.'

Louise Eisfeldt Schultz, Baroness Sievers

"Louise ran business and family with the same firm hand—with such ease and assurance! And just when we all thought Louise had settled into being a doting grandma, when nearly seventy she went off to Europe again and came back the Baroness Sievers. It was quite a sensation—totally unexpected. Baron Richard Sievers, a native of Hamburg, was the emperor's consul to South America, but they were married in London. Naturally there was concern about the Schultz millions, fear that she was senile, he a fortune hunter.

Louise Schultz and grandchildren

"Under German law, a woman's property belonged to her husband. The baron would get it all, if she died first. But, as I said, Louise was solid. She had her expert attorneys draw up a prenuptial agreement. I'll bet the kids were relieved to learn that!

"Louise's son Rudy seems to be the more vividly remembered of the brothers, being 'the type of man that once you met him you would never forget him.' Carl Rudoph was noted in the *New York Times* for becoming 'one of if not the youngest, age 27, bank presidents in the country.' The bank was the Equitable National Bank in New York City. Rudy also served as president of the Carl H. Schultz Mineral Water Company.

Boats and boatman at Homosassa

A photograph of this scene prior to construction of the Schultz summer home appears on the cover of Susan Smith's book, *The First Summer People*.

"Rudy's first wife, Clara Shields, was a favorite of President McKinley. Mrs. McKinley announced their engagement at a White House dinner. Rudy and his brother Carl Walter were 'ardent sportsmen, hunters and travelers who loved life and lived it with zest.' Rudy and Walter were both members of the Thousand Islands Yacht and Country Club, as was mother Louise and her son-in-law Ernest Rubsamen (or 'E. B.,' as we called him).

"Rudy sued Fitz Hunt, the Alexandria Bay builder of his *So-Long II*, because her speed, he maintained, had dwindled from the guaranteed twenty-three miles per hour to nineteen. It was odd, since Fitz hadn't built the boat for Rudy, but for George Hasbrouck who had *So-Longs I, II* and *III* which he raced. I don't recall how the suit came out, but I doubt Rudy had much of a case as second owner of the boat.

"Of the daughters, Elsie Vilas, who married into that other prominent river family, and her sister Orla are best remembered here—although surely Marie and Augusta, like Elsie, her tennis-playing sisters, were better known nationally."

The Rubsamens at Wawbeek

"What was Orla noted for?"

"Oh, Orla?" Julie laughed. "Orla was a character, a 'woman of powerful personality' who married E. B. Rubsamen and built Wawbeek on 'Granny Hill', as that high point had been called and the place once again is called."

"Wawbeek?"

"Another odd name, to go with 'Orla': 'Wawbeek'–that's Algonquin for 'big rock.' Do you know where the house is? It's on the point just below Brown's Bay, high above the water. They built it up on huge stone walls and piers over a great mound of granite. Do you know the place?"

"Yes, but I supposed that house was more modern."

"It looks it, doesn't it? But it was built back in 1904. Leave it to Orla to have an odd house. But by 'odd' I don't mean disagreeable. It's so much more livable and attractive than many of the big barns of houses built at the time. And such a location–what a view–and right on top of the passing parade, yachts, steamboats (or freighters these days).

Elsie Schultz Vilas, right, with friend Vera Auforman aboard the *Lithia*

Wawbeek (Granny Hill), the Ernest B. Rubsamen summer home, is virtually unchanged since it was built in 1904. The house is remarkable for its
unusual design, innovative for the period, and for its spectacular site in an
elevated position on the Wellesley Island point immediately below
Brown's Bay. In the words of an annual visitor, "It's a house to die for."

"Orla was the eldest of the eleven children—quite a bit older than Elsie, the youngest, who was more my age. Elsie, remembered here on the river as Elsie Vilas, Ward's wife, was considered the 'wild, wild one' of the family, but I'd say they were all cut-ups, especially Orla. Wawbeek was a real party house, full of New York City guests. No one ever went to bed before three or four in the morning there. They shipped up the Schultz soda and Vichy water by the barrel and had 'soda fights,' shaking bottles as weapons. Then, to rouse the weary party-makers in the morning, Orla sometimes climbed up on a chair in the hall and through the transom squirted the water into the room with a garden hose—or son Herbert would drop firecrackers down the chimneys into bedroom fireplaces. Then when the alarmed guests tried to escape from the room, they might find the doors tied shut from the outside.

The Rubsamens
E.B. sits at left, next Orla. Son Herbert stands behind his father, next
to sister Pauline (Polly) and her husband, Samuel Cutler. Polly's sister
Orla Louise sits on the arm of her mother's chair.

"Like most women on the river at the time, Orla would come at the end of May and stay into September. There was no heat at Wawbeek other than the many fireplaces. Orla was an avid fisherwoman, as was her daughter Pauline. They went out with guides, but did much fishing right from the large boathouse dock. There was a 'one-holer' outhouse at the boathouse for convenience—it was quite a climb back up to the main house. When fishing with Orla, granddaughter Polly went to use the facility and, looking down through the hole, saw a large pike right below. She called Grandma, who rushed in and landed the fish through the hole.

"The Wawbeek house was full of mounted fish. It was that sort of place—unlike some of the more pretentious and elegantly decorated villas. Wawbeek was no mere camp, however. There were ten or twelve bedrooms in a two-story wing—otherwise the house was all on one floor—very modern for the day. The upper bedrooms opened onto a balcony with a stuffed hawk on the railing, overlooking the grand main hall. At the opposite end was a colossal stone fireplace that took six-foot logs. This big living space opened onto a high terrace overlooking the river—the glory of the house, inviting with wicker chairs and loose cushions. Part of the stone terrace was covered, but there was no conventional porch. The house was unlike the usual Victorian cottages on the river.

"The dining room was up four steps from the main hall and the service wing, with two maids' rooms beyond that. The house wasn't huge but just right for comfort and entertaining. I always thought I'd like to live there. Because the Rubsamens enjoyed big parties, there were extra guest rooms in the boathouse. There was also a three-bedroom caretaker's house where the boat captain and his wife lived year-round. I also recall an icehouse built into that steep hill. The boat captain-caretaker cut the ice during the winter. I think there was a small boathouse in addition to the large one, as well as a pump house where the Delco electric generator was—at least that was a common arrangement for these places.

"Wawbeek was a wonderful place to be at 4:30 every afternoon. Then one of the steamboats that ran from Kingston to the Bay would be saluted with a cannon on the terrace—these 'sunset guns' were found on many islands. The big boat invariably saluted back, and this daily ritual signaled the cocktail hour, which extended two and a half hours until dinner was served at seven—with wine of course, and the evening extending to the wee hours of the morning, with much scotch washed down with Schultz soda.

The main hall at Wawbeek is dominated by a fireplace with a massive granite chimney rising in the two-story space.

Wawbeek dining room

"Orla was quite a rum runner during Prohibition days—for home consumption, of course. They brought back scotch from Canada in twelve-case lots, using the children as decoys. Granddaughter Polly remembers riding with her knees up to her chin, because of all the cases on the deck. The kids always were given ice cream cones as props, the idea being that the agents would never suspect this happy family to be smuggling liquor. The captain dropped the family off at Wawbeek, unloaded the contraband, then went to the Bay to report in at customs. They moved huge quantities of liquor this way and were never caught at their little game.

"The Rubsamens carried lots of liquor back to New Jersey with them, again using the children as shields. On one occasion they placed two rows of bottles under an infant grandson in a basket. The railroad porter commented, 'Boy, this sure is a heavy baby.'

"All the Rubsamens shared the Schultz tennis mania. They had courts at Wawbeek, of course. Orla herself was an East Coast doubles champion and her son E. B. Jr. won several silver cups at the T.I. Country Club.

"Orla was also a bridge fiend. We all played, of course—that was what one did on rainy days, or into the small hours of the morning. When Orla first came to the river in May she would bring three bridge partners with her, and they

E. B. Rubsamen on the Wawbeek tennis court.
The caretaker's house appears at left.

would play all day and evening, since the weather often was not obliging."

"Did the Rubsamens have a yacht?"

"No, they were too busy fishing, or playing tennis and bridge, to be in the trophy boat club. Of course they had boats. We went over in their *#4* at first, then later it was the *Bottoms Up*. That was a Chris Craft that carried about ten people. Then they had what was termed a 'market boat,' used mostly for carrying provisions, but it was big enough to carry eight to twelve wicker chairs. That was the *E.B.R.* I think that one went to Mcnally's along with their boat captain, whose name I recall was Clifford. He was said to be the youngest captain on the river when I first knew him.

"There were only two servants' rooms at Wawbeek, partly because Clifford and his wife lived in their own house on the property, and because some help came in. I remember the wonderful baked goods that Mrs. Booth made. She rowed her boat across Browns Bay twice a week to spend a whole day baking. Everyone treasured Mrs. Booth."

"I would think that these sporting people would have been interested in racing fast boats."

"Oh, you're right. E. B. Jr. raced, perhaps in the Gold Cup events. I believe he won something in some races. But the Gold Cup was the major league. I'd say the Rubsamens were minor league—or perhaps I should say that they were sports enthusiasts who were not so trophy-conscious as some in their class, like the Peacocks, for instance. You see, the Rubsamens weren't new rich. Orla was second-generation; so was Ernest."

"Could the family afford to stay on the river?"

"You keep asking me about people's finances. How would I know? When E. B. Rubsamen died in 1925, Orla continued to come but wanted regular company so she asked her daughter Polly and her family to share her homes, including Wawbeek. I don't think Orla needed assistance in carrying the place, however, since she seemed to be very wealthy until the stock market crash of 1929. That affected many people on the river—like me. The family sold Wawbeek in 1933, during the Depression."

"Did Rubsamen work?" Julie laughed at my supposition.

"E. B. wasn't a fortune hunter. His family was wealthy, and he was making plenty of money in his own right."

"Doing what?"

"He was a silk manufacturer, with factories in Patterson, New Jersey, and in Binghamton, New York. He also served as mayor of a New Jersey borough and was active on the borough council—no loafer, to be sure.

"Orla's sister Irma also married a Rubsamen—Ernest's brother, Louis. Their father was a banker and member of the New York Stock Exchange. Louis himself became a member as an independent Wall Street operator when only twenty-five years old. The Schultz girls married well—probably reflecting their mother's sound influence."

The Foords at Little Watch Island

The Foords' Little Watch Island

"Another of the Schultz girls stayed on the river. Daughter Pauline Schultz married Dr. Andrew Green Foord. They acquired Little Watch Island near Goose Bay where they had a smaller cottage and a houseboat, the *AK*.

"The Foords lived quite simply. Their little houseboat was hardly more than a floating cabin. No Herreshoff yacht for them. The Foords didn't make such a splash in the river, so aren't well remembered. Pauline wasn't such a vivid personality as her sister Orla. But she made a good match. Andrew was quite a handsome man. The Foords were quiet, nice people."

Homosassa boathouse with the Foord's *AK*

"Not so rich as the Schultzes, though."

"There you go again! Dr. Foord owned a very successful sanitarium. I expect they had a very adequate income, my friend. Andrew was a respected physician, a fellow of the American Medical Association. His father, John, was editor-in-chief of the *New York Times*.

The Foords' houseboat *AK* before it was expanded by adding a second story

"The Foords had four children—a lovely family. Again, the Schultz girls made good matches.

"Some of Pauline's seven sisters married stockbrokers who advised mother Louise. She 'played the market and did quite well.' Louise had a fine winter home on the St. John's River at Green Cove Springs, Florida. That's where the Indian name 'Homosassa' came from."

"I know. I've been to the state park there to see the manatees."

"It was an elite enclave of sportsmen back in Carl Schultz's time. He was quite a hunter. I suppose Louise kept the place for her sons, who also were serious hunters.

"Louise traveled often to Europe, invariably crossing after the birth of each of her eleven children. Remember that like the Boldts, the Schultzes were bilingual. I'd imagine them chatting fluently in German with their neighbors the Ritters, and probably the Boldts as well."

"Who were the Ritters?"

"They were at Linden Cove, on the mainland, just above Keewaydin, which is more or less across the river from Oak Lodge, as we call it now. When I knew the Ritters' daughters they called the place 'Lindenhof.' The German name went with World War I, when these folks stopped conversing in German. Frank Ritter built a fine summer home after he retired from his Rochester business, which was making dental equipment. He had the German background in common with Boldt and Straus, but was older. Laura Ritter and the Shumways stayed on at Linden Cove, as they now call it."

Pauline Foord aboard the *AK*

Dr. Andrew Foord aboard the *AK*

"Did the Schultz children inherit wealth?"

"I wouldn't know about their finances, would I? I do know, however, that the company, then known as 'Carl H. Schultz (A Corporation),' went bankrupt in the 1920s, but it was no longer family owned at that time and the Schultz had many other business interests. But, as you can imagine with eleven children, there are many, many descendents today—the pie no doubt had to be sliced into many slivers. With those Schultz genes, however, I expect many of the grandchildren are doing very well."

Carl Rudolph's wife, Minerva Schultz
(standing),with friends visiting Diamond Island

Oak Lodge is still one of the grand houses of the Thousand Islands. With twenty-two rooms (sixteen bedrooms), it was not so large as some very grand villas here, but the house was said to be "one of the most costly in the region" when built. The house is especially distinctive since it is so little changed in more than a century. Oak Lodge has been in the Kincaid-Vars-Breslin families since acquired fully furnished from the Schultz family in 1926. One of two original boathouses remains. The lost one contained mechanical equipment, no longer required. There also was a caretaker's house and an icehouse with separate rooms for meat and dairy products.

Wawbeek, now called "Granny Hill," likewise remains a river landmark, owned by the Schmidt family for several generations. Architect of the remarkable building is unknown, but the design clearly evidences the hand of a designer considerably ahead of his or her time. Very few large houses were built in this one-story manner at the time, 1904, before the bungalow rage. At the time Frank Lloyd Wright was just developing his low, sprawling prairie-style model. The pronounced horizontal lines, banded windows, and hipped roof suggest this precedent—but the midwestern movement had little influence in this region, particularly at such an early date. One notable New York State example, Frank Lloyd Wright's 1904 Martin House in Buffalo, was exactly contemporary with Wawbeek. Closer, we have White Oaks, above Clayton on the mainland (page 306). This house likewise was remarkably "modern" for its time, with some details similar to those at Wawbeek. Possibly both were the work of the same skilled designer.

Schultz boat at Alexandria Bay

Homosassa (Oak Lodge) Interiors

The use of varnished wood on all surfaces—walls, ceilings, and floor—was typical of Thousand Islands cottages, since in unheated buildings plaster proved vulnerable to cracking with large temperature changes in this northern climate.

Looking into the Homosassa dining room

Interlude: "Exciting Struggle with a Muskallonge"

WALTON HOUSE, CLAYTON, Tuesday, July 31, 1860.

Where is Clayton? Asks the reader. It is a small town in Jefferson County, on the St. Lawrence River, formerly called French Creek, and famous as a dépôt for lumber to be rafted down the river. The trade is sparingly carried on yet, some seven or eight schooners making regular trips for oak and pine, to the upper lakes, discharge their cargoes here, to be cribbed and floated down to Montreal and Quebec in larger rafts. Clayton is located at the upper end of the Thousand Islands, and is becoming noted as a fishing-ground for muskallonge, pickerel and black bass. The fishing is generally very good, except during and immediately after a heavy blow; then the water is milky, and the fish are unable to see the decoy at any great distance. Till within two years the accommodations at Clayton were quite indifferent; now there are two other hotels, beside the Walton House, which is kept by STEPHEN DECATUR JOHNSTON. This fishing is peculiar in its character. Your landlord engages your guide, with boat and tackle, for one dollar and a half a day, to serve you from dawn to dark if you wish to fish as early and as late. Wooden rods, supported entirely by the boat, one reaching out upon one side, and the other upon the other, with lines attached about 1000 feet long, with spoons or decoys, and a drag-line from the stern about 150 feet in length, comprises the tackle. A seat is provided for the sportsman, which is generally a cushioned chair in the stern-sheets of the boat, and he sits face to the guide. In this luxurious and easy position he can amuse himself when the fish are not active in smoking, reading, viewing and admiring the quiet scenery of the beautiful islands surrounded by the crystal waters, or, if he so inclines, can sleep, relying upon his quide to wake him when he has a *strike*. The guide rows you over the best ground, if you are not personally acquainted with it, and the most uninitiated are enable to tell when a fish seizes the decoy. They hand over hand with the line, slowly, till Mr. Fish makes his appearance near the boat, and the great skill is in landing him safely. A large one requires the gaff; a smaller one is seized just back of the head with the hand, and a smaller one still is jerked in unceremoniously. A good day's sport gives so many that at night a true sportsman feels ashamed to look upon such murder. The muskallonge vary in weight from 15 to 65 pounds; the pickerel from 2 to 20 pounds; the black bass from one to four pounds. It is not uncommon to see little boys and girls in skiffs rowing about the river trolling. One day last week a small lad was thus engaged in the bay near the vessels lying at the wharf, when he "fasterned" (a local term) to a muskal-longe. Being alone in the boat, with no implements to secure him or kill him, and the fish being about as heavy as the boy, it was a fair and for a long time seemed to be a very doubtfully-resulting fight. The lad, however, had the advantage; for while the fish was being weakened by the struggle, the boy held his own. The boat swayed round and round as the muskallonge struck out right and left, till at last the lad succeeded in getting Mr. Muskallonge's head over the gunwale, and by one sudden convulsion of the fish in he came with the boat. And now the reader may suppose the fight was ended. Not so: for it had but just begun, for the boats sit low upon the water and these fish, averaging about five feet in length, will go overboard, if not prevented, quicker than they come in. The little fellow let go the line, and seized Mr. Muskallonge around the body, and a rough and tumble scuffle ensued upon the bottom of the boat, the fish being first uppermost and then the boy; but he held on, and hollored stoutly for help, when one of the guides, seeing his condition, shot out with his boat from the shore, and towed in the contend-ing parties. But the little fellow never relinquished his hold till the club was appplied to the muskallonges's head, when it was ascertained the fish weighed 48 1/2 pounds. Mr. Johnson, the proprietor of the Walton House, sent the fish to the proprietor of the Everett House, in New-York.

Sportsmen who wish to try their hand at such game can leave New-York at 6 o'clock A.M., and be at Cape Vincent at 8 P.M., where they can get a good night's rest, and the express boat from the Falls will take them up at five o'clock in the morning, and in an hour will land them at Clayton, in time for a day's fishing.

RAMBLER
New York Times, August 10, 1860

Interlude: Julie and Clara

Julie and Clara

Parents, husbands, friends . . . ," Julie sighed. "So many gone—and here I am, still going." She laughed. "Well, good for me. But I miss them—and mostly my little sister, Clara. We were very close. I had so many chapters in my life, with so many people—enjoyed every one of them—but throughout it all there was always Clara. She was my only family, towards the end. And then she went. That was the greatest shock, after losing my parents, brother, husbands.

"I'm sure I've told you how we were 'those Bingham girls' when young—quite a pair, and we cut quite a swath here on the river. Clara was not so tall as I and far prettier. My height was a certain advantage on the stage, but there was always the problem of being taller than the man. Clara was really more the natural belle—quite a charmer.

"I suppose we both were born with happy dispositions. Certainly Clara's sunny nature contributed to her popularity. Maybe we were a bit flighty—I'm sure that some people thought us rather . . . 'liberated' for the time. Of course my being on the stage contributed to

Clara and Julie on the river

that notion." She laughed heartily. "And I did my best to live up to our reputation! We had quite a time, here on the river, back in the days when there was a social whirl. We came on the scene just at the right time, when the children of many island families were our age—and they had lots of sons. Oh, those Peacock and Rafferty boys with their fast boats—sportsmen, athletes, party-goers. Those were the days!"

IV. The Terrys at Woronoco

Woronoco Island

Charles Terry was a corporate lawyer—one of the few professional men to own prominent island establishments. Terry bought Whortleberry (or Huckleberry) Island, changing the name to Woronoco, and constructed a summer home there in 1895 for his family—wife, Marie; daughter, Catherine; and son, Matson.

As a young patent attorney, Charles Terry met inventor George Westinghouse. They became warm, lifelong friends, and Terry for nearly fifty years served as counsel and vice president of the Westinghouse Electric and Manufacturing Company. Terry was central to Westinghouse's battle to establish alternating current as the standard system. Terry obtained patents for many of Westinghouse's inventions that transformed the electrical industry: alternating current motors, transformers, and steam turbines.

Charles Appleton Terry (1858–1939) graduated from Amherst College in 1879 and Columbia University Law School in 1883. As an attorney he had a professional office in New York City, where he resided with his family on the upper west side. Marie Terry was actively concerned with maintaining the visual quality of the Riverside Drive neighborhood. The Terrys were listed in the *New York Social Register,* and he was a prominent club man in the City.

Charles Terry and his family enjoyed their island regularly for many years. They rented it for the 1908 season, however—perhaps because of a trip abroad, which was common. The Terrys didn't open the place in 1911 but stayed at the nearby Murray Hill Hotel instead. Perhaps work was being done on the island. They purchased neighboring Basswood Island that year, perhaps intending to move there. Charles Terry served on the "general committee in charge of affairs" of the Grenell Island Chapel.

The Terrys had an estate at Old Lyme, Connecticut. Charles Terry died at age eighty in 1939, survived by his his wife, Marie E. Cady Terry, and their daughter, Catherine (Mrs. William N. Ross of Nyack, N.Y.), and son, Matson C. Terry of Marmoneck, N.Y.

The Terry yacht, *Woronoco*

The Terry fleet at Woronoco Island, Basswood Island in the distance.

Interlude: THE THOUSAND ISLANDS

SUMMERING IN THE ST. LAWRENCE

BLACK AGAINST WHITE—RIVAL HOTEL RUNNERS— FISHING AND FLIRTING—HOW DIFFERENT PEOPLE AMUSE THEMSELVES—A FOUR-AND-A-HALF-POUND BASS— THE RESULT OF REDUCED PRICES—A PROSPEROUS SEASON

From our Special Correspondent

ALEXANDRIA BAY, N. Y.,
Sunday, July 15, 1877.

At 6:30 o'clock in the morning the stanch old steamer *Passport*, of the Toronto Line—this is her thirty-second season—stops at what is called on the bills Rockport, and passengers for the Thousand Islands are disembarked. Yesterday, together with a dozen other sleepy and not altogether amiable mortals, I landed at the place, and found that it was, indeed, everything that its name implies—a rocky port. Moored to the little dock was a miniature steamer to convey visitors across the St. Lawrence and through the Island Channel to Alexandria Bay; which of late years has become the most frequented Summer resort in Northern New-York. On the boat were two hotel runners, characters in their way and well worthy of a short description. The one, a great, big, hulking Irishman, with an air of indolence and squalor about him that reminded one forcibly of Queenstown and the Cove of Cork, represented, or as he said himself, "riprisinted" the Crossmon House. This, he explained, with that rapid flow of language for which his countrymen are noted, was "the most illigent hotel to be found anywhere for miles around." Continuing he said, "Yis, indeed, ladies an' gintlemen, there's not an establishment in the vicinity like it. Everything nate an' clain as a new churn, plenty to ate, particularly fish, which is served every day, not exceptin' Fridays," this with a sly wink, "and all for $2 a day, an' less if you stay long enough to make it an object." This speech was evidently having its effect upon the tourists, when runner No. 2, a handsome young South Carolina negro, dressed in a natty uniform of blue flannel and gold lace, interrupted it with a contemptuous pshaw! Then, having silenced his Irish rival and gained the attention of the audience, he continued:

A NEGRO HOTEL RUNNER'S ADDRESS.

Ladies an' Gemmens: I represents de Thousand Island House, which de same is de best in Nordern New-York, and dat is beyond disputin'. As for de rival house, which is a place not fit for ladies an' gemmens like you to inhabit, I will say nottin but ask one question, and dat is, How can a fust-class house give board for de miseble sum of $2 per day, an' less if you refuse to pay so much for such poor 'commodations!" Here the gentleman from the Crossmon House interrupted his dusky contemporary with, "Say what you like about your own oppartments, but don't dare to be spakin' agin mine."

"Very well, Sar," continued the negro, not at all disconcerted, "I'll do zactly as you desire; an' for your information as well as dat of de ladies and gentlemen, I repeats de Thousand Island House is de finest in this part of de land'; best table, best rooms, billiard saloon an' bowling-alley attached, an' de new invention in de medical science—a blue grass conservatory—free to guests." This address was greeted with shouts of laughter by the passengers, and as they neared the landing there was more than one anxious inquiry for "de blue grass conservatory." Whether it was the wonderful speech of the gentleman from South Carolina, or a desire to see that "newest invention in de medical science," I am, of course, unable to say, but it is certain that on disembarking, nearly all the passengers took their way to the Thousand Island House. The negro representative of the place did not exaggerate its advantages; it would be impossible to say too much regarding the beauty of its surroundings. The house, a noble structure, having a capacity to accommodate 700 guests, is situated upon a rocky point, which extends far out into the bright green waters of the beautiful St. Lawrence, and from the high tower by which it is surmounted, can be obtained one of the finest and in many respects the most peculiar views of natural scenery to be had on the American Continent. Far in the west can be seen the stupendous sweep of the mighty river flowing languidly from its great reservoir, Lake Ontario. Nearer, but still far in the distance, rises a thickly wooded island miles in length. Situated in the midst of the stream, rock bound, dark, and silent, it almost seems to dispute the river's right of way. Still nearer, but still far away, the eye rests upon Clayton, its glittering church spire and modest one-story houses reaching down to the water's edge. Then comes island after island, some of them mere specks, other miles in extent and crowned with imposing dwelling-houses. Here they are thrown together in heaps, almost, the water finding scant room to struggle on between: in other places the river forms what appear to be great lakes surrounded on all sides with rock shores, through which there is no outlet; and so the scene continues for scores of miles down the river, ever varying, ever attractive, always disclosing some new beauty, some fresh and strange combination. At night the view from the tower is even more striking than in the day. On many of the islands—there are really 1,800 of them—summer-houses are erected and on hundreds of others young men have camped out. From all these inhabited spots lights flash and twinkle through the darkness around them; boats and miniature steam-yachts bearing lanterns are continually darting in and out; from some of the rocks at a certain hour each evening fire-works are let off, and to heighten the effect, many of the cottage owners illuminate their places with Greek fire; soft music floats out sweetly from the dark recesses and wooded glens; the river ripples gently past, reflecting back the rays of many lights and the great trees swing to the gentle evening breeze "themselves make harmony which no man can imitate." At such times the scene is beyond description; it is enchanting, fairy-like.

Keewaydin
Painting by Theodore Gegoux

Thousand Island House

LIFE AT THE THOUSAND ISLAND HOUSE

But in this prosaic age people don't come to watering-places to have all their senses ravished by fairy-like scenery; they seek rest and quiet or, if they are young and giddy, an opportunity to dance the German by gas-light in the day-time. Both classes can be accommodated at the Thousand Island House. Indeed, there have always been two distinct classes of society here. Those who compose the most numerous set come to catch fish, and they devote themselves almost entirely to that pursuit. The other class is made up of young ladies and gentlemen from Watertown, Utica, and a number of the small cities of New-York and the West. They come here for the beautiful scenery, they say, but it is noticeable that they dance a great deal, and "they do say, them as know," that dancing leads to flirtation in row-boats, and that this sort of thing is very frequently concluded late in the season by a trip to some secluded island, where, because she is "all alone, so far from home," &c., the young lady says "yes," and puts the youth out of his misery—the whole drama being ended some months later by a plain gold ring and four bridesmaids. There is more than one of the Thousand Islands that could tell a romance not unlike the above. But I must not forget the fishermen. They are here just now in scores. At 5 o'clock in the morning, sometimes earlier, they get into their light boats and are paddled across the river to some favorable position. There they remain until evening. They come back with empty lunch-baskets and boat-loads of fish. Last evening one gentleman returned with a pickerel weighing 12 pounds. A bass which turned the scale to the tune of four and a half pounds was caught the same day after a determined struggle which lasted nearly an hour. It will thus be seen that all kinds of people can come here and be happy. There are dancing and other dangerous pastimes for the young ladies, plenty of fish for the fishermen, quiet and re-pose for those who seek the, and noise, music, and gas-light for the foolish people who cannot get out of the habit of turning day into night. I may say in conclusion that these varied attractions are well appreciated by a discrimi-nating public, and while other watering-place hotel-keepers are complaining of the hard times, the proprietors of the Thousand Island House are pros-pering as they have never done before. A marked reduction in prices has doubtless largely contributed to the success of the hotel. Transient visitors are charged only $3 a day, and permanent boarders are taken for $17.50 a week.

H. C. [*New York Times*]

St. Lawrence Park
The Lotus Hotel made the community, now merely a collection of cottages, a steamboat destination. The dock, turf of the "Dock Rat Association," was mentioned in the article, "Bob's Case," about Robert Gotham.

South Boulevard.

Grenell Island

One of many island and mainland cottage communities, Grenell was not so large as nearby Thousand Island Park, but similarly had a hotel, the Pullman House, that served as a social center. Steamboats made frequent scheduled stops at the community dock. Although Grenell has a lovely landmark chapel, it was not a sectarian development like several larger river cottage colonies. A phenomenon of the last decades of the nineteenth century, these flourishing villages of cottagers reflected new middle-class prosperity combined with improved railroad access.

St. James Place.

Interlude: Demise of the Thousand Islands Yacht Club and Decline of "Society" on the River

I was about fourteen years old when I read in the *Thousand Islands Sun* that the Thousand Islands Yacht Club–Welcome Island, that is, with the large clubhouse—was for sale because of unpaid taxes. The amount due seemed, even then, to be so laughably small as to be virtually negligible—a matter of merely hundreds of dollars, as I recall. I didn't laugh at that, but my parents did when I suggested we become owners of the Thousand Islands Yacht Club.

In retrospect I can't imagine what we would have done with that barn of a building, with its huge, empty spaces. But what a bargain! Welcome Island for a few hundred dollars—I couldn't believe it at the time and still find it difficult to imagine.

But, to put it in perspective, that was the summer of 1944, shortly after D Day. The Allies had just landed on the coast of France in June, and few people were thinking about summer real estate. Because of gasoline rationing, fewer visitors were driving to the river or operating powerboats. Of course help was scarce, because so many women as well as men had left their regular employment for work related to the war effort. The distressed sale of the Thousand Islands Yacht Club property was merely typical of the state of affairs on the river after more than a decade of hard times—the Great Depression followed by the war years.

I recall the late Jean Chapman Hammond talking about the last days of the Yacht Club. Her husband's father, J. H. Hammond, had been commodore back in the twenties, before the stock market crash of 1929. The new golf club facility that Ed Noble and Gus Miles (Clover Boldt's first husband) built nearby on Wellesley had siphoned off much of the activity and prestige of the older club, but many families retained a sentimental loyalty to the Yacht Club—even into the Depression years of the thirties. The number of those families gradually diminished, however, partly because of natural attrition of old-timers passing away, partly because of a younger generation's preference for the newer golf culture, but largely because of the economy and then the war.

Eventually the handful of members trying to keep the place going simply had to recognize that the growing annual cost was becoming excessive. They stopped paying taxes on Welcome Island, which meant that the property was confiscated and sold at auction in order pay the delinquent taxes.

The grand old building remained during the dozen years it was owned by Albert Madlener, Jr. After Milton Wier purchased the property in 1962 the structure was demolished.

The Thousand Islands Club on Wellesley Island succeeded as the social center, largely subsidized by Edward John Noble, who had acquired the Miles interest in the property. The T.I. Club was not a club in the same sense, since it was the property of Noble, who was its proprietor. Although touted as "exclusive," in reality the continuing operating losses of the facility resulted in its becoming increasingly a commercial inn. The nearby Chalet served to expand the number of rooms, but even so the scale was never sufficiently large for operating efficiency. Noble eventually sold the facility to a hotel chain. When its operation proved unprofitable, they threatened to close the club, so Noble stepped back in and repurchased the property to keep it operating. Again, to keep it running, the Thousand Islands Bridge Authority, under leadership of its visionary chairman, Vincent J. Dee, bought and held the property until another owner could be found. Since that time there have been a succession of owners and operators. The Thousand Islands Club retains much of its glamour, if less lavishly operated than when subsidized during the tenure of Ed Noble.

With decline of the clubs, the late Clover Boldt Baird observed, "There's no cementing that binds the community together." The late Andy McNally seconded, saying, "There's no meeting place anymore." Alice Arnot agreed that "it used to very gay. . . . The social life at present is very dull."

Well, perhaps—or at least the social regime has changed. Probably when the sun is over the yardarm as many cocktails are consumed today as a hundred years ago, but the venues have changed. As Betty Haxall said, "One sticks to one's group of islands" (hers the head-of-Grindstone neighborhood).

Bob and Nikki Pfeiffer, whose Hickory Island is in that group but across the border, lament passing of a custom there. Neighbors used to cruise in front of one another's porches with the cocktail pennant flying, tooting to announce, "Our place." With increased border security today it's no longer lawful to disembark on the other side of the border without first checking in with mainland authorities on that side—and then reporting to officials on one's own side before returning home.

During his Hickory Island tenure, the late Dr. Raymond Pfeiffer served his legendary VO Manhattans on the rocks daily on the terrace promptly at 5 P.M. Neighbors were always welcomed. Jack Andress, the Hickory caretaker for thirty-nine years, often would stay for cocktails before heading home to Gananoque. Dr. Pfeiffer's friends often speculated that his daily Manhattan contributed to his longevity. He was 101 years old in June 2002 when he passed away, after fifty-three summers hosting cocktail hours on his terrace.

A few benefit events, such as an annual outing of the Thousand Islands Land Trust, draw a larger representation of islanders from up and down the river. Increasingly, however, two-income families spend less time here, often regarding their commuter cottage or condominium as hardly more than a hotel room or a temporary investment. As an old-timer observed, "A lot of them don't put down roots or have a stake in the community here."

Retired people often volunteer and support local institutions like the hospital and cultural groups; younger newcomers tend to cherish limited weekend days spent with their own families and guests. But even families on the river for many generations no longer seek to "belong" to the "right" set. That went out (fortunately) with that outrageous notion of "good breeding."

The new rich built the Thousand Islands Yacht Club. Their great-grandchildren, if still on the river, have acquired a different culture. They are less concerned with costly trophies and mannered rituals. Old money here, such as it is, has come to be more like the second- and third-generation wealth that built the isolated great camps of the Adirondacks—as places to retreat far from urbane social life, hiding far from the public eye, living more intimately with family and friends, and living closer to nature.

V. The Resort Begins

The 1840s, the First Decade

Today, when our sense of geography is conditioned by a network of arterial highways, it may be difficult to imagine the isolation of the Thousand Islands when the first fishing fraternity convened here. There were no good overland roads. The first plank road in Jefferson County appeared in 1848, running from Watertown to Sackets Harbor. That was the year that Charles Crossmon took over his inn. Many families still occupied log cabins. Most of the Canadian islands (881 of them) were still property of the resident Mississauga Indians. This was not a total wilderness, however, since the river had long been an international highway, connecting the Great Lakes and the sea. Queens University was founded at Kingston in 1840, and Kingston became the capital of Upper Canada in 1841. The monumental City Hall was completed in 1844. The Martello Towers were built there in 1846, supplementing Fort Henry, completed in 1837. Across the river, twenty-four miles away, Clayton (until recently called "French Creek") had a ship building industry since 1832. No doubt Alexandria Bay, a smaller village farther downstream from these towns, seemed more romantically "wild" to visiting fishermen of the 1840s.

A Cottage Colony Develops

The 1840s were a decade of growing appreciation for unspoiled nature. A romantic wilderness mystique already was developing—mainly in growing cities far from the primitive conditions still endured by residents of hinterland log cabins. Pioneers hardly romanticized their frontier life. The first lengthy account of the nearby Adirondacks, viewed as a remote retreat for hunters and fishermen, was published in 1839. During the 1840s an English author, writing as "Frank Forester," published a series of books popularizing outdoor recreation. The notion of the "gentleman sportsman" was imported from Britain. Enough time had passed since the Revolution and War of 1812 for Americans to ape English aristocratic manners once again. Here in the United States, Andrew Jackson Downing in the 1840s wrote eloquently about country living on the shores of the Hudson River, as did *Harper's* editor Donald G. Mitchell in the next decade.

The first visiting fishermen didn't build summer homes, however. They didn't bring wives and families often, since access was so difficult and accommodations were so rustic, mainly in raucous taverns. Fishing was a stag affair, and the first summer colony was one of male cronies "roughing it."

The cottage that Seth Green built on Manhattan Island often has been called the first island summer home on the river. Why did Green break from the prevailing practice, deciding instead to built a summer home? First of all, Green was not one of the political elite that congregated at Crossmon's tavern and Walton's store. Surely Green was familiar with this group and admired, but he was more fully involved in his study of nature and his work with nature. Probably he had other things to occupy him on the river, beyond socializing in the Bay.

Cornwall and Walton, the firm succeeding Azariah Walton as owner after he died, sold Manhattan Island to Green in 1855. Green's cottage was not the first island home, however; many families occupied farmhouses on larger islands. One of the first island residents was the hermit Ezra "Old Man" Brockway who lived in a shanty on Cedar Island in Chippewa Bay between 1838 and 1876. A veteran of the Mexican and Civil Wars, he made "Brockway Salve," which he "peddled all over the North Country." Green may not have been the first summer cottager on an island either, as Louis Hasbrouck of Ogdensburg already was summering on Huguenot Island in 1855, the year Green bought Manhattan Island.

Accounts of early residents by Alexandria Bay writers seem to consider only their immediate neighborhood. Clayton writers identify Dr. Whedon as the pioneer island cottager. Certainly he acquired his Round Island property later than these earliest island settlers, however. Henry Spicer had a very early cottage, Fernbank, on nearby Hemlock (Murray) Island about the same time as Seth Green, in the 1850s.

Cornwall & Walton's Stone Store, built 1866 on the Alexandria Bay waterfront.

Arrival of the railroad at Cape Vincent in 1852 made the river more readily accessible. Steamboats transported visitors to Clayton and Alexandria Bay. Clayton was a larger commercial village, while Cape Vincent had a population of more than twelve thousand the year after the railroad arrived. By 1990 the number of residents there had dwindled to some nine hundred. Clayton remains the largest Thousand Islands community on the U.S. shore.

About 1860, wood began to be supplanted by coal as fuel for steamboats, so even the islands that had not been clear-cut had less immediate value to the Cornwall and Walton firm. The notion of developing here a major resort—"a famous watering place" now more than a decade simmering, became more than an idle dream. With Seth Green's and a few other island summer homes as precedents, Andrew Cornwall offered islands for sale at very reasonable prices, requiring purchasers to erect cottages within three years.

Sales were not brisk, however, and the first cottages were "of a rude sort." Cherry Island, just above the Bay, had one of these—a "small, rough cottage"—as early as 1860, "irregularly occupied by fishing parties." Before the envisioned resort could materialize the Civil War intervened. All of the steamboats were converted to war use, and few men had leisure for summer sojourns on the river. In 1862 Cornwall and Walton asked five dollars apiece for Occident and Orient Islands, near Fishers Landing. But the next year Powder Horn and Shot Bag islands near Clayton (Calumet and Governor's) sold for three hundred dollars. In that year, despite the Civil War, Charles Crossmon enlarged his ten-room inn for the first time.

George M. Pullman

President Ulysses S. Grant

About this time the Pullmans discovered the Thousand Islands. One of several brothers, James Minton Pullman graduated from nearby St. Lawrence University in 1861. Proximity may have introduced the whole Pullman family to the Thousand Islands. The mother of the siblings became a devoted islander, and several brothers established island summer homes. One of them, George M. Pullman, put the place on the map, initiating the Thousand Islands as a long-envisioned resort—a story of another chapter in island history, more fully related in my preceding book, *Fools' Paradise.* In short, however, entertainment of President U. S. Grant, together with Civil War heros Generals Sherman and Sheridan, triggered a boom in the resort.

Cornwall and Walton sold Sweet Island to George M. Pullman for forty dollars in 1865. Pullman soon became a millionaire, the first of many to acquire islands for summer homes. Although the first of the Thousand Islands castles would rise on Pullman Island twenty-three years later, earlier buildings

Gen. William T. Sherman

on Pullman's island were less grand. This was still a "camp," with simple frame cabins supplemented with tents. Festivities on receiving the presidential party here in 1872 were widely reported in the national press.

Gen. Phillip H. Sheridan

Pullman Island Awaiting the President

The turning point for development of the Thousand Islands as a famed resort occurred in 1872, when George M. Pullman welcomed to his island President U. S. Grant together with a large party that included the Civil War heroes Generals Sherman and Sheridan. As evidenced by this photo of the place decorated for the party's arrival, cottage life in the 1870s was still fairly simple and unpretentious. Note a larger house partially obscured by trees at the upper left and the red carpet unfurled on the steps, awaiting the presidential party.

The railroads provided more comfortable and rapid access to the St. Lawrence River from cities of the East Coast and Midwest. Wives and children now came with the fishermen. Grand hotels accommodated families, but many families didn't care for hotel life, preferring more private summer homes. A cottage colony would provide less casual socializing. New friends of youngsters would be known to parents. Boosters actively recruited members of the summer community, particularly from New York City. Building of the cottage colony is another chapter in island history. The first phase of the summer community, most notable for the male fishing cronies who assembled annually at small inns and boardinghouses of Alexandria Bay, had passed by the time of the Civil War.

First among a long line of famous Thousand Islands regulars was U.S. senator and New York State governor Silas Wright. The governor didn't have far to come to fish, when not occupied by, and finally retiring from, politics. Declining several offers for honorific positions in the cabinet and on foreign missions, Wright returned to nearby Canton, New York, after his defeat for reelection as governor in 1846. Although he enjoyed honest, hands-on farming again, Wright continued to be a prominent national spokesman, particularly in opposition to the spread of slavery into new U.S. territories.

Silas Wright, 1795–1847

Silas Wright, "a plainspoken man of the people," Democratic leader of the U.S. Senate and chairman of the Finance Committee, was devoted ("almost to idolatry") to Presidents Jackson and Van Buren. He became the confidant, "best friend," and right-hand man of Martin Van Buren. Wright was considered a possible presidential candidate himself for 1848, but he died unexpectedly the year prior to the election. Walt Whitman, who had proposed his presidential candidacy, said, "We loved Silas Wright as a true democratic friend of the people."

Charles Crossmon

Silas Wright was a fisherman. Politicians often had time during summer legislative recesses to undertake the long journey through the Erie Canal and across Lake Ontario to visit the Thousands Islands. Wright's personal and close political association with President Martin Van Buren brought that fellow New Yorker to fish on the river in the 1840s. Alexandria Bay was a mere hamlet at the time, not nearly such a business center as Clayton. But the Bay was closer to Wright's Canton, and Charles Crossmon took over his father-in-law's small tavern and ten-room inn at Alexandria Bay in 1848, becoming a famous host. Crossmon's descendants, now the Thomsons, have continued to be notable innkeepers there for more than a century and a half. Governor Silas Wright had appealed to the Canadians for clemency for prisoners of the Patriot War

(1837–1839), among whom was young Crossmon. Although two prisoners were executed and many sent to the British penal colony in the South Pacific, some never to return, because of his youth Crossmon was freed.

Silas Wright, fond of his liquor and his food, was an amiable fishing companion (although he gave up drinking in his last years, when some considered him to be a problem alcoholic). Although Wright was the nucleus of the first sum-

Crossmon's Inn, 1848

mer colony on the river, his tenure as leader of the fishing tribe was brief. Before he died, however, Silas Wright foresaw the Thousand Islands becoming "the greatest summer resort in the United States." That vision was not lost on landowner Azariah Walton and his younger partner, Andrew Corwall. The notion of creating a major resort here apparently was taking hold in the 1840s. The recreational development of the Thousand Islands really began when Silas Wright's presence attracted other leading political figures of the day. President Martin Van Buren's time on the river is memorialized by Van Buren Island near the foot of Grenadier, where he enjoyed shore dinners.

Martin Van Buren
President of the United States

President Martin Van Buren–"Matty," the "Little Flying Dutchman," the "Little Magician," or the "Sly Fox"–was "small, fiercely energetic, dandified." Although he had not the rhetorical flair of his son, "Prince John," Van Buren was astute and shrewd. "With Van Buren the age of American machine politics opens." Van Buren was the most prominent fisherman on the river prior to the Civil War, but it was said that "if a list had been kept of the names of visitors, it would have embraced nearly all the prominent statesmen during the administrations of Jackson, Van Buren, Polk, and Buchanan." Martin Van Buren's court included his son, "Prince John," and others in the "Albany Regency" that "for a third of a century dominated the political life of New York and not infrequently exerted a controlling influence upon the politics of the nation." Martin Van Buren as a U.S. senator became a friend as well as loyal supporter of President Jackson. He resigned the Senate to become governor of New York State in 1829, resigning as governor to become secretary of state in Jackson's cabinet. He subsequently was elected Jackson's vice-president. Then, "hand-picked by Andrew Jackson as his successor," Van Buren was nominated as the Democratic candidate and elected to the presidency in 1837.

Silas Wright and Martin Van Buren were known well enough to locals to be characterized differently: "Old fishermen tell of the generosity of Silas Wright in quietly slipping into their hands, on returning from a trip, a liberal 'tip.' While Mr. Van Buren, less thoughtful, to put it mildly, never exceeded the exact sum stipulated in the contract by dispensing the expected *doucer* to his boatmen."

Vying with Charles Crossmon's little inn as clubhouse for the fishing fraternity was Azariah Walton's general store. Fishermen gathered there to exchange tall tales and enjoy Walton's yarns. He was something of a poet, composing political campaign songs—one of them for the "Son of Kinderhook," Martin Van Buren.

Azariah Walton was a patriarchal sort of figure locally, but a genial peer to visiting fishermen. One of them recalled:

"The Waltons stood high in social distinction throughout that section. . . . Mr. Azariah Walton I regarded as a grand old man, by whom I was always treated with kindness and courtesy. At his store, I frequently saw his massive figure seated behind the counter employed in thumping some refractory substance into use for trolling spoons. The shelves in the rear were garnished with lines, hooks, bright brass spoons and other fishing tackle. In on corner was seen a forest of fishing poles, some of these being suspended by wooden supports overhead."

Azariah Walton

Walton and a partner bought most of the U.S. islands between Round Island, near Clayton, and Morristown for $3,000 in 1845. Walton subsequently acquired the partner's interest, becoming the major landowner of island property. Although some of the larger islands supported farms, generally the rocky terrain and thin soil had little agricultural potential. Walton's commercial interest was lumbering timber to sell as fuel for passing steamboats. Once cleared, the rocky islands had little financial value—until the vision of a summer resort began to take shape in the 1840s.

Walton paid about fifty cents an acre for the islands. In his later years he took in a younger partner. Andrew Cornwall joined him in 1852. The following year the old frame store building

Walton House, Alexandria Bay

was demolished and a new stone store erected on the Alexandria Bay waterfront—now a historic landmark of the region. Cornwall and Walton, as their business was known, purchased nearly all of the remainder of Wellesley Island not included in the original purchase. Andrew Cornwall was an astute businessman with vision. He embraced the notion, then in the air, of a major resort developing on the river.

Chaplain to the pre–Civil War fishing fraternity was "genial and talented" Rev. Dr. George W. Bethune, who began coming in 1845. An avid fisherman, the "first fly caster of the St. Lawrence," Bethune edited the American edition of Izak Walton's *The Compleat Angler* (1847). In 1846 he recognized the need for a church at Alexandria Bay and was a major donor of the fine Stone Church that remains a major landmark of the community and region. If the denomination of the congregation, Dutch Reformed, seems odd for the North

Rev. George W. Bethune

Country, it may seem less so when recognizing the connection to Martin Van Buren of Kinderhook, likewise from the Hudson Valley—the last president to speak Dutch. Van Buren's family belonged to the Dutch Reformed Church. Rev. Bethune was pastor of a congregation at Rhinebeck, in the Hudson Valley, but also at New York City, Brooklyn, and Utica.

The Stone (Reformed Protestant Dutch) Church, Alexandria Bay, 1848–1851

Fishing was not Rev. Bethune's only sporting interest, as he "kept an excellent span, took great delight in driving, and kept a colored man to groom and take care of them." Bethune was not a poor clergyman, as evidenced by his summer sojourns on the river. His father was a Philadelphia merchant and philanthropist; his mother was noted for her charitable work. Rembrandt Peale painted his portrait, and Rev. Bethune spent his last year in Italy. President Polk wanted him to accept a professorship at West Point, but he declined. He also declined chancellorship of the New York State University. Bethune is remembered as a poet and author of hymns. His two-volume work, *Guilt, Grace, and Gratitude* remains in print, as does his *British Female Poets* and his edition of *The Complete Angler*. One of his last and most memorable public appearances was at a great rally in New York's Union

Square, when "with extraordinary fire and eloquence he urged the duty of patriotism in the trying crisis that then threatened the nation." A marble mosaic portrait memorializes Rev. Bethune in Rutger's Sage Library at New Brunswick, New Jersey.

George Bethune's contribution to the region went beyond building a village church. He was a well-connected booster. It was said "the figure of the sportsman parson is a prominent one in all that pertains to the welfare of this region, and in bringing its rare beauties and pleasures to the knowledge of the public."

Reference to the "Democratic Party" of the early nineteenth century ought not to suggest identification with the modern Democratic Party. Martin Van Buren "jockeyed to displace John C. Calhoun in the favor of Andrew Jackson" leading to a splitting of the Democratic Party into northern and southern factions. Calhoun then defected to the Whigs, leaving Van Buren to lead the Democrats. Van Buren himself, although conciliatory to the South in the interest of unity, in 1848 became the candidate of the anti-slavery Free Soil Party (the "Barn-burners"). The factional split among Democrats, some defecting to the antislavery Free Soil Party, gave the presidential election to Whig Taylor. Some of these Democratic defectors, including Preston King, a member of the early fraternity on the river, became founders of the Republican Party as the Civil War approached.

Preston King was a native of nearby Ogdens-burg. Guardian of young orphan Preston was Louis Hasbrouck, an associate of Silas Wright who followed him to the U.S. Senate and who perhaps built the first island cottage on Huguenot Island. Preston King in 1830 established an Ogsensburg newspaper, the *St. Lawrence Republican*. King was marginally involved in the Battle of the Windmill, the ill-fated invasion of Canada launched from Ogdensburg. A lawyer and close friend of Silas Wright, King was allied with the other Free Soil

Preston King

opponents to the extension of slavery. King was one of the first to recognize and publicly state that a civil war might be inevitably required to keep the South in the Union. King then became founding member of the Republican Party. Preston King served as a U.S. congressman and senator and was appointed customs collector of the Port of New York. That position,

Frank Blair

in the post–Civil War climate of political corruption, apparently was too stressful for King, who committed suicide by leaping from a ferryboat in the New York City harbor.

Frank (Francis Preston) Blair was another founding member of the Republican Party. A Kentucky newspaperman, his opposition to South Carolina's attempted nullification of a federal tariff brought him to the notice of President Jackson, who invited him to Washington to found the pro-union *Globe*, recognized as the Democratic Party organ. Blair, like Van Buren, was an ardent supporter of President Jackson. Subsequently President Polk removed Blair from his editorial position—a victory for Jackson's southern opponent, John Calhoun. Blair became a Van Buren supporter in 1848. Blair presided over the 1856 convention of the new Republican Party and was one of the leaders of the 1860 convention that nominated Lincoln. Frank Blair had considerable influence in the Lincoln administration.

Dick Taylor

Political affinity of these members of the early fishing fraternity suggests a common tie, but motivation of others who joined them here is less apparent. Dick Taylor, son of President Zachary Taylor, was brother-in-law of Jefferson Davis and a Confederate major general during the Civil War. Of course, the fishing club convened prior to the war. At that time Taylor probably had merely social rapport with the northern politicians. His inheritance made him a wealthy southern planter himself. He also married well, further enabling an aristocratic lifestyle.

William L. Marcy

William L. Marcy, a "ponderous, dogged, and yet cultured" lawyer and judge, was elected to the U.S. Senate as a Jackson supporter. Silas Wright filled his seat when Marcy became New York State comptroller. Marcy served as New York governor

Seth Green's Cottage, Manhattan Island, "restored" in 1868 by Judge Spencer.

when Van Buren was president. Both were confronted with the international crisis with Canada, the "Patriot War" with hostilities here on the river. Marcy served three times as New York governor, serving also as Polk's secretary of war and Pierce's secretary of state. Governor Marcy appointed "Pirate Bill" Johnston Rock Island lighthouse keeper.

Not all of the early fishing cronies were politicians. In addition to the group's chaplain, Dr. Bethune, Seth Green was the fish authority. Of course there were local guides or "oarsmen," as known at the time, such as "Old Man" Griffen, Ned Patterson, and Alph and Tom Comstock. Seth Green, however, was the scientific fish expert.

Seth Green

Seth Green was a born outdoorsman. He never outgrew his boyhood passion for woods, field and stream. Operating a fish and game market in Rochester, he thought about increasing supply by artificial propagation of fish. Green developed propagation methods for his own business use. As a result of his remarkable success several states asked him to conduct experiments for them. Green became New York's superintendent of fisheries but worked nationally. As a result of his innovations more than a million shad were marketed on the West Coast in 1885. Green not only propagated but also hybridized species of fish. He wrote two books about his work and was awarded with international medals. Locally Seth Green was revered as an accomplished angler, vying with Rev. Bethune for introducing fly-fishing to the river.

William H. Seward

Another luminary among the early visitors was William H. Seward of Auburn, governor of New York State. Seward may not have been so integral to the earliest group of political cronies since he was a Whig, not a Democrat. The Whigs opposed Van Buren's presidential candidacy. Seward played a role in formation of the Republican Party, however—which connects him to a second generation of politicians on the river. Seward served in the U.S. Senate and as Lincoln's secretary of state. He is remembered for the purchase of Alaska and for his abolitionist stance. "Intellectually adventurous, cheerful, and convivial—though somewhat vain," Seward would have been a boon companion in the small summer fraternity.

The Breckenridges seem like unlikely cronies for the northern fishermen. Like General Dick Taylor, the Breckenridges were southerners allied with the Confederacy. Not merely politics but fishing makes strange bedfellows. John C. Breckenridge, best known of this southern political dynasty, was Congressman and vice president in the Buchanan administration. In opposition to the new Republicans so well represented on the river, Breckenridge ran as a candidate for president against Lincoln. Losing,

John C. Breckenridge

he served as senator until expelled for supporting the rebellion. Then he became a major general and secretary of war for the Confederacy. After defeat, John C. Breckenridge resided in Europe for years until final returning to Kentucky. Preston K. Breckenridge also was a contemporary U.S. senator.

These nationally prominent figures were recalled as early visitors at Alexandria Bay. Clayton, if more a commercial town and less a rustic fishermen's

"Old Salt" Alvord

destination, attracted anglers at any early date as well. Thomas "Old Salt" Alvord, identified early with Clayton, came to the river in the 1840s. His published recollections, however, refer to the next and subsequent decades, and he mentioned going to Alexandria Bay, "that Mecca of fisherman," with his brother-in-law in 1852. In fact he observed that Clayton was "headquarters for square timber cutting and no boatmen or fisher folk hailed from there until some years thereafter."

Some Post–Civil War Visitors

Roscoe Conkling's name may not be recognized today as belonging to one of the powerful political figures of his day, but Conkling was a major force in the U.S. Senate and American politics. He was born into a political family. Presidents John Quincy Adams and Martin Van Buren were guests in his boyhood Albany home. Although of a later generation than President Van Buren, like his son, "Prince John," and others who gathered here, Conkling was instrumental in the 1854 founding of the Republican Party. When as mayor of Utica he

Roscoe Conkling

moved to national politics, Conkling was a strong supporter of President Lincoln. After the Civil War, when he became a U.S. senator, he was an equally strong supporter of President Grant. Conkling's political power derived in large part from his personal control of the political patronage system in New York State. Control of the New York Customs House was Conkling's major political tool. As mentioned, islander Preston King became collector of customs but committed suicide, probably in large part due to the stress of that position. President Chester A. Arthur, who also fished here in later years, had been a Conkling appointee to the same position

Roscoe "Sandy" Conkling "was a man easy to dislike. His caustic remarks and strutting physicality managed to offend even his closest political allies." He had a scandalous affair with another senator's wife. He was an arrogant wheeler-dealer in an era of gross political corruption.

Clayton about 1860 with the Hubbard House on left side of James Street.

Hubbard House proprietor James T. Hubbard ("Captain Jim") stands in front of the window, chatting with fashionably attired guests, their trunks on wood plank sidewalk, while others (probably including some local oarsmen) lounge outside the bar room.

Idlewild Island
The Eggleston house supplanted this Robert Packer cottage.

"Little Eva"

For all his flaws, Conkling persisted in the ideals of the Radical Republicans, staunchly advocating the rights of African Americans. After retiring from politics to become a highly successful New York lawyer, "he would put aside other matters to serve the needs of the poor and powerless."

Roscoe Conkling was more a fixture of the resort in the 1880s than in the pre–Civil War period. He accompanied President Chester Arthur when he came to fish. Despite the four-decade interval, the lineage from Silas Wright, who died in 1847, was recalled in 1890 when it was observed that Roscoe Conkling "possessed Mr. [Silas] Wright's kindness of thought and action, and his suavity of manner. He might perhaps more nearly than any othe, have kept that mantle."

John Cardinal McCloskey

Contrasting as the sacred to the profane was another distinguished visitor of the post-Civil War era, John Cardinal McCloskey. The Roman Catholic bishop of Albany and Archbishop of New York in 1875 became the first American Cardinal. Cardinal McClosky considered the 1879 completion of St. Patrick's Cathedral in New York City to be his greatest achievement.

His biographers don't tell us whether his eminence enjoyed fishing, but probably it was not diocesan business that brought him to Charles Crossmon's Alexandria Bay inn.

Another contrasting visitor of the period was the British philospher Herbert Spencer, "a major figure in the intellectual life of the Victorian era, . . . one of the principal proponents of evolutionary theory in the mid nineteenth century [whose] reputation . . . rivaled that of Charles Darwin." Again, biographers don't confirm that Spencer was a fisherman. Probably he didn't come to the Crossmon House to philosophize, however.

Herbert Spencer's now often castigated "Social Darwinism" or, as popularly characterized, "survival of the fittest" in the social realm, is offensive to many today. At the time his views were congruent with the widely shared notion of success as the re-

Herbert Spencer

ward for ability, effort, and achievement. Probably Spencer would appreciate the great trophy houses and yachts of the Thousand Islands.

If not so famous afar as these notable visitors, another islander of the period needs to be recognized for his contribution to the resort. Reverend George Rockwell in 1854 began a long tenure as pastor of the Dutch Reformed Church at Alexandria Bay. He succeeded Reverend George Bethune as not merely a spiritual leader, but a community leader as well. Rockwell was an author, publicist and cartographer in addition to his pastoral duties. He wrote at least five booklets and articles about the Thousand Islands, anonymously or using a pseudonym, providing valuable maps and directories of

Rev. George Rockwell

island properties and their owners. Andrew Cornwall gave Rev. Rockwell Cherry Island. He built a cottage at the head, where Nelfred now stands. The Rockwell cottage was the only improvement on the large island for many years.

Due to advancing deafness, Rev. Rockwell resigned his pastorate at Alexandria Bay in 1887 after thirty-three years, moving to Fulton, New York City and finally Tarrytown, New York.

Andrew Cornwall

Together with George M. Pullman, who brought national attention to the resort, Andrew Cornwall was one of its primary developers. A local boy who went to work at thirteen, Andrew Cornwall became Azariah Walton's partner and acquired the Walton interest in the firm of Cornwall and Walton. We don't know whether Cornwall and Pullman together plotted the presidential visit of 1872, having it coincide with the visit of newspaper editors, and initiating the resort's boom. Cornwall had foresight, however, and was astute to sieze the moment. Immediately he gave valuable riverfront property in Alexandria Bay for the grand Thousand Islands House, constructed during the winter following the presidential visit. Cornwall's vision was rewarded by sales of islands at rapidly escalated prices. Rightly Andrew Cornwall was called "the most useful man on the river."

To Andrew Cornwall was "due the greatest credit for the movement which has developed the Thousand Islands." With partner Walton he was said to be the "practical founder of the now world-famous Thousand Islands as a watering place." Cornwall served as a New York State legislator but failed to win a congressional seat. The "patriarch of the American Side of the Upper St. Lawrence" was a leading stockholder in the Alexandria Bay Steamboat Company, one of two major rival lines of excursion steamers. He was president of the village, served as town supervisor and was president of the Angler's Association. Andrew Cornwall's four sons continued the family business as Cornwall Brothers. Andrew Cornwall "can be truly said to have made the Thousand Islands what they are."

For many years the Pullmans did not keep a yacht on the river. Consistent with their unpretentious establishment in the early years, they chartered one of the rental yachts, usually the *Valletta*, shown here with Royal Pullman on board, probably at his Camp Royal on Wellesley Island, next to Pullman Island.

Pullman Island's skiff house supplemented a boathouse. The latter had slips allowing boats to enter while in the water whereas a skiff house such as this had a ramp allowing smaller craft to be pulled out of the water. Although this photograph was taken shortly after Castle Rest was completed, we see a tent still in use on the island. Despite the grand new structure, this was still a "camp."

One of the most famed and admired regular visitors to the Thousand Islands was Clara Barton. When the Red Cross flag was flying over Royal Pullman's Wellesley Island Camp Royal, neighbors and excursionists knew that the founder of the American Red Cross was visiting. Rev. Royal Henry Pullman, brother of George M. Pullman, was Clara Barton's secretary. Royal Pullman spent most of the summer on the river, so she was often here as well. Clara Barton was a teacher and then a government clerk in Washington when the Civil War broke out. She requested permission to serve at the front and became superintendent of Union nurses. After the war, traveling to Europe to recover from exhaustion, she learned about the Red Cross. On return she founded and became president of the American Red Cross.

Other Early Islanders

"One of the first to discover the beauties of the Thousand Islands" was William Green Deshler, known as "one of the most prominent and wealthy Thousand Islands residents." For fifty dollars the Columbus, Ohio, banker bought fifteen-acre Deshler Island, now known as Harbor Island, close to Heart Island. Deshler, who was already in his seventies when construction began on Boldt Castle, sold his property to younger Boldt after having there for many years "one of the most picturesque cottages" on the river.

The Deshlers were very close friends of the Crossmons at Alexandria Bay. In fact, the family usually stayed at Crossmon's hotel, while their caretaker occupied the island cottage. Probably the food was better at the hotel, where the table was famous. Five-year-old Bessie Deshler had her birthday party at the Crossmon House in 1880. Deshler bankrolled Charles Crossmon's purchase of Crossmon Point adjoining his hotel property. Deshler had a major stake in an Ohio railroad, of which Peter Hayden of nearby Fairyland was a co-investor and president. Probably the Haydens were attracted to the river by the Deshlers.

William G. Deshler was longtime president of the National Exchange Bank in Columbus, retiring in 1892. He was a noted investor and was listed in *American Millionaires* that year. Deshler served in the U.S. Treasury and was president of the Central Ohio Natural Gas Company, treasurer of the Corning Oil Company, and for many years served on the Executive Council of the American Bankers' Association. He built the well-known Deshler Hotel in Columbus, where he is also rememberd by Deshler Avenue. Here on the river, William Deshler served on the Executive Committee of the new (1875) Thousand Islands Association.

"One of the best known summer visitors" who first visited the river in the early 'forties was Herbert Ray Clarke. He was one of its most durable and long-lived River Rats, after some seventy years of loyal visits. Whereas the Deshlers were habitués of the Crossmon House, the Clarkes were among the first patrons of the Thousand Islands House when it opened in 1873, and they remained regular visitors for many decades thereafter. Clarke was particularly important to the development of the resort, since he brought many others to the river including, it was thought, the Boldts. Perhaps he also introduced Abraham and Straus to the islands, since he was in the wholesale dry goods business. Confidence of his firm, Teft, Weller & Company, had enabled Nathan Straus's father to begin his retail operations. Apparently Clarke was close to the Boldts, since he gave young Clover a small island as a gift.

Herbert Ray Clarke was widely known as a fisherman on the river, where he had "the name of being the best fisherman at the Bay." Vice president of the Anglers' Association, his active work in the interest of conservation was noted in the press. He camped in June and September at Brewers Mills on the Rideau. Mrs. Clarke was also a noted fisher-woman. For three years in the 1880s she caught the largest bass taken in the region.

The Clarkes of Jersey City had a son and two daughters, Herbert B. Clarke of New York, Mrs. Charles Cooper of Jersey City, and Miss Grace Clarke, also of Jersey City, who became Mrs. A. J. Thomson. In later years the family tired of hotel life and acquired a summer home near the Bay. Herbert Ray Clarke was known not merely for his longevity on the river, but was respected for his contribution. As an islander he "earned all the honors that can be awarded him."

Stephen Decatur Johnson

Vying with Charles Crossmon as the pioneer resort proprietor was Stephen Decatur Johnson, who
began his inn-keeping at Clayton in 1849, only a
year after Crossmon started at Alexandria Bay. His
Izak Walton House was named after the famed
British angler, whose work Rev. Bethune brought to
America. Like Crossmon, Johnson acquired a small
country tavern and developed it to become a resort
hotel for an elite clientele, one of several in Clayton
catering to fishermen and their families. The chief
competitor at Clayton was the Hubbard House,
across James Street. Acquired by John Hubbard in
1850, it likewise had been a village tavern and country inn before becoming a
resort hotel.

If not the first resort
proprietor on the river,
certainly one of the most
notable and successful was
Col. Orin G. Staples, initial
proprietor of the grand
Thousand Islands House at
Alexandria Bay. A real entrepreneur, he had started a
patent medicine business in

Walton House, Clayton

Watertown at age seventeen. He sold that company to an Albany firm and
used the proceeds to build fifty-seven fine houses in Watertown. When the
nationally publicized presidential visit triggered the "Rush of '72," Staples
siezed the opportunity, rushing to completion the huge Thousand Islands
House for the next season.

As mentioned, Andrew Cornwall donated the land, which proved to be
in his own interest as the major landowner of other island property. With
this large waterfront parcel as collateral, Stables was able to finance the huge
construction project. Financing proved precarious in future years, but Staples, with the substantial contribution of Cornwall, in six months built the
landmark icon of the Thousand Islands that, probably more than any other
feature, denoted the region as a major national resort.

So successful was Staples' venture that after ten years, sale of the Thousand Islands House enabled him to purchase the famous Willard's Hotel in Washington, D.C., with which he was identified for decades. He then acquired a second hotel in the capital and other real estate investments. Eventually he owned four large hotels in the city and was considered "one the wealthiest residents of the capital."

Col. Orin G. Staples

Staples, the largest stockholder in the Columbian National Bank, served as treasurer of the Washington Board of Trade. He served as director of banks in Washington and New York City. After leaving home with sixteen dollars Col. Staples was supposed to have become a millionaire at a relatively young age. In 1909 he sold some Washington, D.C., property at the foot of Penn-

Col. Staple's *Neried*

sylvania Avenue to the government for one and a quarter million dollars—back when a million dollars was a lot of money. On the river, he had the fine Herreshoff steam yacht *Neried*. Subsequently Staples owned two yachts on the river, after acquiring the *Idler*.

Col. Staples was a natural entrepeneur. As John Haddock said of him, "Taking him all in all, his many business reverses and his way of overcoming them, his tenacity of purpose after he has struck a business for which he had a liking, and the democracy of his manner under great success—he must be regarded as an exceptional character. There has never been another like him within the remembrance of the writer and his successful career may be pointed out for the encouragement of young men of our time."

Orin Staples had taste—he was "a connoisseur of art"—combined with an aggressive entrepreneurial instinct, a winning combination in the hotel business. In addition to his other enterprises, he was co-owner of the Lotus Hotel at Central (St. Lawrence) Park, where his wife and daughter stayed. He also managed hotels elsewhere, such as the Ocean House at Watch Hill, R.I. Recalling that preeminent hotelier George Boldt, Staples was an attractive and likeable man whose extensive social network was an asset for his business and for the Thousand Islands. He entertained many dignitaries here aboard his yacht while being generous to local neighbors. The young people of the Bay presented him with a silver claret pitcher "in appreciation of the privilege of the hotel extended to them each season." Probably this referred to his welcoming them to dances and other functions. He donated the main stained-glass window to the Episcopal Church of the St. Lawrence at the Bay.

Staples in 1900 built the casino on "Staples Island," as it was then called, a short distance off the channel waterfront of the village now connected by a footbridge to the village park. The "casino" (a term common here at the time) did not imply gambling, but referred to a recreation pavilion. Although clearly a driving force on the local scene and elsewhere, Staples didn't build the great Thousand Islands House single-handedly. In addition to Andrew Cornwall's contribution, C. A. Nott was also involved in planning and building the facility. Staples was a promoter of local events, such as the annual Water Carnival at the Bay. He was an organizer of the St. Lawrence River Yacht Club, to which he donated a trophy. Ever the promoter of the region, he offered islands to President Taft. He was regarded as the "one man who then read correctly [our river's] grand future."

Staples invested in other business on the river, such as the company owning the steamer *Unique*. His freewheeling financial operations came under scrutiny eventually. He was indicted in 1905 for making a false financial statement of the Inter-State Live Stock Insurance Company.

Orin Staples remarried late in life. He surprised even his many friends when, at age sixty-five, he married his nurse, who gave her age as thirty years younger. Nurse Kinnear was well known in the summer community, and the 1913 wedding at the Church of the St. Lawrence was a major event locally. It may not be surprising that Staples avoided remarriage until retirement age. Like Boldt, he was "married to his work," and lived the financially precarious life of a financial adventurer, at times "not worth a dollar clear of his debts," while at others being a millionaire.

Col. Staples apparently was admired but regarded with mixed feelings on the river, due to his financial ups and downs and run-ins with the law. He probably organized the St. Lawrence River Yacht Club because he was not admitted to the prestigious Thousand Islands Yacht Club. One had to own a substantial summer home to be eligible for regular membership. Staples had hotels and yachts, but that might not have qualified him. Nathan Straus, who did have a magnificent island residence, and other Jewish islanders and patrons of the Thousand Islands House participated in events of the alternate club. Admired and shunned, Col. Orin G. Staples was one of the most prominent but controversial figures on the river, in retrospect one of the most important contributors to development of the resort.

If less flamboyant, another popular host on the river was "Genial Jim" Hubbard, proprietor of Clayton's Hubbard House. As mentioned, this was a favorite venue for the theatrical crowd. James T. Hubbard, "Captain Jim," expanded and operated his hostelry for decades and then was succeeded by his widow, Eleanor M. Hubbard, in the 1890s. She was known for packing fine lunches for fishing parties.

President Chester Arthur

Another president's visits brought national attention to the Thousand Islands, where he "always fishes." One of President Chester A. Arthur's fishing expeditions was documented by famed photographer Mathew Brady. The president's alliance with Senator Roscoe Conkling connected his political lineage back to Martin Van Buren and Silas Wright a half century earlier. President Arthur stayed at the Crossmon House, which probably was the choice of more distinguished guests than the rival Thousand Islands House nearby. That grand hotel had an affluent clientele, but the Crossmon House probably was considered more the elite establishment at the time, prior to opening of the New Frontenac Hotel near Clayton. Contrary to the *New York Times* report quoted previously, in 1904 the Crossmon charged four dollars a day, the same rate as the Frontenac, whereas the Thousand Islands House rates varied from three to five dollars. The Crossmon House survived the longest of any of the major historic hotels on the river. It was demolished in 1962, supplanted by a motel.

Interlude: J. Walter Thompson and the New Age of Marketing

Until about the time of the Civil War, farmers and others focused on production. They produced in order to use their crops or wares themselves; then they hoped to produce a surplus to sell for cash. The industrial revolution increased production to the point where disposing of surplus became critical. Few islanders' wealth derived primarily from manufacturing industries. Most businesses produced something, but the remarkable success represented by many new fortunes at the islands was based more on innovating new methods of marketing and distribution.

William Browning of West Point (Hopewell Hall) after the Civil War created one of the first national chains of clothing stores. William O. Wyckoff of Carleton Villa was the salesman for Remington typewriters who expanded markets and took over the company. Commodore Bourne of Dark Island developed perhaps the first great global marketing and distribution system for Singer sewing machines.

Advertising was critical to develop mass markets. The patent-medicine men (Fulford, Warner, Comstock, and others here) knew this, as did manufacturers of products such as cigarettes and whisky (Emery, Bradley) having few distinctive qualities.

J. Walter Thompson

J. Walter Thompson was one of the pioneers of the advertising industry in America. Thompson founded his famous advertising agency in 1878– not the first in America, however; Ayer founded his agency in 1869. Nevertheless the JWT company claims to have "literally invented advertising." Advertising copywriters are prone to hyperbole. Thompson actually went to work as an accountant for an advertising "broker" in 1864. Thompson bought the business in 1877. In 1899 he opened a London office. The J. Walter Thompson Company now is a global corporation with 8,500 employees in 86 countries.

John Walter Thompson did not have pretentious tastes. He rented the Wrens' Dixie Cottage at Round Island. Thompson entertained clients at his purported "costly summer home on the northeast coast" of Round Island. Although he had a "very large steam launch," Thompson preferred his "natty looking" little naphtha launch *Aphrodite*.

VI. A Visit to Julie's

When she wasn't visiting us at Steele's Point (or over at the Heineman's on Picton Island) I regularly called on Julie at her third-floor walk-up apartment over Corbin's (above John "The Bear" Amo's barber shop, actually, but the stairs went up between them). Clayton hasn't changed greatly in sixty years, but fires have left a few holes in the commercial wall of Riverside Drive. The voids open the view to the river but make the street less coherent.

Clayton, 1942

Riverside Drive, as I remember it at age twelve, had more buildings, some subsequently lost to fire. Seventy-five tons of scrap was coolected in the street for World War II.

One of Julie's friends was a lady about her age, Mrs. Dillenback. I don't recall her first name. There are lots of Dillenbacks in the town of Clayton. Mrs. Dillenback was from Depauville (which she pronounced with the accent strongly on the first syllable, *De*-po-ville). This sprightly lady's tête-à-têtes with Julie often coincided with mine. The two older women made an odd couple, the one seeming so tall, articulate, and sophisticated (at least to this youngster), the other less so if not totally the opposite. Whereas Julie's syntax and diction were finely honed, Mrs. Dillenback offered homespun wit, wisdom, and strong opinions in a Yankee twang. I remember one of her lines, "I don't canter to nobody." Julie would never laugh at Mrs. Dillenback's malapropisms. Julie was too much the gentlewoman, and she treasured Mrs. Dillenback's friendship. Probably Mrs. Dillenback, like me, re-garded Julie as someone from another world, a privilege to know.

The entrance to Julie's apartment, because it was on the third floor, up two flights of stairs, was into the kitchen, at the rear of the commercial building. The living room was on the street side, and to get to it, one had to pass through the bedroom-bathroom area in between. One advantage of the top floor location, compensating for the long climb, was a skylight illumining the center of the apartment, which otherwise would have been dark. Both the living room and kitchen were commodious, since the dimensions were determined by the commercial space required on the ground floor. I thought the quarters utopian and often think how nice that apartment would be as a retirement haven. Julie paid forty dollars a month, including utilities (or Social Services paid it, after she became destitute).

In the center of the linoleum-covered kitchen floor was a large ta-ble—round, I think, covered with oilcloth. There Julie and I would most frequently converse, since it provided the best place to lay out and inspect her big scrapbooks. From there we could also watch the big freighters passing by—I could, at least. Julie could barely make them out with her failing eye-sight. There was a porch beyond Julie's two kitchen windows. To get to it, I had to use a door at the head of the stairway. Otherwise one would have to climb over a windowsill. The bottoms of the windows were not high above the floor, but with screens in the open sash, climbing out that way would be a nuisance. Julie didn't like me going out on the porch, where she never went, since she didn't trust her failing vision and hence was unsure of her

Clayton Waterfront. Julie lived on the top floor, under the flag.

footing. But it was a glorious spot to watch the marine activity on the docks below and far off on the river. I couldn't stay out there long, however, as Julie kept urging me to come back in.

Calumet Castle was the central feature of the panorama from Julie's kitchen windows. We talked about it often. Julie remembered it when it was open and occupied by the Emerys. I had explored the shuttered stone structure and shared a fantasy of acquiring it (or, at that age, having my parents buy it. It was then for sale).

"But Paul," Julie protested, "the main reason the Emerys abandoned the place was the cost of operation, or so I suppose. Frank Emery talked about selling the place within ten years after his father died—but his dad's will didn't allow it. Charles Emery had set up a trust fund providing income to carry the property, but Frank said it was inadequate. The annual taxes ran more than seventy-five thousand dollars a year back when that was a lot more money than today, or so they said. That's hard to believe, but even today the taxes, at about a third of that, I hear, are a burden. I think that the locals here are trying to kill the bird that laid the golden egg. That establishment employed a lot of Clayton people. Now the Emerys simply aren't paying the taxes, I hear. I think they'd be content to have the property taken off their hands to be auctioned for back taxes."

Yes, I conceded, it would be very costly to maintain and operate, but I would (or so I imagined) simply camp out there, enjoying the romantic splendor of all those empty rooms. I envisioned descending the curved staircase into the dark ballroom carrying a candle. Julie, being theatrical herself, enjoyed my fantasies but couldn't repress laughter.

"Oh, Paul," she reminded the youthful dreamer, "this place is not all sunny days and summer daydreams. We have horrible weather sometimes, and tragedy. You should look out that window in the winter, during a storm. The day after Christmas one year Ed Rogers, who was Emery's caretaker, living in the big frame house on the island, had to take a young visitor back to her home on Grindstone. Minerva Robbins had come over to play with the Rogers children during the holiday school recess. Ed never should have tried to cross, because the river was at that treacherous stage when it's partly frozen, full of great slabs of floating ice.

"Mrs. Rogers was rightly concerned and watched from the porch of the frame house as Ed, little Minerva and their son, Frank, left in the ice punt, headed for Grindstone.

"One of our lake-effect squalls came up suddenly, as they do. The punt disappeared from view. The total whiteout sometimes lasts only five minutes or so, as it did that day. When suddenly it was over, and the sun came out, under the blue sky there was no punt."

Julie stopped. That was the end of the story, I supposed. "They disappeared?"

"Searchers the next morning found the empty punt, drifting in the open water. There was nothing in it but little Minerva's fur muff."

Julie didn't go down to the street often, because of her limited eyesight and the steep stairs. She would usually walk with the aid of her cane every week or two to Melba Churchill's to have her hair done. Julie, ever the actress and always aware of her persona, dressed for the occasion with jewelry and a hat. She had her white hair tinted blue, a fashion of the older generation.

Julie ate like a bird, and friends, aware of her financial plight, would often stock the cupboard. Often I would bring up two ice cream cones from the wonderful soda fountain of the Ellis drug store, a few steps up the street. I frequently brought new postcards or a souvenir booklet I would purchase from a stand on the sidewalk. That was how my collecting began. Julie would hold each image up close to the one thick lens she could see through (the other lens covered by a piece of paper, affixed with Scotch Tape). Usually she would have some comment about the place pictured, or it would suggest a series of recollections. This was the beginning of my research in our local history, which has been going on now for sixty years.

Ma Irwin

"You remember May Irwin," I inquired, "–was she the most famous person here?"

"Not more famous surely than the presidents who came, but I suppose more people were interested in theatrical celebrities, and May was the best known, nationally and internationally. All sorts of anecdotes were passed around, since she was such a funny lady. Cap' Gould had a store of tales he'd relate on his boat tours. He was pretty funny himself. Here's one of his stock commentaries:

The little place on the point is owned by May Irwin, the actress. May is my age, just 40. May is F.F.F.—Fair, Forty, and Funny. She has several hobbies. She has fifty Jersey cows. We get milk of her. There is only one objection to it, and that is when you get the milk out of the bottle the cream is so thick that you have to use a corkscrew. She raises Angora cats and Airedale puppies. I was over there lately and helped her raise some rye. I remember distinctly not long ago there was a sweet young bud there, and she asked May if she ever went out in a canoe. May looked at her and said, "Dearie, if you ever see me in a canoe, you will have to look quick." If you've ever seen May, she is not much on longitude but she is considerable on latitude.

"It was Fred Remington—the famous artist, you know—who put the bee in May's bonnet, even suggesting Clayton as the place to go. May had already heard of the river, since many theatrical folk had come to Clayton for years, but mostly men, here to fish. Fred, although not a theater person, knew the river well since he was a North Country native and loved Chippewa Bay. That's a long way from Clayton, but Fred knew our village as an actor's hangout. Fred was a boon companion of James K. Hackett, the Broadway star who had a Clayton estate, Zenda.

"May loved to tell the story of her first visit here. It seems a bit improbable. Here was May, coming up supposedly to provide her ill sister with rest and recuperation. May would have us believe that, immediately on arrival, she put sick Flora in a rented boat and started rowing, with no idea of where she was going or any destination in mind—out from Clayton into that open water, into a rainstorm and the darkness. Because of the storm she had to find shelter in an unoccupied boathouse on Bartlett Point, wrapping poor, wet Flora in a blanket, while May stood watch until morning. Do you believe that? Well, maybe.

"What makes me more skeptical is her telling us that when the sun came up, she just headed out across the river to find an island—any island. After four hours (she must have been pretty slow) she crossed the channel to arrive at Club Island. She fell in love with it, found the farmer who owned it, and bought it. Really? I know for a fact that she bought the island from an actor friend, Hugo Toland. And why, I ask you, was May rowing from Clayton, with night falling, headed for Hugo's island? Hmmm.

"May built a grand summer home on Club Island, but never really cared for it. She wasn't one to luxuriate in splendor, being served by others. May was far happier when she bought her mainland farm, where she could get her hands dirty. She was an earthy woman at heart–down to earth–and she had a big heart and joyous personality.

"On her farm, May's bungalow—that's what we called those low, one-floor houses—was far smaller than her Club Island summer home. 'Cozy' was more the word to describe the mainland place. It was full of comfortable furniture and piles of books. It wasn't built for entertaining. Although May had close friends like Geraldine Farrar as house guests, the only social events that I remember (or that I heard about, even if I wasn't invited) were her afternoon coffee klatches. May wouldn't be one to have an elegant 'tea,' you know. Instead, she poured the steaming hot coffee, even on the hottest afternoons, out of a big, white ironstone pitcher. No silver tea service for May. With it you got crackers–period. Or maybe some cheese to go with the crackers–or if you were really lucky, some cinnamon coffee-cake. But that was May's style of entertaining. Who cared, when she was the real entertainment?

"Oh, but May wasn't trying to discourage visitors. Not at all. For many years she used to hold an annual barn dance on the farm. She invited hundreds of people. It was to benefit the Clayton Golf Club, one of many local organizations she supported. There would be a single fiddler—no borrowed hotel orchestra for May. You had to come in costume—that was the rule. Something seedy, you know. Imagine the society matrons trying to find and borrow down-home attire! Can you picture the Arthur Brisbanes, he in worn coveralls and she in gingham apron? Oh, but they would do it, for May—and she would do it for the social set, so long as they brought money to contribute to the golf club.

Geraldine Farrar

"Unlike many of the island people, May participated regularly in village community events. She always showed up at the Catholic church fair, going home with big shopping bags full of purchases. Even in her seventies she took her horses to the county fair at Watertown. May was an excellent sulky driver, proud of her fine horses. May was one grand lady.

"But I suppose in later years Jerry—Geraldine Farrar—was better known, especially among a younger generation, than May. Although world renowned as an opera star, Jerry went to Hollywood, which created her large following.

"And we had another well-known star here in more recent years, Irene Purcell. She was primarily a Broadway stage actress, but also went to Hollywood in the early thirties. She was in a dozen or so films within a few years, pictures like *Just a Gigolo* in 1931 and *The Crooked Circle* the next year. In 1939 she was in the famous Broadway production, *The Women*."

"Where was her place?"

Irene Purcell
with co-star George Montgomery

"It's Fancy Rock, a Canadian island over by Rockport. She's not there anymore, however, since she recently married Herbert F. Johnson, the chairman of the Johnson Wax Company, and moved out to Wisconsin. She's his third wife, current mistress of a stupendous house–14,000 square feet–designed by Frank Lloyd Wright, who's done those other world-famous buildings for the Johnson Wax Company. Marty Zonnenberg, over on this side of Grindstone, has Irene's beautiful boat, the *Show Girl*.

"There's quite a story here. You see, Irene Purcell came to the river as a gentleman's 'fiancée' [Julie winked]. He was Yves de Villers, a Montreal businessman. Irene, of course, was based in New York and Hollywood. I believe Yves gave Irene little Fancy Rock Island. It was their pied-à-terre here, but the idyll soured and they quarreled. One afternoon, when Irene came back to Fancy Rock in her long deck launch, she was astonished and horrified to see the house vanished, only the chimney remaining. Yves had the building completely taken down. That was the end of the affair.

"But not the end of the story: you see, Irene went back to the city and forgot about her island until a war bond benefit event at the Waldorf–Astoria. Sitting at the same table, Joan Marlowe, an actress friend, mentioned her fondness for the Thousand Islands and dream of owning one. Irene casually said to Joan, 'Well, I'll give you mine.' And so it was that Joan came to the river. She married Ward Morehouse, a famous *New York Times* columnist. He writes the 'Broadway After Dark' pieces and does books as well. He tells the story of Fancy Rock in his book about the Waldorf-Astoria. The Morehouses subsequently divorced,

Joan Marlowe

and Joan married Roderick Rahe. Joan is copublisher of *New York Theater Critics' Reviews* and *Theater Information Bulletin*.

"But glamorous as all these theater people were, in the last analysis they weren't as truly significant as some here, even if those others weren't such celebrities."

"Actors and actresses weren't so rich," I ventured.

"Oh, Paul. There you go again. Spending money is no accomplishment. The Boldts probably spent the most, but surely they weren't the most important people here. They couldn't compare to the Bournes or Pullmans for wealth or power. The Boldts were merely big spenders. But none of those plutocrats could compare to the one really great man here."

"Who was that? Frederic Remington, the artist?"

"A good guess, my friend, and maybe Fred's name will be remembered after all the others are forgotten. But no, I was thinking of someone who gave most of his money away and devoted most of his life as well as his fortune to helping others. That was Nathan Straus."

"He was at Cherry Island—one of the Twin Cottages."

"Yes, with his dear friend and partner, Abraham Abraham, in the house next door. Nathan used his large place less after Abraham died—I think I told you that. I've heard that Nathan then used a smaller cottage on Cherry Island, but if so I never visited it."

"Straus had Macy's—the biggest department store in the world."

"The family owned it. Nathan and his brother Isidor ran it. Isidor went down on the *Titanic*, you recall—his wife with him, when she refused to leave his side. The Straus family was partner with Abraham in Abraham and Straus, another huge department store over in Brooklyn. But Nathan Straus's name is on other things in New York City—a public school, a library, a community center, a public square, a park. One of the cities over in Israel is named for Nathan—Nathanya. You see, he was a great philanthropist and public benefactor. I've read that he saved the lives of more than 445,000 babies in New York City. That's the sort of accomplishment that people remember, long after they've forgotten big trophy castles and colossal yachts."

"How did he save so many babies' lives?"

"Well, that's not what he set out to do, particularly. Nathan was simply a good man who was concerned about other people. There was a horrible humanitarian crisis during the winter of 1892-1893. That was the winter when

Boldt opened his Waldorf and had a nervous breakdown because his venture seemed doomed. There was a financial collapse, with people thrown out of work. Straus distributed food to those who couldn't afford it. For two winters he subsidized coal for fuel, selling a million and a half buckets of coal at five cents each the first year, two million the next. The tickets could also be used for food and lodging. Nathan set up housing for the homeless, offering bed and breakfast for five cents. That's how he got started in his humanitarian philanthropy.

"At the same time, in 1893, Straus learned that many of the infant deaths really were not caused by poverty. He was astonished to learn that almost a quarter of new babies in New York City died before their first birthday. He was sufficiently concerned to ask why—that's the way he was, you see. Medical experts suspected the cause was largely lack of pasteurized milk. The pasteurization process cost money, of course, which was why it was slow to be widely used. Nathan made up his mind to change that. He set up nearly three hundred milk stations, first in New York City and then elsewhere around the country. Within four years, the number of babies who died dropped from 241 per thousand to a mere 4 per thousand. That's what I call remarkable!

"But not everyone thanked Nathan Straus. He was Jewish, and we had plenty of anti-Semitic bigots like Henry Ford—we still do. It's hard to imagine aversion to a great man like Nathan Straus—and his wonderful wife, Lina Gutherz Straus, who was so supportive of his humanitarian work and so knowledgeable about it. She was a cultured and highly educated woman. Lina wrote a definitive book you'll find in

Nathan and Lina Straus

medical libraries, called *Disease in Milk: The Remedy Pasteurization, the Life Work of Nathan Straus.*

"Nathan was generous in many ways. During the Spanish-American War he gave the army refrigeration equipment to preserve food and maintain health of our troops. His greatest generosity was to Israel (then Palestine). Nathan gave more than two-thirds of his fortune to establishment of a Jewish homeland, and he worked vigorously during the last fifteen years of his life to make this happen.

"So you can see why Nathan was not so rich as some of his neighbors, and why his house is not so grandiose. He did have a fine summer home and yacht, of course, but he gave them up. His real trophies were intangible, like Chief Justice Taft's heartfelt tribute: 'Dear Old Nathan Straus a great Jew and the greatest Christian of us all.'

"Probably Nathan Straus's greatest memorial, however, are those 445,000 babies whose lives he saved—and all of their millions of descendents today."

"How do you know so much about so many people?" I asked.

Julie laughed. "Well, I'm nosey—and an incurable gossip, I suppose. Because we never had a place of our own on the river, I depended on a network of acquaintances to provide my entertainment (and indeed my upkeep) here when I was young. And I had to entertain them—gossip being the main amusement. Getting to know people became a modus vivandi. I associated with a lot of other gossips, some professional, like Nanette Lincoln, the river correspondent for the *New York Times*. You could learn a lot from local people, too, since with so many servants on these little islands people led rather public lives. Living on a small island surrounded by this floating world of sociable islanders is like living in a glass bowl. I remember one place where a new owner couldn't imagine why there wasn't a big picture window to take in the stunning view from the dining room. They tore out the sideboard and put in a huge show window. That didn't last long. When dining, especially when entertaining prominent guests—or worse, having a discrete tête-à-tête with an intimate visitor—there was a gallery of boats outside enjoying the proceedings."

"Was that at Cherry Island?"

"No, not the Straus place. They were so high above the water, nobody could look in."

"Did you visit the Strauses at Cherry Island?"

The Nathan Straus Family

"Not often. Their daughter, Sissy, was my age, but the Strauses didn't belong to the yacht club set. They did have their own tennis court on that little island, connected by the lovely arched bridge, however, and we were invited to play there. Sissy might also be allowed to visit some islands where a friend's parents were known, but the Strauses seemed very protective. Certainly Sissy wasn't one of the 'fast' set at the club."

"Mr. and Mrs. Straus sound strict."

"Oh, but they were good-humored, really. I recall dining there, which was amusing. Before sitting down, Nathan would ask his secretary if she would earn her meal. Smiling, she'd say, 'Yes, Mr. Straus,' and go to one of the windows at the end of that big dining room where she'd toss out a handful of breadcrumbs for the gulls. At their suburban home at Mamaroneck the birds would actually fly into the dining room, some perching on Nathan's shoulder. Our gulls up here were rather large to be swooping over the dining table, however. They make such a messy nuisance of themselves, you know. Once the birds were fed, everyone could be seated.

"Oddly, Mr. Straus had a menu propped up in front of him at the head of the table. No one else did, and he didn't order anything from it. The food just came automatically from the kitchen. But Sissy thought that her dad wanted to know what was coming, so that he could gauge his intake, saving room for whatever might be coming later. He was always dapper, never overweight. As we ladies left, he would be taking out a big cigar, clipping off the end with a fancy tool he had, just for that purpose."

"How was the food?"

"Oh, marvelous. I have some recipes from the Strauses's wonderful cook, Anna. She was the German-born wife of their yacht captain, Fred Stowell. The Stowells were with the Strauses forever. They went from the Bay to New York City. Anna was a widow cooking for Nathan after he was a widower, until he died. Then she went with Gladys Straus' family."

"Did you know the Abrahams next door?"

"Not really, as their children were a bit older, married at the time. Next to them on Cherry Island the Marx family was at Casa Blanca. Eugenie Marx was Lina Straus's sister. The Marxes had a daughter, Mary about my age—but she got married there, in quite a gala wedding, so afterwards I didn't see much more of her. Her father, Señor Marx—talk about glamorous figures on the river! Although reputed to be a sugar plantation baron, he really was the largest tobacco grower in Cuba, producing the wrappers for cigars. He also was a very rich property owner in Havana and the Washington lobbyist for Cuban tobacco manufacturers. He also raced automobiles—he had a Darracq, I recall. The Marxes added a cosmopolitan tone to the resort, even if they weren't members of the Yacht Club. They were Jewish, of course. Unfortunately Luis's wife, Eugenie, died at Casa Blanca in 1903, only a few years after they rebuilt the place."

It seemed at the time incredible that Julie's memory could reach back sixty years to a past that seemed to me remote and lost forever. It seems less surprising today, as I can recall these visits with Julie. Those conversations occurred sixty years ago. They are as remote now as events on the river at the beginning of the twentieth century had been to Julie.

Interlude: Anna's Recipes

Anna Ruff Stowell, the German-born cook for the Straus family, created many of the dishes served at the Straus's Cherry Island summer home. Recipes of "our Anna" recall some memorable meals. The recipes were published in a cookbook written by Gladys Guggenheim Straus, wife of Nathan's nephew, Roger Williams Straus. Roger Straus, Jr., the publisher, partner in Farrar, Straus & Giroux, is son of Gladys and Roger. Mrs. Straus said in the book, printed privately for friends, "All of you know our Anna—Anna who cooks by genius and by ear." A representative dish is Anna's fairly simple but very rich (and cholesterol laden) lobster chops:

LOBSTER CHOPS ANNA

Chop up the meat from two medium size lobsters. Make 1/2 c. rich cream sauce (see below); mix with lobster, 2 egg yolks, 1 t. finely chopped parsley, a little grated onion, salt and pepper to taste. Shape into chops, dip in egg and bread crumbs and fry in deep hot fat.

CREAM SAUCE:

2 T. butter, 2 T. flour. Let boil up and stir—don't let get brown. Gradually add 1 c. thin cream. Stir until it thickens. Salt and pepper to taste.

Although Nathan Straus was "conspicuously and outspokenly a Jew," ham was served at their summer home. Lina went to the temple regularly, but ardent Zionist Nathan did not, even though he was close to their rabbi. The family was not regarded as "observant." Anna's ham recipe is characteristically simple in terms of ingredients but at the same time is labor-intensive:

VIRGINIA HAM ANNA

Soak ham for 2 days in lukewarm water, changing water at least 3 times. Take ham out and wash very well, scrubbing the under part and black edges; then skin. Lay in a dish and sponge with a cloth dipped in a mixture of red or white wine, 1 T. sugar, 1 T. mustard.   Sponge 4 or 5 times a day.   The next day put ham in a roasting pan with leftover mixture and 1 pt. cider.   Cook in a slow oven 4 or 5 hours, basting frequently.   When done, skim off the gravy, add 1 glass of wine, 1 t. sugar, 1/2 t. cornstarch, juice of 1 lemon, 1 T. ketchup. Boil up and serve with ham.

LIVER TIMBALE ANNA

1 1/2 lbs. Chicken livers   little paprika, salt

1/2 pt. cream   1 t. Worcestershire sauce

5 egg yolks

Put liver through a very fine strainer, add yolks and seasoning and mix well.   After this has been done, add cream.   Put in well-greased mold and cook in medium oven for 3/4 hour in a *bain-marie*.

SAUCE

1 T. chicken fat or butter   paprika

1 T. flour   little sherry

1 c. strong broth   little sour cream

1 onion

Put butter or fat in saucepan with flour and onion and brown;   then add broth and other ingredients, strain, and add sherry last.

VEAL RAGOUT ANNA

2 lbs. Veal cut up; cook in chicken fat in pot roast pan; brown all over. Take out meat. Put in cut-up onions, parsley, 1 shallot, celery. Cook this until soft; then add 1 T. flour, 1 1/2 c. strong stock or gravy. Boil up and strain. Put veal back into strained liquid. Put on side of stove and cook very slowly until meat is soft. A few minutes before serving add sherry to taste and 1/2 c. cream. Boil up and set aside until ready to serve. Pepper and salt to taste; add chopped parsley.

SHAD ROE RING ANNA

1 1/2 shad roes (or 1 very large one)	3 egg yolks and 1 whole egg
1 1/2 baby halibut (or filet of sole)	1/2 pt. heavy cream
	salt and pepper to taste

Put fish through very fine sieve—it should then weigh 1/2 lb. Scrape the inside out of the roes (do not sieve)—this should weigh 1 lb. Mix together with the cream and the egg and yolks, salt and pepper. Put in well-greased mold decorated with truffles. Cook in *bain-marie* for about 30 minutes. When cooked turn out on platter.

SAUCE:

Cook bones of fish and skin of roes in chicken broth. Add to the broth a cheesecloth bag in which you have put parsley, 1/2 onion, a little tarragon, a tiny pinch of saffron and some peppercorns. Simmer well; there should be 1 cup. In a double boiler put 3 T. butter and 2 T. flour. Cook until yellow, then add 1/2 pt. heavy cream and the broth. Salt to taste. Keep very hot in double boiler but do not allow to boil. Just before serving, add 2 egg yolks, 3/4 c. good sherry, and a grated truffle. Pour over fish. For six.

VII. Yachting at the Thousand Islands

Boats and boating have been central to the history and character of the Thousand Islands for centuries. Many ship and boat builders produced sailing vessels, steamboats, and our famous rowing skiffs–and Rushton his famous canoes–on the St. Lawrence. Builders continued to craft noted powerboats of the twentieth century. Some grand steam yachts were built locally, such as the Nichols' *Nokomis*. But the most magnificent private craft were designed and constructed by America's leading yacht builders, the Herreshoffs of New Bristol, Rhode Island, and by a few other internationally prominent boatyards.

Perhaps the first in a series of outstanding pleasure boats on the river came from Bristol via the Erie Canal in 1881, built by Herreshoff for one of the most prominent summer residents of the time, the author and editor J. G. Holland of Bonnie-Castle, who was said to have "initiated yachting at the Thousand Islands." Holland had an earlier steam yacht, the *Bonnie-Castle*, that had been "creating many a ripple nowadays," according to the *Watertown Daily Times*, which added, "She's a daisy." That was in 1880, the year before the new Herreshoff yacht arrived. C. E. Hill of Chicago bought *Bonnie-Castle* and renamed her *Wauwinet*, the name of his island, later acquired by the Wheelers, as mentioned elsewhere.

The Herreshoffs' *Camilla*, costing Holland $8,000, "is the finest craft yet put on the river," observed the *Watertown Daily Times* when she arrived in May 1881. The *Camilla* promptly won her first race, "badly beating the *Island Wanderer*, no mean competitor." Although we may think of small boats, like the later internal-combustion Gold Cup racers, as being faster than large yachts, generally the big steamboats like the *Wanderer* had the advantage over smaller steam yachts, since the larger vessels carried much larger and more powerful steam engines. The *Camilla* was said to do 14 m.p.h. But the reporter observed that although the new *Camilla* "is a nice boat, . . . many may do not fancy her." Holland enjoyed her, however, albeit too briefly. After taking an August cruise down the river to Montreal he died in October of that season. Although the Holland family continued to summer at Bonnie-Castle, someone from Sing Sing bought the *Camilla* during the winter after Holland's death, taking her to the Hudson River.

Lotus Seeker and Other Famed Boats

Lotus Seeker

E. R. Holden's 72-foot Herreshoff steam yacht, *Lotus Seeker,* was medium size here but was the largest at Thousand Island Park and fastest on the river for a decade. This view shows Hart Island in the distance, with the original house of Congressman Hart, before the Boldts enlarged it, then replaced it with Boldt Castle.

The steam-yacht speed title was much contested during the nineties, the last decade before internal combustion engines dominated speed races. In 1893 the anxiously awaited new boat of W. B. Cogswell was "guaranteed" thirty miles per hour, capable of beating the "three speediest steam yachts in the world," *Stilleto, Norward,* and *Vamoose.* That year C. Oliver Iselin came on his Burgess-built *Helvetia,* "pride of the New York City Yacht Club [*sic*]" and raced the *Lotus Seeker* but "could not wrest the title." By 1897 some thought the fastest boat here to be Luckenbach's *Now Then* (an article about which follows) but when Gillespie's *Jean* (mentioned previously) arrived that year, others thought the boat to beat was still Holden's *Lotus Seeker.* Two years later the *Lotus Seeker* still vied with the *Jean* as fastest on the river, both doing better than thirty knots per hour.

Edwin R. Holden of New York City was vice president of the D.L.&W. Railroad. The Holdens were benefactors of Thousand Island Park, building the fine library there in 1903 and contributing to other civic improvements such as the lawn tennis court on St. Lawrence Avenue. The landmark steamboat dock pavilion had a large letter "H" on its roof. The Holdens had a large house at 113 Coast Avenue West. Holden built a large boathouse for the *Lotus Seeker* in 1888, using its roof as a bandstand. The Holdens, unlike many more reclusive Methodist cottagers at Thousand Island Park, were socialites, belonging to the Thousand Islands Yacht Club and listed in the New York *Social Register.*

Now Then

When she arrived in 1895, the *Now Then* challenged Holden's *Lotus Seeker* (preceding page) as the fastest boat on the river. Herreshoff built the 92-foot commuter craft in 1888 for the New York publisher Norman Munro, who sold her after a year. New owner Commodore Lewis A. Luckenbach and his family favored the grand Frontenac Hotel. The *Now Then* had a speed of twenty-one knots, logging more than twenty-four statute miles per hour—very fast for a steamboat of the 1880s. Her "beaver-tail" or "cruiser" stern, an affectation thought to suggest speed, proved impractical, as on reversing the ramp scooped water onto the aft deck. The masts were another affectation, fairly useless except to recall traditional schooners.

Lewis A. Luckenbach had built "probably the largest privately owned steamship line in America," a fleet of more than twenty large cargo ships. Luckenbach began with the novel notion of owning several Hudson River barges, served by a single tug. Lewis Luckenbach died in 1906, succeeded by his son, Edgar, and grandson, Lewis. The Edgar Luckenbachs were friends of the Orcutts of Wyanoke Island in Chippewa Bay—quite a distance from the Frontenac, so the fast boat would be appreciated. Calvin Orcutt had a major shipyard in Virginia, probably building cargo vessels for Luckenbach. The Luckenbachs where said to be "very *nouveau riche*," the ladies so "very dressy they could hardly walk." The steam siren on the *Now Then* could be heard for miles—considered *gauche*.

Say When

After owning the *Now Then* for a year, Norman Munro sold her and launched the *Say When*, built for him by Herreshoff in 1889. The new yacht was not merely another fast commuter but was a larger 138-foot cruiser, providing cabins below. She was equally fast, however. The *Say When* came to the river when acquired in 1891 by W. J. White of Cleveland. He sold the yacht in 1909 to Frederick K. Burnham, who leased Boldt's Chalet and is remembered especially for his Gold Cup winner, *Dixie III*. Burnham enjoyed the *Say When* until 1914, when she disappears from *Lloyd's Register*. Most of the steam yachts disappeared from the river about that time, many taken by the navy for use in World War I.

A newspaper account in 1907 mentioned Jacob Jacobs of Montreal as an interim owner who paid "a high price" for the *Say When*, the "fastest boat on the river," and kept the yacht at Abraham's yacht house. According to that account, the *Say When* had logged twenty-eight miles per hour. That report may be mistaking the older *Say When* for a new *Say Now*, a 139-foot Herreshoff yacht about the same size, acquired by S. A. Jacobs of Montreal, according to another 1907 article.

The High Cost of Yachting

A yacht in the class of Laughlin's *Corona* (frontispiece illustration) or Emery's *Calumet* (article follows) might cost some fifteen million dollars today. Converting late-nineteenth-century figures into today's dollars, the annual insurance alone on such a vessel would be about $273,000. Depreciation would be about a million dollars a year.

Other operating costs, for a forty-day season, would be about three hundred thousand dollars. The largest of these, for forty days' service of a crew of fifteen, would be somewhat more than a hundred thousand dollars. The next largest operating expense would be for maintenance and repairs, seventy-five thousand dollars. The third largest bill would be for coal, forty-two thousand dollars, if cruising constantly throughout the forty-day season. Most trophy yachts on the river, of course, actually were used infrequently—although occasionally longer cruises were taken elsewhere.

If a great yacht like the *Corona* or *Calumet* were fully used for a mere forty-day season, the total cost for operating the fifteen-million-dollar vessel one summer might exceed one and a half million dollars. As J. P. Morgan famously answered, when asked about the cost of running a yacht, "If you must ask, you can't afford it."

Stroller

Gilbert T. Rafferty of Isle Imperial brought a Herreshoff yacht, *Consuelo*, to the river in 1896. In 1900 Herreshoff built a fast 81-foot commuter craft for Rafferty, the *Stroller*, designed for day-sailing rather than having cabins below, required for cruising. The photograph, taken from the Rafferty yacht house, shows the square tower of Rafferty's Isle Imperial.

Calumet

In 1902 Charles Emery sold his lovely Herreshoff steam yacht, *Nina,* for $30,000 to D. M. Clemson and Alexander Peacock. This was the year the Peacocks first arrived on the river. They stayed at the Frontenac before renting Boldt's Belle Isle summer home, which they bought in 1905. Originally Clemson and Peacock intended to take the *Nina* to Florida, but Peacock acquired Clemson's interest. He renamed the yacht *Irene,* and she stayed on the river for several years, until he replaced her with the *Irene II,* built in 1910. Both *Irene*s appeared in the previous volume, *Fools' Paradise.*

During the summer of 1902, the year he sold the *Nina,* Emery visited the great yacht designers and builders, the Herreshoffs, at Bristol, R.I., to discuss construction of a far larger yacht. Not the Herreshoffs, however, but George Lawley and Sons of Neponset (South Boston), Mass., designed the second *Calumet* in 1903, built by A. S. Chesebrough, powered by a Lawley steam engine.

The *Calumet*, said to be carrying a crew of seventeen (although the plans show berths for fifteen), came by way of Halifax, Nova Scotia, arriving on the river in the summer of 1904.   Charles Emery enjoyed the grand vessel for a few years, but his ailing wife died in 1907 and thereafter the yacht was largely in dry dock on Washington Island while Emery used a smaller yacht.   With her crew of fifteen (or seventeen), the cost of operating the *Calumet* was similar to that of a typical large yacht, mentioned previously, likewise with a crew of fifteen.

After Charles Emery's death in 1915, his estate in 1916 sold the *Calumet* to James Farrell, president of the United States Steel Corporation, who re-named her the *Kehtok*.   The United States entered World War I in April 1917.   In September of that year Farrell free-leased the vessel to the navy. She was commissioned in December 1917, with Ensign J. J. Phelps, USNRF, in command.

Kehtok served as a harbor entrance patrol and shore guard vessel. She as-sisted East-Coast shore convoys, screening submarines.   The *Kehtok* was de-commissioned at New York in January 1919 and returned to her owner, James Farrell.

The *Kehtok* (ex *Calumet*) served again in World War II.   The navy in March 1942 acquired the vessel, now renamed *Tourist,* from Edward Baletti of Weehawken, N.J.   She retained her civilian name, *Tourist,* in service as a patrol craft (but the navy also designated her as *PYc—32*).   The vessel was found unsuitable for this duty, however.   The navy returned the *Tourist* to her owner after two months.

A few months later, however, in August 1942, the navy reacquired the ship and classified her as a miscellaneous district auxiliary.   Although still called *Tourist*, the navy now designated her as *YAG–14*.   Conversion work began at the Frank McWilliams Shipyard, Staten Island, N.Y., and pro-gressed until she was 98 percent complete, when the remainder of the work was undertaken at the Bethlehem Steel Co. yard in Brooklyn, N.Y.   Her beam was increased from 17.6 feet to 26.1 feet.

Tourist (YAG–14) was placed in service in December 1942.   In January she went to Miami, via the inland waterway system.   She was recommis-sioned USS *YAG–14,* in April 1943 at Fleet Sound School, Key West, Flor-ida.   She was decommissioned and struck from the Naval Register in August 1944.   The navy transferred the *Calumet-Kehtok-Tourist* to the Maritime Commission, which sold her in 1945.   Her fate thereafter is unknown.

Magedoma

The last of the great Thousand Islands steam yachts, Fulfords' *Magedoma*, is a gorgeous museum piece. "Her clipper bow, low-slung sheer, and dashingly raked masts and stack all beautifully reflect the great age of sail then just winding down," says Captain Ben Ellison, a contributing editor to *Power and Motoryacht* in an article in that magazine.

Ross MacTaggart, in his book, *The Golden Century*, says, "There are only two other yachts in the world that compare." The *Magedoma* alone remains in eastern America. The others are continents away: one of the yachts, the *Medea*, is in San Diego, California. The other, the *Ena*, is in Australia. The "magnificent" *Magedoma*, MacTaggart observes, is "one of the very few extant steam vessels from the Golden Century of motor yachts."

In 1901 builders Pusey & Jones of Wilmington launched the *Magedoma* in the Delaware River, christened the *Cangarda* by her owner, Michigan lumberman Charles Canfield and his wife, Belle, one of the New York Gardners. Ben Ellison tells us, "It was not an auspicious beginning, as on the very first cruise, Mr. Canfield engaged in some 'indiscretion' with a young female guest, causing 'shocked indignation' amongst others onboard and eventually America's most expensive divorce (to date). ...Canfield only got in that one cruise before selling his lovely yacht to the colorful Canadian Senator George T. Fulford."

New *Cangarda* at Delaware shipyard, 1901

The Fulfords and their splendid villa, Fulford Place, at Brockville were featured in the previous volume of this series, *Fools' Paradise*. The almost new *Magedoma*, as they rechristened her, was their boat through the early twentieth century, until World War II.

The name, *Magedoma*, derived from those of his wife and children—Mary, George, Dorothy, and Martha. Like the first owner, Senator Fulford enjoyed the grand yacht briefly, for he was killed in a 1905 automobile accident—perhaps the first motor car fatality in Canada.

The Fulford family continued to enjoy the *Magedoma* for more than three decades, entertaining on board the Prince of Wales, Duke of Kent, and the prime ministers of both England and Canada during the summer of 1927. The family turned the yacht over to serve as a training vessel during World War II.

After the war, the *Magedoma* returned to the Fulfords, who sold her to J. Gordon Edington of Toronto and London, England, in 1948. He in turn sold her in 1955 to F. Burtis Smith of Rochester. For eighteen years the *Magedoma* served as Frederic B. Smith's suburban residence, moored most of the time at the railroad dock of nearby Charlotte. Smith changed her name back to the original *Cangarda*. Richard Reedy of Gloucester, Mass., acquired the vessel in 1983, towed her to Boston, and disassembled her. Reedy spent $850,000 restoring the yacht extensively in the 1980s. The hull was replated to ABS standards; the Kew Bridge Steam Museum in London rebuilt the main steam engine and six auxiliary engines, while much joinery work was renewed in Boston. Reedy was unable to complete the project, however. In 1999 the gutted hull sank. The Massachusetts Port Authority was about to scrap her when Elizabeth Meyers, "the renowned savior of classic yachts," came to the rescue. Her firm, J-Class Management, Inc., bought the distressed vessel that year, raised the hull and gathered the disassembled *Magedoma* parts in a shipyard warehouse at Fairhaven, Massachusetts. There they remained four years, awaiting completion of the project.

Meyers in 2003 sold the *Magedoma* (ex. *Cangarda*) to a well-known American yachtsman, holder of some world sailing records, whose previous boat restoration work has been published but who prefers to remain anonymous. He has bases on both coasts, but is shipping the *Magedoma* across the continent since his restoration team is located in California. On completing the restoration, the owner intends to sail the yacht in Alaskan waters before bringing her around to the Atlantic coast, where she may be exhibited at the Herreshoff Museum, in Bristol, Rhode Island. Thereafter the owner intends to sail her up the St. Lawrence. We may give her a rousing welcome when she returns home!

Magedoma, dining saloon about 1960

Magedoma's lavatory basins

Magedoma's disassembled woodwork in storage

Magedoma's hull, weeds growing

Magedoma's engine crank

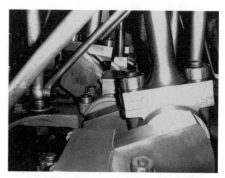

Capt. Steve Cobb of Camden, Maine, has been a passionate advocate for restoration of the *Cangarda-Magedoma*. A 1972 graduate of the Maine Maritime Academy, Steve has served as a captain of yachts, tall ships, passenger schooners, diesel and steam tugs, museum vessels, and more. He also has managed refits and advised maritime organizations. Steve Cobb is the authority on the history and technical details of the *Cangarda-Magedoma*. Ben Ellison, after interviewing Cobb for hours, asked if there is anyone else alive who knows so much about this boat. Cobb's reply: "Not on the face of the earth." That was the somewhat exasperated response of a man who has spent much time in research and an attempt to finance restoration. Cobb estimates the cost of finishing the job as $2.5 to $5 million, depending on options. That includes Meyers' half-million asking price for the dismantled vessel, now seventy percent restored.

Steve Cobb explained to Ellison that the *Cangarda-Magedoma* is a "bell boat." She had no prominent brass fixture that we associate with steamboat pilothouses, the device that indicated "full ahead" to "full astern" control positions, transmitted by wire to the engine room. Instead, the captain and engineer communicated by means of a large bell, a little bell, and a code. Cobb knows the codes as well as the stately cadence of steam power. Down in the boiler room, the chief, the fireman, and the oiler began, hours before departure, to get "a head of steam up." A coal fire would be built the proper size, and when ready steam would be slowly eased to the yacht's seven engines, opening petcocks here and there to drain off condensation until all machinery was warm and ready.

This was tricky, requiring skill learned through experience. If the timing was off, the huge room-size boiler would reaches its maximum 250 pounds of pressure before needed. Then some of the coal fire would need to be quickly ejected through the grates, to be cleaned out later. Otherwise, the captain should blast steam out the stack—an embarrassing public admission of miscalculation when guests like the Prince of Wales were coming aboard.

When navigating, the captain needed to know the behavior of his craft instinctively. Cobb estimates a full twenty seconds required to get the five-foot-diameter prop to shift from 175 rpm full ahead to full astern, much longer for *Cangarda-Magedoma* to actually stop.

Magedoma's rudder

Magedoma's hull

Magedoma, Engine Room

The *Cangarda-Magedoma* has a 300-hp Sullivan triple expansion yacht engine and matching Davidson auxiliaries that push air and water through the system and handle the anchors. Cobb notes that there is no internal combustion going on in the engine room. "At full speed ahead, you should be able to hold a normal conversation down there," he says. "It's like being inside a giant sewing machine. What you hear and see is the wonderfully complex linear and rotational motions of all those parts." All working parts are exposed—push rods, camshafts, oiling systems, and such.

Ellison explains that the "triple expansion" aspect of the engine means that steam runs through three cylinders, one after another, each larger than the previous in order to salvage power from the diminishing energy. *Magedoma*'s high-pressure piston is nine inches in diameter, her low pressure one is a whopping two feet. This arrangement increases fuel efficiency, allowing the yacht's range, with her 15-ton coal bunkers full, to be about 300 miles. Cobb reminds us that "You don't just push a button and drive away. Steam is organic; you become a major part of the engine." While elegantly clad passengers recline above, stokers below shovel coal into the boilers.

Photographs reproduced in this series' preceding volume, *Fools' Paradise,* conveyed luxurious life aboard Fulfords' *Magedoma.* In addition to the spacious aft deck, covered with awning and furnished with cushioned lounge chairs, there was a Cuban mahogany saloon (or "drawing room") and a dining saloon where the steward could lay out dinner service for twenty.

Ben Ellison recalled Capt. Cobb's evocation of being skipper of a restored *Magedoma,* hearing "the slight hiss of steam behind him as he imagines preparing to take her off the dock from the open bridge on her forward house. In his mind's eye, the fitting-out is now complete. Steadying sails are neatly furled to the pennant-topped masts, and the enormous ensign snaps to the breeze aft. Fine small craft sit between the pairs of tapered davits, and the full set of white canvas awnings are stretched out on their frames to protect smartly dressed passengers from coal dust and smoke. That bituminous smell mixes with the odors of manila rigging and red leather-encased furniture arranged on oiled-pine decks. Cobb is wearing the appropriate white-brimmed hat and dark-blue, narrow-labeled, high-buttoned outfit; his deck and engine hands are in white, almost in defiance of the coal."

Magedoma, interior passage

Looking forward a few years to her coming up the St. Lawrence, we envision the restored *Magedoma* visiting her historic home, Fulford Place, now a property of the Ontario Heritage Foundation. Like that splendid mansion, and like Boldt Castle, Dark Island, and *La Duchesse*, the *Magedoma* is a dazzling icon of a Gilded Age in America and a golden age of the Thousand Islands. The alluring 126-foot masted yacht, with her clipper bow and fan-tail stern, would be a stellar feature on the American as well as the Canadian shore. At the Antique Boat Museum she would be a glamorous mate for the 110-foot Boldt-McNally houseboat. They would be a pair of magnetic attractions, confirming the status of a world-class maritime museum and of the Thousand Islands as a historic international resort.

Ross MacTaggart provides an article on the *Magedoma* (ex. *Cangarda*) *in The Golden Century: Classic Motor Yachts, 1830-1930.* Much of the material here is from Ben Ellison's article, "Cangarda: A Classic Megayacht Kit, and a Man Who Could Put Her Back Together," which appeared in *Power and Motoryacht,* February 2003. Capt. Steve Cobb provided additional illustrations.

Poor Man's Yacht

Alberta

Alberta

Commodore Fredrick G. Bourne of Dark Island was in a class by himself at the Thousand Islands. Henry Laughlins's *Corona* was the largest yacht regularly on the river, but Laughlin did not own the largest vessel, by far. Frederick Bourne, commodore of the New York Yacht Club, had not one, but several magnificent yachts that surpassed the *Corona* in grandeur. The *Alberta* had belonged to the king of Belgium. She was built in 1896 as the *Margarita* for Anthony J. Drexel, the Philadelphia banker. Bourne passed her on to serve in the Russian Navy in 1918. She also served in the British Navy as HMS *Surprise*, flagship of the Mediterranean fleet in World War II.

Not only Bourne's 278-foot *Alberta* surpassed the 150-foot *Corona*. The commodore also owned two more vessels larger than the *Corona*, the 189-foot *Colonia* and the 253-foot *Delaware*. Bourne had as well a large fleet of smaller boats. He didn't bring the largest yachts to the river for several reasons—one being their draft, 15.4 feet for the *Alberta*. The big ships were, moreover, ocean going vessels intended for taking large parties on long cruises around the world, whereas Commodore Bourne's Dark Island residence was merely one of his smaller homes, this one used for relatively short visits. The larger yachts were based at Indian Neck Hall, the Bourne estate, which was the largest on Long Island. Frederick G. Bourne is subject of an article in *Fools' Paradise*, the preceding volume in this series.

Nina

Although both Charles Emery and Alex Peacock traded her for larger yachts, one of the loveliest boats ever on the river was the *Nina,* which Peacock called the *Irene*. The yacht appears in many photos, some reproduced in the previous volume in this series, *Fools' Paradise*.

August on the "Fifth Avenue of the St. Lawrence"

Calumet

Second only to Laughlin's *Corona* as the most magnificent yacht regularly on the river, Charles Emery's 140-foot vessel had a "Drawing Room" with a piano in the aft deck house while a "Dining Room" occupied the forward deck house. An adjoining pantry was connected to the galley below only by a dumb waiter. Service required many hands. Crew cabins between the galley and crew mess room accommodated six men in double cabins, plus the captain in a private cabin. Eight more men shared the forward hold. A large owner's room and three guest staterooms and two baths occupied the stern. Eight passengers were served by a crew of fifteen men. Photograph from Frontenac attributed to Robert Gotham.

Klotowah

The Edson Bradleys' 117-foot steam yacht was one of the larger on the river. It is seen moored at their summer home on the north shore of Wellesley Island, now Wellesley Island State Park. The yacht burned at an Alexandria Bay shipyard in 1916. Their huge house at Arcadia Farm burned in 1922.

Wau Winet, 1892 summer home of Chicago merchant C. E. Hill.
The main house was enlarged after purchase by Thomas Wheeler
and the 1888 boathouse rebuilt.

Viola

The photograph of the large steam yacht appears in a Wheeler album,
probably taken when visiting Wau Winet Island.

Commodore, Columbia Yacht Club, 1912

VIII. Tom Wheeler

When John D. Rockefeller became acquainted with young Tom Wheeler, the shrewd operator must have recognized a kindred spirit. Rockefeller took on twenty-nine-year-old Tom, who retired forty years later as the millionaire secretary of Standard Oil.

After his mother died, ten-year-old Tom ran away from his home at Phelps, New York, going to work as a grocery clerk, apprentice blacksmith, then farm-hand. A few years later, an adventurous sixteen-year-old Tom

Private Thomas H. Wheeler, 1863
Company I, 23rd Regiment, New York State Volunteers

was one of the first to enlist in the Union Army, two days after Lincoln's call for volunteers.

Wounded in the second Battle of Bull Run, Tom was captured and put to work making shoes for Confederate soldiers. He returned to the Union Army in a prisoner exchange, allowing him to fight in later battles of the Civil War. After mustering out, enterprising Tom became a "sutler," selling troops provisions unavailable as regular supplies. He adopted an escaped slave as a helper, an older man garbed in mixed Union and Confederate uniforms.

Sutler Tom and his sidekick, Yorktown, Virginia, 1864

After the war, Tom went to Pennsylvania to sell lumber for his Michigan uncle. There was great demand there for wood staves, used for barrels—which in turn were used to transport petroleum from the new oil fields. In the boomtown of Pithole he met John D. Rockefeller, who was just beginning to build his great petroleum monopoly, the Standard Oil Company.

When twenty-nine years old, Thomas H. Wheeler went to work for Rockefeller, starting in Cleveland in 1873. From his initial service, providing barrels, he became chairman of the corporation's "cooperage" committee, concerned with the transport of oil. In the early years, prior to the advent of automobiles, petroleum was largely used in the form of kerosene for lighting and cooking, shipped across the nation and abroad in wooden barrels.

Fifteen years after Tom joined Standard Oil, company executives held a retreat at the Crossmon House in Alexandria Bay. Wheeler was not yet an officer of the company but joined the executives on this sojourn. Tom was hooked, falling in love with the river. He returned every year of his life.

In 1884 Wheeler moved to the New York City area, in 1887 becoming president of the Oswego Manufacturing Company, a Standard Oil subsidiary, and the following year he was assigned to the Standard Oil's Transportation Committee.

Tom Wheeler, 1873

Probably Wheeler acquired Standard Oil stock early, holding it during the period 1882-1906 when it returned an average of 24% per year. Prior to income taxes, one could double a fortune in about four years, holding Standard Oil stock. For the ten years ending in 1906, moreover, the dividends were even more, ranging from 30 to 48 percent.

After serving as "the outstanding figure" in the Cooperage Committee from 1885 to 1890, Wheeler became the chief purchasing agent for the company, acquiring everything from oil to paper clips and a fleet of tankers. By 1902 Thomas Wheeler had become secretary of the Standard Oil Company and a director of the corporation. He was listed in *American Millionaires* that year, when he bought Wau Winet Island.

In addition to his several yacht club memberships and positions, Wheeler belonged to the Union League Club and served several terms as president of the Twenty-third Regiment Association of New York Volunteers.

Tom Wheeler

"He was known . . . as a jolly young fellow with lots of pluck and trifle of cheek."

As mentioned more generally about fortunes of islanders at the time, surprisingly few were made by industrial entrepreneurs like George M. Pullman, who originated and manufactured railroad cars. Towards the end of the nineteenth century more islander wealth derived from marketing existing products. This was the moment in our history when the focus moved from production to consumption. The marketing and distribution of goods became the major engine of wealth.

Like Dark Island's Bourne, who amassed probably the greatest wealth on the river from building a worldwide distribution of sewing machines, serving consumers directly, Standard Oil (represented here by Wheeler, Pratt, Vandergrift, and Bird) was one of the first businesses to sell directly to consumers, eliminating middlemen. By 1898, Standard Oil was refining almost eighty-four percent of the nation's oil. Monopoly by the Rockefeller "trust" was, of course, controversial, as was the cigarette monopoly of Emery's American Tobacco Company.

Distribution networks of retail outlets owned by producers became a device to capture large segments of the national market, as early demonstrated by Browning and Dewey (of Hopewell Hall and Friendly Island) in their ready-made men's clothing business, and internationally by Bourne's Singer sewing machine company. Browning's company may have made the uniform Tom wore in the Civil War, sewn on Singer machines. After expanding production to serve the war need, Browning required a much larger outlet for his ready-made clothing, to keep his plants busy. He devised the nation's first chain of clothing stores, allowing him to take his product directly to consumers.

Tom Wheeler married Orcelia Roberts, daughter of Thomas Jefferson Roberts of Leslie, Michigan. They were married forty-four years. After the death of her husband in 1926, Celia received more than five million dollars. She survived her husband by three years, dying of diabetes in 1929.

Branches of the family have descended in four lines, one from the son, Emmett Wheeler, and others from

Orcelia Roberts Wheeler
Portrait by the English artist Frank O'Salisbury

the three daughters. Mary Louise became Mrs. W. T. Dewart of New York City. Stella became Mrs. Roy N. Bishop of San Francisco. Leita became Mrs. Charles P. Nelson of New York and subsequently Mrs. Henry G. Pearce of Philadelphia.

The Wheelers' only son, Emmett, married Julia Wilshusen, whose family had immigrated from Germany. They had two sons, Thomas Henry Wheeler II and Robert Leroy Wheeler. Julia died when her sons were young boys. Tom, the elder brother, "became progressively hostile and unmanageable, . . . prone to fits of rage and violence." Tom was sent away to school. He had inherited his grandmother's diabetes, which was not diagnosed until he was a young man, after breaking many bones. His diabetes was incompatible with his drinking. Tom "just bummed around" for a while and was living in the Syracuse Y.M.C.A in 1920. His diabetes took him to the Los Angeles County Hospital where he met his wife, Peggy Sturgis. He died at age forty-three, leaving two young sons, Emmett and Thomas H. Wheeler III. The younger remembers his father as "quite a drinker, who often became violent and beat his wife. . . . When the Japanese attacked Pearl Harbor he destroyed the breakfast room and destroyed the china. [His wife] told him it

Robert LeRoy Wheeler and Thomas Henry Wheeler II,
"Two 'flash' young 'gentlemen' at Keewaydin, 1924."

was china and he said that was close enough." The boy "thought [his father] was truly crazy. . . . He remembers his mother and him hiding under the table to get away from him."

In 1931, "as Emmett Wheeler lay dying upstairs in his house in Beverly Hills, his two boys threw a party downstairs to celebrate coming into the old man's money. In the confusion $200,000 of Emmett's money vanished. It is thought that his mistress made off with it. This story was confirmed by Robert L. Wheeler himself to his grand-nephew Michael Stephen Wheeler in 1986, who then told me" (Frederick B. Gleason III).

The last Thomas W. Dewart saw of his cousin Robert. L. Wheeler (who appears in the illustration above) was around 1940 when he was working as a uniformed guard at the gate of one of the major Hollywood studios.

The three daughters of Thomas and Celia Wheeler, Mary Louise, Stella, and Leita, survived their husbands, living past the mid-twentieth-century mark. Stella married Roy N. Bishop, a world-class mining engineer. They had two children, Richard and Celia Bishop. Leita was briefly married to Lt. Charles P. Nelson, U.S.N. Frederick Gleason recalled that "'Juggy' Nelson was a crack destroyer captain and a colossal alcoholic. Once, when told his ship was aground, he said, 'The hell it is,' and dived off the bridge, swam under the keel and came up the other side." The Nelsons had a daughter, Leita. Her mother, Leita Wheeler, then married Henry G. Pearce, "an altogether quieter person" who was considerably younger than she and a world-class cricket player.

Tom Wheeler resigned from Standard Oil at age sixty-nine. After fifty-nine years of work, he enjoyed thirteen years of retirement. In March 1903 for $26,500 he acquired yacht builder Herreshoffs's personal boat, the three-year-old *Eugenia*, which Wheeler renamed the *Empress*. She was 84 feet long with a beam of 17.7 feet. After the 1929 death of

Widows Leita Wheeler Nelson Pearce, left; Mary Louise Wheeler Dewart; and Stella Wheeler Bishop in Mamie's Park Avenue apartment, 1948.

Celia Wheeler, Mrs. William Leslie Gilmore bought the yacht, replacing the triple expansion Herreshoff steam engine with a gasoline motor, reducing the crew required. In 1941 Leo J. Omelian of Erie, Pennsylvania, bought her, changing the name to *Princess*.

Tom Wheeler and granddaughter Mary Dewart, center, with guests, Mrs. James and Louise Moorhead.

Memorializing Thomas H. Wheeler, the 10,000-ton Esso tanker SS *Thomas H. Wheeler* was 438 feet long (10,450 tons). She carried five million barrels of oil on seventy-five voyages during World War II, surviving many passages through "Torpedo Alley," where forty-one ships were sunk by torpedos and two lost to mines. The huge Esso oil tanker traveled from the tropics to the Arctic and "helped make history in World War II."

SS Thomas H. Wheeler

SS *Thomas H. Wheeler* Launching Party, 1920

This is the only photograph known to show the whole Wheeler family together. Left to right: William T. Dewart, Mary Wheeler Dewart, Emmett Wheeler, Celia Roberts Wheeler, Robert LeRoy Wheeler, Thomas H. Wheeler, Stella Wheeler Bishop, Roy N. Bishop, Leita Wheeler Nelson Pearce, and Henry G. Pearce.

Wheelers' *Meteor* carrying the burgee of the Columbia Yacht Club,
of which Wheeler was commodore. Below is a smaller Wheeler boat.

Interlude: T. H. Wheeler Characterized

Tom Wheeler

Like many of his contemporary islanders, Tom Wheeler was a self-made man. He was "new rich," proud of the trophies that symbolized his achievement. From all accounts, he was an amiable but no-nonsense sort of fellow, liked and admired by his contemporaries. Here are a few characterizations:

"I had always a very real and warm affection for Mr. Wheeler. He was remarkable in many ways. In his early life he earned his living by the strength of a good right arm. Some years after he had made his fortune, which was after his retirement from the oil business, he was motoring through upper New York when he passed a blacksmith shop in which he once was employed. The Commodore laid aside his hat, gloves and fine coat, put on an apron and proceeded to make by hand some perfectly beautiful old-time horseshoe nails."

George H. Jones, Chairman, Standard Oil Company of New Jersey, 1926

"He was known . . . as a jolly young fellow with lots of pluck and trifle of cheek. . . . Such success . . . ought to be an example to all of you boys still there. [He] began with little except . . . brains and pluck and you must do the same."

Charles W. Tufts, letter from Berlin to a Leslie, Michigan, newspaper, about 1890

"The late T. H. Wheeler's life was an excellent illustration of the rewards of industry. Starting without any special advantages of birth or education, and making his living for many years with his hands, he achieved eventually a very responsible position with the Standard Oil Company [and] was a real factor in building up the Standard Oil organization."

W. C. Teagle, President, Standard Oil Company of New Jersey, 1926

They've stowed away the things they bought,
  Or hung them up for show,
Until there's scarcely left a spot,
  Where anything can go:
And when Tom settles down to smoke,
  And sees the incense curl,
He's satisfied he is not broke,
  Nor is his gallant girl.

Stanza XV, "The Wheelers at the Waldorf," Anonymous, 1896

"And when Tom settles down to smoke"

Interlude: Letter from Father to Son

In April 1901 Thomas H. Wheeler wrote to his twenty-seven-year-old son (on Standard Oil letterhead):

Dear Emmett,

I enclose herewith check to your order on Mechanics national Bank for $100.00.

I am sorry to learn that you have been unable to find employment. I was afraid you would not find it an easy matter to get work to your liking.

However, you must persevere in that direct, and perhaps not be too particular as to what work it is so that it is honorable. It may be necessary for you to take a position further down the ladder and build up to a solid foundation, and when you get started in again remember a man must always stand on his own feet, and to succeed, you must make yourself indispensable, and not set a limit to the time of your working hours, but do your work to the best of your ability, and let pleasure be of secondary importance. The right type of man finds pleasure in his work and employers are offering premiums for that class.

Emmett Wheeler

Men who compel recognition by their work cannot be restrained from forging ahead. It is not always the man who is most brilliant or smartest who makes the greatest advancement in business; it is he who by bulldog tenacity, he who cannot be discouraged and never gives up, but by perseverance, push and energy, gets there, by surmounting all obstacles.

Your Father

William Thompson Dewart

IX. William T. Dewart and His Family

William Thompson Dewart was born in 1875 at Fenelon Falls, Ontario, now a resort village north of Toronto in the Kawartha Lakes on the Trent-Severn Canal. His grandfather John had come to Canada four years before his father, William, was born in 1836. William T. Dewart was one of eleven children. His father was said to be "a Scotch economist who promoted railroad construction in Canada." While not necessarily false, that characterization may have been intended to enhance the family status. Dewart ran a general store in a remote Canadian village and wrote letters to newspapers recommending developing rail service to the hinterlands and tariff protection. When he was six, his family moved to Rochester, New York.

After attending the University of Rochester, William and one of his brothers started a button manufacturing business that failed. William then served as an accountant for the publisher Frank A. Munsey with whom he was associated for a quarter century, becoming general manager in 1903, before Munsey's death in 1925. Munsey was a friend of George Boldt and an occasional visitor to the river. On Munsey's death, the publisher left assets of his enterprises to the Metropolitan Museum of Art. Munsey's assistant, Dewart, became president of the businesses. During that year, 1926, Dewart purchased from the museum the *Sun* and the *New York Telegram* for thirteen million dollars. Dewart also ran the Mohican chain of grocery stores and, like many men of means, was invested in many businesses, serving as director of corporations, largely Munsey banking and real estate businesses.

William Thompson Dewart   Mary Louise Wheeler Dewart

Portarits by the English painter Frank O'Salisbury

William Dewart married Mary Louise Wheeler in the Collegiate Church on Fifth Avenue in 1908. Frank Crowinshield, blueblood editor of *Vanity Fair,* was Dewart's best man. In 1931 the Dewarts acquired a 102-acre estate that they named Willmary Manor, located on the highest point of Greenwich, Conn. There they enlarged a fine Tudor-style country house, now on Dewart Road. The residence, presently owned by Mark Fisher, remains a notable landmark of the community. The T. W. Dewart estate sold the last twenty acres of land in 2003 to Mr. Fisher.

William T. Dewart, Sr., died at age sixty-eight in 1944 at his Park Avenue residence. Direction of his business interests passed to his two sons. A family holding company (C. W. H. Merlis Corporation) had interests in real estate and banking. Widow Mary Louise Wheeler Dewart died in 1958 at Willmary Manor in Greenwich.

The two Dewart sons, William Thompson, Jr., and Thomas Wheeler, successively assumed leadership of the newspaper business. The elder brother was killed in a 1946 plane crash while taking flying lessons. He and his younger brother were well known in sports-car racing circles. Mary Dewart married Frederick B. Gleason, Jr. She died in 1997. Thomas W. Dewart died in 2001. All three Dewart siblings had children.

William T. Dewart, Jr., 1909-1946   Thomas Wheeler Dewart, 1910-2001

By 1920, when the Dewarts acquired Keewaydin, almost all of the great steam yachts had disappeared from the river. Jackson had built two of the tall yacht houses, incorporating quarters for the yacht's crew—captain, engineer, and two seamen. New motor yachts did not require either the tall yacht house or such a large crew. The Dewarts disposed of the 75-foot Jackson steam yacht, *Amabel,* shortly after acquiring it with the Keewaydin property. They retained the *Empress* until 1930. Thereafter they had no large yacht.

After her husband's death, Mary Louise Wheeler Dewart in 1946 sold her parents' island, Wau Winet. She sold Keewaydin in 1948 to John K. Wallace of St. Louis, president of the Cupples Manufacturing Company, a leading producer of metal window units and curtain walls for commercial buildings. Wau Winet Lodge became a restaurant, but after a few years there was a fire, closing the restaurant for an interval. Mrs. Helen Bolton reopened her restaurant in 1959, but it burned to the ground in 1976.

Wheeler granddaughter Mary Dewart's husband was a New Yorker and Yale man, Frederick Brockway Gleason, Jr. He became a business executive, moving to Rye, New York, and Portland, Maine, where Mary died in 1997. She was survived by her husband and two children. Frederick Gleason died at Portland two years after his wife. Their daughter, Laura Gleason Edgar, resides in Maine. Their son, Frederick B. Gleason, III, married Ann Powell Lackey of Tennessee. They reside in Savannah, Georgia. Frederick Gleason has contributed much family material to this book.

Frederick B. Gleason III and
Ann Powell Lackey Gleason, 1981

Mary's brother William T. Dewart, Jr., married Catherine Smith. They had two children. After serving during World War II in the Army O.S.S., William was killed in 1946 while taking flying lessons. His younger brother, Thomas W. Dewart, first married Elinore Irwin Hoelzel. They had four children. After a divorce, Tom married his Thousand Islands' boyhood sweetheart, Libby Fox Landman. Both wives survived Tom, who died at his Greenwich home at age ninety, in 2001.

The *Aurora* approachng Keewaydin dock, 1924

Interlude: Automobile Racing at Alexandria Bay

The Dewart brothers, avid sports-car racers, were among the founders of the Automobile Racing Club of America. The brothers brought automobile racing to the river. For five years before World War II interrupted the series, an annual ARCA was a major event of the season at Alexandria Bay.

The third annual "Round the Houses" Race, Alexandria Bay, Saturday, August 6, 1938. Tom Dewart is in the lead in his MGTA, followed by Lem Ladd in a Ford V-8 Special. The granite bank building and the Cornwall Stone Store are still standing, but the Marsden House, appearing at the right, has disappeared.

Although both Thomas and William Dewart raced their MGs, younger brother Tom was a real moving force in the ARCA and in racing at the Bay. He recalled that initially "it was very loose, not really an organization as much as an idea, just . . . friends and probably no more than a dozen of us at most." Races were sometimes held at the large Dewart estate at Greenwich, which had many private roads and several garages. Tom was recognized as winner of more races than any other MG driver before World War II.

Recalling the origin of the annual Round the Houses Race at Alexandria Bay, Tom said, " We had been energetically searching for a street race . . . as our main event for 1936. . . . Our family had a summer place, Keewaydin . . .

where we normally spent much of July and August. . . . The village, looking to boost its summer activity, decided to hold a Centennial Celebration . . . but had not come up with a major event to cap off the affair. . . . I proposed a race through the streets as the prime attraction. . . . They seized on the idea very quickly . . . but [were] concerned about accidents, spectator safety and village liability, all concerns I had to deal with." Tom accepted personal responsibility to the village for any problems or damages. As Tom observed, "In many respects the village was relying on its confidence in . . . the Dewart family." He realized that "I had placed my family in a potentially awkward position."

Since Tom also had "promised the village a high-class event," he controlled entry, wanting "to eliminate the junky cars such as stock Austins with their doors removed, stripped 'stock' cars, or anything that looked like a passenger car. My idea . . . was to make it an invitation-only race for the best cars and drivers [and] to eliminate the hotheads and difficult ones. Above all, we wanted drivers who represented ARCA's idea of amateur gentleman racers, obeyed officials' signals, had the right sportsman's attitude and got along well together." Tom's admonishment to the fourteen invited entrants to RSVP promptly reflected the gentlemanly nature of the event: "We are particularly anxious that you will treat this with the same courtesy which you would any social invitation." Suggesting that the race would be well mannered rather than raucous, a postscript to the letter of invitation noted (with tongue in cheek) that "rumors current that a prize will be offered for the noisiest change into third are unfounded."

The course was a 1.4-mile clockwise circuit extending from the start and finish line near the school on Bolton Avenue around the Monticello Hotel. An elaborate system of handicapping allowed entry of small as well as big cars. The largest vehicle, a Ford V-8, would be required to average 63 mph to match the smallest, a side-valve "baby" Austin, if its average speed for the race was 46 mph. In practice, the handicap system proved flawed, however, giving too much advantage to the small cars.

Businessmen in town were delighted with the crowds that appeared the evening before the Saturday afternoon event. Conservatively, the race drew more than eight thousand spectators. They were not disappointed, since many exciting events enlivened the afternoon, some caught by a Metrotone newsreel photographer lying flat in the road, grinding his camera. Viewers "hung out of windows, were packed on porch roofs, stood in doorways and store windows in the genuine European manner." So pleased were sponsors as well as spectators that they hoped the Round the Houses Race would become an annual event at Alexandria Bay.

The region sorely needed a shot in the arm in 1936, during the Great Depression. In addition to drawing a big weekend crowd to the Bay, the event provided national exposure, since Metrotone News had many photographers around the course, depicting "Madcap Millionaires" who "risked their necks in search of a new thrill." The sportsmen found this sort of coverage "pretty galling," but it did project perhaps the last vestige of Thousand Islands as a playground of the rich and famous.

The racers enjoyed dinner at Keewaydin after the event, then went to a ball at the Thousand Islands Yacht Club. One recalled that "Tom and his brother Bill both have fast speedboats, there is a large express cruiser owned by the father and also a smaller boat used for fishing. It would be, I suppose, illegal to use any of the other boats to fish from. We stayed at the Club until quite late, most of us drivers simply relaxing in our chairs and letting the others cavort. Before returning, we went on a fast ride up the river and back. It was black as night, and was night in fact, and we went quite fast. Tom certainly knows the river like a book. The next day we slept late, went in swimming, had lunch, and went for a really long boat ride with Tom."

After the event someone in the ARCA observed, "You members can justly increase your compression tenfold to know that never in the history of the Club has a race been organized and run off in such an efficient manner. We gained a tremendous amount of prestige. And right here and now I want everyone to know that it was through all the hard work and diplomacy of Tommy Dewart. The crowd behaved, the policing was excellent and the nine entries made up the best-appearing field that has even been entered in any ARCA race."

The Round the Houses Race became the club's premier event every year until terminated by World War II. More than two hundred newspapers reported the event. Pathé News provided coverage at motion picture theaters. The village engaged a New York public relations firm to promote the event. Lowell Thomas, then America's most prominent radio commentator, urged his audience to attend. In 1940 the fifth and last ARCA race at Alexandria Bay was avidly reported in Britain as Hitler's bombs fell on London.

Tom Dewart in his MG J2, Alexandria Bay, August 15, 1936

Tom Dewart was known for his "very dry, sharp wit and playfully sarcastic comments, as well as an astute business mind with a close attention to detail." Neither Tom nor older brother Bill went on to college after prep schools (St. Paul's and the Hunn School)–which was supposed to prepare them for Princeton. Instead both decided to go directly into their father's business, preparing by a year at the Empire State School of Printing in Ithaca, and apprenticeship with several upstate New York newspapers (not their father's).

World War II interrupted the brothers' careers as well as terminating automobile racing at Alexandria Bay. Bill went into the U.S. Army, Tom the Navy. Shortly after the war, following the death of their father, William T. Dewart, his widow, Mary, sold Keewaydin.

Joel E. Finn provides a lengthy account of the five Round the Houses Races at Alexandria Bay in his lavishly illustrated book, *American Road Racing: The 1930s*, the source of material quoted here.

X. Keewaydin

Main entrance gates, now lost to Keewaydin State Park highway entrance.

"The road leading in from the highway to the river front is sided by loose moss stone work four feet high. The entire length of the road is landscaped with white cedars and flowers. About 35,000 white cedars have been set out on the grounds and intricate bridle paths wind in and out.

"There is a bit of Indian lore told about the spring on this property. It was here that the Indians used to camp and to use the water from this spring. Mr. Dewart has had an artistic covering built over the spring and it is known as Indian Spring. All large ledges about the place have been cleared of underbrush and are a part of the landscaping.

"The buildings on the property consist of the large summer home, two large yacht houses and a small doll like cottage, which the family uses in the spring and fall. Mr. Dewart also maintains a farm, and a modern up to date farm house is located about one fourth mile from the main house."

Thousand Islands Sun, 26 March 1936, courtesy of Jeanne Snow, editor.

Keewaydin entrance driveway

Keewaydin roads and bridle paths, stables in distance

Stone bench along driveway, Keewaydin

Keewaydin lawns, flower garden at left, touring car on driveway at right

Keewaydin, main house, garden side

Yacht houses from main house, Keewaydin

River-side detail, Keewaydin

Keewaydin yacht houses

Keewaydin lane

Keewaydin grove

Garden path, Keewaydin

Keewaydin herd

Keewaydin

The estate landscape was highly developed by the Dewarts, intricately weaving roads, walks, and bridle paths. The arrangement contrasted rectilinear geometry with organic forms of granite outcroppings and groves of trees.

Keewaydin

Tennis courts appear at the bottom edge of the photograph. Bella Vista Lodge is seen on the wooded point across the bay from the Keewaydin boathouses.

Keewaydin

Like most island establishments, the Dewarts' support facilities, especially related to the water, were larger and more ambitious that the large house itself. Two yacht houses supplanted the Jacksons' original boathouse. The internal slips of each building were augmented by large quarters for staff, service, and recreation.

Rowing the skiff *Stella* from Keewaydin to Wau Winet

William T. Dewart

A characteristic pose, at the Arizona Biltmore Hotel,
Phoenix, Arizona, 1936. The rosette in his lapel is that of
an officer of the French Legion of Honor.

Interlude:
Pickerel Trolling on the St. Lawrence, 1866

"If you can't spend six or eight weeks on the Saguenay and have to take your fortnight's vacation so late in the Summer that reason and law forbid your following trout streams, take my word for it that you can do nothing better than to spend as long a time as you can get, if it is only six or eight days, trolling for pickerel among the Thousand Islands. There is reason in this, certainly, and what is more, there are high precedents for the adoption of such a course. Dr. BETHUNE rarely let a Summer pass without spending some weeks at Alexandria Bay, and he was certainly an eminent fisher of fish as well as of men. The oarsmen at Alexandria love to tell of his exploits to this day, and one can hardly spend twenty-four hours at the Bay without being reminded that the Doctor bore the larger part of the expense in the construction of a Reformed Dutch church in the town. Whether the structure was consecrated to the memory of the pickerel and musckallonge the distinquished divine slaughtered there, I cannot say, but I suspect that the completion of the structure quieted his conscience, and that if he had lived to this day he would have felt that he had secured the right to take as many pickerel from the St. Lawrence each Summer as he could entice upon his hooks. Then WILSON ROOT—or WILSE, as he is called 'for short'—one of the oldest and best among the fishermen at Alexandria, although he is still a young man, relates with pardonable pride that he rowed Dr. BERRIAN, Summer after Summer, until years pressed so heavily upon the venerable old man that he had to be helped into and out of the boat, even requiring assistance finally to haul in the fish which he could feel tugging at his line. And more than all, in looking over the register at Crossmon's, I noted the names of sundry distinguished Wall-Street financiers who had tried their luck in the St. Lawrence the present Summer—the JEROMES being well represented among others. The facts quoted prove that pickerel fishing, besides being orthodox, for I suppose no one would charge either of the lamented divines I have named with the slightest tinge of heterodoxy in any article of their creed, also has charms sufficient to entice the money kings from their thrones, and it will, therefore, be safe for anyone to venture a dash at it. . . ."

From Our Own Correspondent
New York Times, September 23, 1866

XI. Carl H. Schultz and His Family

Elsie Schultz Vilas Towne recalled that "my father had a wonderful mind. He used to play chess blindfolded against three boards. Someone would tell him where the men were and he would make his decision. He had a photographic memory."

Carl Heinrich Schultz remarkably combined the reflective characteristics of the scholar and scientist with the activist instinct of the adventurous entrepreneur. As observed previously, Schultz was similar to George Boldt in many ways, not least of which was mental acuity combined with ambitious industry. Graduating from the Gymnasium of Lissa with a Ph.D. degree and from the University of Breslau with an M.D. degree, Carl's first love remained chemistry. He taught briefly and might have pursued an academic career had he not been attracted by opportunity in America.

Carl Schulz came five years after the failed liberal movement of 1848. He was part of the wave of "Forty-eighters" who migrated to America after it became apparent that Germany would not modernize on the English model but would remain a Prussian autocracy under the reactionary leadership of a new kaiser and conservative Bismarck, an agrarian Prussian landowner. Carl Schulz arrived when twenty-six years old, in 1853.

Carl's first engagement was briefly to assist Benjamin Silliman, the Yale professor who was then organizing the chemical presentation at the New

York World's Fair of 1853-1854. Shortly thereafter Carl assisted Dr. John Torrey at Columbia University's College of Physicians and Surgeons. When Torry became the government's chief assayer he took Carl with him as his assistant. Three years later the government sent Carl to Europe to study the assaying and coinage practices of other governments. Many of his report recommendations were adopted. While on this European sojourn in Hamburg, Germany, Carl Schultz met Louisa Eisfeldt, who became his wife.

During the seventeen years Carl Schultz worked with the Assay Office he also did research for the Manhattan Gas Company, installing a laboratory that he used. Professor Silliman, with whom he had first been associated, was not forgotten, however. That association was fortuitous. The Yale chemistry professor in 1807 had bottled and sold seltzer water. Sweetened and flavored carbonated drinks had become popular in the 1830s. Carl's familiarity with European spas, together with his medical experience, led him in a slightly different direction. He became interested in the healthful aspects of natural mineral waters, long regarded as curative or therapeutic.

Carl's intellectual curiosity led him to pursue independent research. His instinct to actualize opportunity directed him to apply his research. Carl's major business venture began in 1862, in partnership with Thomas Warker. After chemical analysis of natural mineral waters that Europeans regarded as having curative or healthful properties, the partners filtered and distilled New York water, adding similar combination of chemicals, charging the water with carbonic gas and bottling it. Warker had brought the novel seltzer bottle from France.

Schultz in 1872 bought out Warker's interest in the partnership, reputedly for eighty-thousand dollars–a considerable sum in those days–and devoted himself fully to his company. The business employed some 250 men who regarded Carl Schultz "more as a father than an employer." Because he retained loyal and experienced men, after his death they were there to assist his widow to continue operation of the business. Carl Schultz left an estate reported to be about five million dollars–again, a huge fortune at the time.

The Schultz family lived in the Washington Heights section of Manhattan when it was still fairly rural. They had a large estate that extended from the boulevard (now Broadway) to the Hudson, where they enjoyed a beach and boat dock. In addition, Carl Schultz in 1874 purchased four hundred acres in New Jersey and built the first summer home in the area. In time the Schultz family gave up the Manhattan property. They added two stories to the summer home and around it developed a large family compound in New Jersey, founding a community that Schultz named Murray Hill.

Although Carl was a homebody, he and Louise enjoyed company and entertained lavishly at Murray Hill—which the locals and train conductors, because of the many parties, called "Merry Hell."

As his daughters married, he built each a fine house and barn on fifty to seventy-five acres of the estate. At the time each of these properties was valued at $20,000 to $50,000—considered high in those days. Many of these houses remain fine homes today. Bell Telephone Labaratory was constructed on two of the estates. Schultz also built the D.L.&W. Railroad station for the community.

The Schultz children acquired their fondness for the outdoors from their parents, who enjoyed walks and drives through the surrounding countryside. Carl was also an avid hunter, an interest acquired by his sons. The estate had a swimming pool and tennis courts, where the children's interest and proficiency in the sport developed.

Although the Schultz family seems–and probably was–in the main a happy and contented one, tragedy struck when the eldest son, Carl H. Schultz, Jr., was fatally injured in a railroad accident while travelling to the New York City factory. He was twenty-four years old, a handsome and exceptionally promising young man who was expected to take over his father's business. He had been married only about a year and left a wife and infant son. His father never fully recovered from the tragedy.

Carl H. Schultz died suddenly and unexpectedly of pneumonia in 1897 at age sixty-nine. Louise Schultz survived Carl by twenty-five years and outlived her second husband, Baron Sievers, as well. Louise (like many an islander) died at her Thousand Islands home in July 1921.

Carl and Louise had eleven children. Son Carl Rudoph Schultz ("Rudy") and his first wife, Clara Shields, divorced in 1910. Within a few days Rudy married Minerva Huntington Chappel. They had a son, also named Carl Schultz; and a daughter, also named Louise Schultz. Rudy, who was president of the Carl H. Schultz Mineral Water Company, died at age fifty-six, survived by his wife and children. His grandson, like his son also named Carl Schultz,

Carl Rudoph Schultz

has contributed most of the Schultz family material for this presentation. Carl and Janice Schultz live in Lisbon, Connecticut.

Son Carl Walter Schultz was vice president of the Carl H. Schultz Mineral Water Company when he died young of a heart attack at age forty. Carl Walter, a large man with light brown hair and gray eyes, was the big-game hunter.

Another son, Carl Herman Schultz, died even younger, at age twenty-six, of complications after an operation. He was at the time only two years older than his brother Carl H. Schultz, Jr. who had been when killed in the train accident.

Carl Walter Schultz

The eldest Schultz daughter, Orla, married Ernest B. Rubsamen, a silk manufacturer. Orla's sister Irma married Ernest's brother, Louis C. Rubsamen, who had become a member of the New York Stock Exchange at age twenty-five. Augusta Schultz Hobart, a national tennis champion herself, married Clarence Hobart, an international tennis champion. Marie Schultz Aufermann Kast was another proficient tennis player. In addition to Pauline Schultz VonBernuth Foord of Little Watch Island there was still another sister on the river, Elsie Schultz Vilas Towne, as mentioned previously. The remaining sister was Heda Schultz Brigham.

Ready to Depart
Keewaydin appears in the distance at the left, Bella Vista Lodge at the right.

Apache

Rudy's small steam yacht was distinctive in design. Her low profile with little sheer was thought to be modeled after a German "torpedo." Her trawler bow and cruiser stern were contrary to the prevailing fashion for clipper bows and counter sterns.

Carl Rudolph Schultz, left, and friend at Homosassa.

Rudy, son of Carl H. and Louise Schultz, was a well-known member of the family on the river.

EMPIRE STATE.
Formerly SYLVAN STREAM.

BUILT 1863, at NEW YORK

HULL, OF WOOD, BUILT BY THOMAS COLLYER. Length of keel 148 feet; over all 157 feet; width of hull 26 feet; over guards 44½ feet; depth of hold 8 feet 6 inches; draft of water 5 feet 8 inches. JOINER WORK by DE-CKER & BROWN, N.Y.
ENGINE, VERTICAL BEAM, CONSTRUCTED BY FLETCHER, HARRISON & CO., NEW YORK. Diameter of cylinder 40 inches; stroke 8 feet
BOILER, LOBSTER RETURN FLUE, OF IRON. Total grate surface 62 feet; total heating surface 1363 square feet. Built by FLETCHER, HARRISON & CO.
WHEELS. Diameter 26 feet; 22 buckets to each wheel, 6 feet 8 inches long and 20 inches wide; dip 31 inches.

TONNAGE: Gross 349 ⁴⁴   Net 240 ⁶⁴

The SYLVAN STREAM was built for the route on the East River, between New York and Harlem. Speed 17¾ miles per hour. Sold 1865 for service on St. Lawrence River. Name changed 1873 to Empire State.

Point Vivian

Several competing lines of steamboats linked many cottage colonies and mainland communities. They made scheduled stops to deliver residents and provisions, and also served as excursion boats for tourists.

XII. German American Families on the River

The Boldt, Schultz, Straus and Ritter families were prominent, first-generation German Americans at the Thousand Islands. Probably the families were acquainted, at least on the river, although the Ritter-Shumways came from Rochester whereas the other families were New Yorkers. The three families built summer homes nearby, a short distance from Alexandria Bay. Abraham Abraham, also a close neighbor, was second-generation; his father, a prosperous Brooklyn merchant, had come from Bavaria, now in the south of Germany.

George Boldt immigrated from Prussia, from a northern island in the Baltic Sea, whereas the Straus family migrated from Bavaria in the South. Although their regional cultures and dialects differed, both Boldt and Straus, and their wives as well, spoke fluent German. Their experiences differed in other respects, however. George came alone; Nathan came with his parents, two brothers and sister—not directly from Germany, but by way of Georgia, where Nathan lived for eleven years before moving to New York City. Nathan was three years older than George. Straus had come to America at age six, while Boldt was thirteen on arrival. Nathan moved with his family to New York City the year after George arrived there. While George began in Manhattan as a teenage kitchen helper, young Nathan's father was a successful merchant whose family had been affluent in Bavaria.

Carl Schultz came from Austria with a slightly different cultural background. His parents had been poorer than Straus's, but he had the more extensive education. Schultz came alone, like Boldt, but as an adult far better prepared for success in a professional career. Like the Boldts and Strauses, both Carl and Louise Schultz revisited Germany often, both speaking fluent German.

The major distinction between the German American families was between those that were Jewish and those that were not. The Straus and Abraham families, like the neighboring Marx family at Casa Blanca—and like many other prominent New Yorkers on the river—were Jewish. They did not belong to the Thousand Islands Yacht Club. They tended to keep to themselves, and particularly did not encourage their children to socialize with non-Jewish young people—or, indeed, with the "wrong kind" of Jewish children, particularly those from non-German family backgrounds.

Nathan Straus

The Straus family became aristocratic in American Jewish circles. Although not prestigious bankers, the Strauses belonged to a select elite that intermarried—to Guggenheims, Sachs, Sulzbergers, Lehmans, Kuhns, and the neighboring Abrahams. Leon Harris in *Merchant Princes* characterized the Strauses as an American Jewish family like the Rothschilds in Europe, known for a "lifestyle as notable . . . in terms of luxury, of generosity, and of service." He noted that a few Jewish banking families in America may have been richer, but none set such an example. Cleveland Amory regarded the Straus family as "foremost among the inner circle of the 'Jewish Grand Dukes.'" Stephen Birmingham likewise characterized the Strauses as "grand dukes," noting that a group of German Jewish families comprised "the distinguished "Old Guard—families who migrated to America between 1837 and 1860," forming "a closed, cloistered social order." Seen from this perspective, pity for the poor Strauses, excluded from a discriminatory Thousand Islands Yacht Club, may be misplaced. Probably they didn't miss associating with these "new people," the new rich—and wouldn't have wanted their daughter Sissy associating with the likes of young John Hayden, arrested in 1902 for kidnapping the McIntyre girl (an unsavory episode recalled in *Fools' Paradise*).

Although Nathan Straus became revered for his good works, he ought not be envisioned as unworldly. His Herreshoff yacht, *Sisilina,* was almost a hundred feet long; its successor, the *Vitesse,* was 125 feet long (the Abraham yacht, *Wana,* was even larger, at 132 feet, sleeping twelve plus a double crew of eleven. It replaced his earlier yacht, *Rose*). Nathan liked fast boats as well as fast horses. In 1909 he bought the "show boat at the New York Motorboat Show," the 35-foot *Ostrich* (which "Straus" means in German). She would do 23 miles per hour, very fast for the time. Nathan, who loved horse racing, owned champion horses and was "a recognized figure in the world of sport." Nathan was nicknamed "King of the Speedway." He also was a boxing fan, counting among his close friends famed prizefighters, with whom he liked to play cards.

Nathan is fascinating because of the differing aspects of his personality. He was no ascetic saint, but on the contrary was said to be vain, a "natty dresser," tending to the "flashy or faddish" in his attire. He whistled a lot (which must have annoyed George Boldt, who would fire an employee for whistling). One of Nathan's favorite tunes was "There'll Be a Hot Time in the Old Town Tonight"–which may tell us something. Nathan was a live-wire, an extrovert who constantly cracked jokes—hardly "Saint Nathan," as sometimes called, fitting our stereotype of the saintly do-gooder.

Like George Boldt, Nathan "made friends with everyone." He was "democratic in his notions," and "hates illiberal or pretentious persons," although "he devotes considerable care to dress and follows the fashions closely." He was not so much a populist as to refrain from acquiring splendid yachts and a showplace summer home. He traveled in princely manner, taking with him a famous horse, Defendum, on some of his annual trips to Europe, so as to drive around France and Germany in style.

Sisilina

Nathan and his brother, Isidor, were a "study in contrasts." Whereas Isidor was more the sober businessman, Nathan, "a nervous, energetic man," seemed lightweight, impulsive, avoiding details, with a short attention span. He could be formal in manner only by making a special effort, which usually didn't last long. "Gay and jaunty" was how one writer characterized him. Another observed that although he "lacked discipline," he was gifted with "a quick mind and lively imagination," with "flashes of brilliance."

Nathan, "strong in his likes and dislikes," was said to have "an individuality which is elemental, almost primitive in its loves and hates," but a personality "far too delightful and picturesque to be forever buried" under the image of the noble philanthropist. He was "an original, original in word and act, in every interest, in every association, in every understanding of his life." If Nathan Straus evidenced contrasting traits, as said of him, "perhaps no man will ever achieve the same perfect combination again."

The Strauses and their local help were on cordial terms. Nathan threw a big banquet at the Thousand Islands House for everyone who worked on building his cottage when it was completed, attended by 300 workmen and their wives. He engaged the Kingston Band for the occasion. The Stowells were key persons on the local household staff—Fred was captain of the yacht and his wife, Anna, was in charge of the kitchen and housekeeping. Anna was German-born, so able to chat in her native language. The Stowells named their son Nathan Straus Stowell, and their grandson also was named Nathan.

Nathan was keenly interested in politics. Like George Boldt he was considered a possible candidate for mayor of New York. Straus actually turned back the Tammany Democratic nomination in 1894 after it was given. Tammany was the consummate, corrupt political machine. Nathan probably could not work within it. As observed at the time, "He is of a temperament so independent of control that quite likely he would break with Tammany before he had been long in office." Nathan did not break with Tammany, however, and not only subsequently became a member of the society, but became one of its sachems. He served on its Committee of Public Affairs and was a delegate to the Democratic State Convention.

Why did Straus support the Tammany machine, so reviled by history? Most important, Tammany's political strength derived largely from its tangible support of the less privileged, particularly the large immigrant and ethnic population of New York City. If the Tammany programs may be regarded as buying votes, they also may be viewed as providing social service at a time of need. This, of course, would have been Nathan's strongest affinity with Tammany. Second, Straus hoped to influence the Democratic Party for the better from within. He became somewhat disillusioned after being denied an opportunity to speak at a state Democratic convention. He was particularly disheartened because, as he said, "I have always prided myself on being a straight Democrat. . . . Why did I vote for Bryan? Because he was nominated in the regular way by the Democratic Party and though I disagreed most emphatically with his platform, I know the man was sincere and honest and had a big heart. And when a man is honest, my friends, he will come pretty near to doing the right thing when placed in power." His comments seem highly revealing of Nathan's political views, somewhat sentimental and naive, perhaps, colored by a sense of loyalty even "though I disagreed most emphatically." With Nathan it was a matter of heart. When asked why he thought Bryan could have prevented bank failures, Nathan replied, "Well, Mr. Bryan would have found a way to prevent it somehow. When the appeal is in the heart, legal technicalities should not be permitted to become obstacles. It's all very well to talk about the inability of the law to reach these evils, but if you go down into the streets, the cries of these women and children will wring your heart, and if there is any humanity left in you, you will start to brush aside these obstacles and get through a law that will be effective." His comments presaged Nathan's subsequent affinity for F. D. R. and his controversial policies.

Nathan's loyalty to the Democratic Party was at odds with the political orientation of all the rest of the Straus and Abraham families. Abraham Abraham observed emphatically that "Nathan Straus stands alone among the voting members of the Abraham and Straus families. Sixteen out of seventeen votes will be cast for Hughes," the Republican presidential candidate in

Nathan Straus and Franklin D. Roosevelt
at Democratic National Convention, 1924

1916. Nathan was, as always, the maverick individualist.

Although declining to become embroiled in elective politics, Nathan continued actively in public service. He served on the New York City Board of Education, served as president of the city Board of Health and as commissioner of parks. Of special relevance to us in the North Country, Nathan was instrumental in the 1893 formation of the state Forest Commission, so critical to Adirondack conservation and wilderness preservation. He served as its first chairman, resigning with a letter of protest to Governor Live P. Morton, stating, "I regret exceedingly that three of the Forest commissioners granted, during my enforced absence, the right of way through the forest preserve to the Adirondack Railroad Company. . . . I desire to record a most emphatic protest." He concluded with the recommendation that "when you select my successor you name a gentleman who has no interest in lumbering."

Nathan Straus is most often remembered as he appeared in later life, either as a compassionate friend of the people or, more cynically, as "Lord Bountiful," a naïve do-gooder—a "bleeding-heart liberal"—characterizations especially familiar during the New Deal era but not unfamiliar ideologically today. If compassionate, Nathan was no sentimental pacifist, however. "Peace does not mean that nations must weakly yield rather than fight," he said. "The power to prevent war can be achieved only by the most thorough preparedness. . . . America should have a powerful navy and a strong army."

And Nathan was not merely a privileged dilettante. As a young man he spent arduous years on the road as a salesman, sometimes "penniless and half-frozen" because of his characteristic generosity. When he wearied of this hard life on the road, wanting to stay with family, he approached Roland H. Macy about opening a concession in the basement of the Macy store. It was Nathan who initiated the family acquisition of the institution that was to become the largest department store in the world.

Macy's

Brother Isidor was more active in day-to-day management of Macy's, but Nathan was the more creative partner, innovating new departments and services. He was in charge of advertising and was especially involved in civic promotions for which Macy's became known, such as the Thanksgiving Parade. The famous Macy's window displays were his introduction.

It might seem that some striking epiphany changed Nathan's character at midlife, but he always had evidenced contrasting characteristics. If at times he appeared flighty or frivolous, he was always considerate of others, even displaying special empathy for their problems. He had a sincere personal interest in employees, those of his stores as well as his homes, winning their "loyalty and affection." Nathan and Isidor were pioneers in America in providing employee welfare programs. Macy's Mutual Aid Society for employees was first in the nation. Learning that two sisters were going without lunch in order to support an ailing mother, they opened a dining hall at the store, providing full meals for five cents. During a time of hardship, an anonymous advertisement in New York papers offered free turkeys for Thanksgiving. Thousands were given away. Only after many years was Nathan's generosity discovered. Because of his impulsive and "unpredictable individualism," brother Isidor had to restrain Nathan's "quixotic generosity." Nathan, however, "utterly independent in judgement and in action," was "willing to stand alone for great causes." Because of this characteristic, the great man in Nathan Straus emerged from the charming but apparently lightweight man-about-town.

Nathan's sense of duty became apparent during the severe depression of the 1890s. Seeing the human suffering in New York City, he provided unemployment relief, establishing workrooms to employ unskilled laborers. With the help of J. P. Morgan (the only time he accepted aid), Nathan set up coal stations offering fuel free to the needy, selling 25 pounds for five cents to others, distributing a million and a half buckets of coal. He opened lodging houses for 64,000 persons, providing bed and breakfast for five cents. He set up soup kitchens for the aged, blind and other handicapped persons, giving 50,000 meals for one cent (or accepting work instead). Nathan didn't believe in making gifts, feeling that total charity destroyed people's self-respect. But undercutting prices of other providers, impairing their incomes in hard times, did not win their approval. With the "zeal of a fanatic" he ignored protests, alienating many other retailers by dispensing provisions to the needy at lower prices.

Nathan Straus, as later recognized, was "among the first to see the true dimension of the acuteness of the panic which left 39,000 families without means of sustenance. . . . His amazing organizing abilities . . . immediately set into motion a tremendous relief machine. Nathan Straus was becoming "the Great Giver."

Straus's concern and generosity responded to many needs, as diverse as sending an ice and water distilling plant to Cuba to support U.S. troops during the war, and supporting families of coal miners that companies refused to reemploy after a coal miners' strike. He sent relief supplies to Italy after an earthquake. On Arthur Brisbane's farm he established a facility to build resistance of children in families struck by tuberculosis. He gave buildings to Trudeau's Adirondack and California sanitariums. He contributed to construction of a Catholic church at Lakewood, New Jersey, where he had built a hotel open to all, after being refused registration at another because he was a Jew. He gave the Red Cross use of the facility during World War I.

Nathan Straus may have abandoned his grand Cherry Island house, not merely because his friend and neighbor Abraham Abraham died, but because he resolved to dispense with such costly trophies, dedicating himself instead to public service and philanthropy. There never was a single, sudden epiphany, changing the course of his life, but tragic events during the second decade of the twentieth century had profound impact. His close friend, neighbor in the other Twin Cottage, and his business partner, Abraham Abraham, died unexpectedly while fishing in 1911. In 1912 his brother, Isidor, and his wife, Ida, went down hand-in-hand on the *Titanic*, she refusing to leave his side to be rescued in a crowded lifeboat. Those were the years of the great fires at the Thousand Islands that marked the end of the resort's heyday. Nathan Straus retired from business in 1914, as World War I erupted. He devoted himself fully thereafter to charitable causes. In 1916 Nathan sold his large yacht, and gave the proceeds to feed war orphans. He also sold both Twin Cottages that year.

Straus was known not merely for his major public philanthropies, but for his personal generosity as well. Nathan was a big tipper who told his secretary to have messenger boys deliver telegrams to him personally, so he could shake their hands and dispense one-dollar tips, considered highly extravagant at the time.

The first Straus Milk Station, 1893

Straus was not universally praised, however. He was a Jew. Nathan was, moreover, "conspicuously and outspokenly a Jew." And as many retailers had objected to his subsidizing low-cost provisions for needy consumers, so his campaign for pasteurization of milk was vehemently opposed by much of the dairy industry, which rightly foresaw that pasteurization would become compulsory. The influential publisher of the *New York Herald*, James Gordon Bennett, launched a smear campaign to discredit Straus and his project. Henry Ford supported Bennett's rabid anti-Semitism, writing and publishing notorious rants that sounded much like Nazi propaganda. Discouraged by the adverse reaction, Straus in 1910 decided to discontinue his milk project in New York City, concentrating on other major American and Europan cities. An overflow crowd at a Cooper Union rally in support of Straus heard him lauded by physicians and others, including the nationally syndicated columnist Arthur Brisbane who became a regular visitor and then resident at Cherry Island.

Nathan Straus contributed to other causes, such as setting up health stations for victims of malaria and trachoma. He was one of the first to respond to the need for war relief. He will be remembered for all these things, but most of all he will be remembered as the "Great Giver" for his contributions to Israel. Much of his fortune was spent in support of Zionism, particularly to assist farming pioneers, the Hebrew University, and health facilities in Israel (then Palestine). It was said, in his time, that "no living Jew, rich or poor, statesman or scholar or philanthropist, commands the love which Jews everywhere delight to show Nathan Straus."

Ten thousand people clogged the streets at Nathan Straus's funeral, hoping to view the plain coffin without flowers. Theodore Roosevelt said of Nathan Straus, "He was one of the finest citizens this state ever had. I feel that I have lost a very close personal friend." James Waterman Wise characterized him as "the rarest of things, a legend in and to his own generation."

Nathan Straus "never recovered" from Lina's death in 1930. He lived only eight months longer. Nathan died in 1931 at age eighty-three. He was survived by three children, Nathan Straus, Jr., Hugh Grant Straus, and Sissie S. Lehman. Another son, his eldest, had died of illness just after being admitted to Cornell University. Another son and daughter died at ages three and one. The surviving Straus children received bequests that were not enormous, since their father had given away most of his multi million-dollar fortune while he was alive. Nathan had protested when his name was included on a published list of America's wealthiest men. The Straus family was not exactly impoverished, however. Lina herself left more than two million dollars when she died shortly before her husband. Nathan may have exaggerated slightly about his literal intentions to die poor, but considering the extent of his generosity during his long life, it rang true when he said, "I wish to die a poor man, for then I shall be rich in happiness and good works." Nathan also said, "There is no greater pleasure in life than giving; give while you live and then life becomes truly worthwhile."

Abraham Abraham

As one might expect of such a close friend, Abraham Abraham shared Nathan Straus's values. Said to be "foremost" in Brooklyn in working for Jewish causes, he was nevertheless supportive of Catholic and Protestant charities as well. Abraham served many Brooklyn institutions–even as an officer of the local S.P.C.A. Abraham was lauded for his compassion: "his heart and his means were always at the command of the poor and afflicted." Revealing his culture as well as his generosity, he funded Cornell University's purchase of the Eisenlohr collection of ancient manuscripts and publications relating to Egyptology and Assyriology. A man of great character, Abraham Abraham was a personal friend of Presidents McKinley, Roosevelt, and Taft.

Abraham and his wife, Rose, had one daughter, Edith. From his previous marriage to Isabel Hyams, who died in 1873, he had three other children–a son, Lawrence, and two daughters, Lillian and Florence. Lillian married Simon F. Rothschild and Florence became Mrs. Edward C. Blum, while Edith married Percy S. Straus, son of Nathan's brother, Isidor Straus.

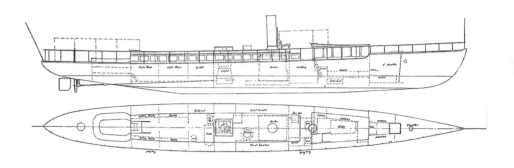

Sisilena

The Hart Nautical Collection at M.I.T. retains twenty-five original Herreshoff drawings, dated 1905-1910, used for construction of the Nathan Straus yacht.

Lindenhof (Linden Cove), summer home of the Ritter-Shumway family, demolished by subsequent owners.

Frank Ritter and the Shumways

Frank Ritter, said to be "a wealthy retired German of Rochester," purchased a mainland point from L. Keppler in 1889 and built a cottage there that year. This house was supplanted after a few years by Keewaydin, when the property was sold to the Jacksons. In 1900 Ritter purchased Clark's Point, where he built a finer summer home, "Lindenhof"– the German term meaning "Linden House." Frank Ritter was seven years older than George Boldt. He was closer in age to Nathan Straus, being two years younger than Straus. Ritter was seventeen years younger than Carl Schultz.

F. Ritter Shumway

Frank J. Ritter (1844-1915) was born at Astheim, Germany, where his father was burgomaster. Coming as a young man to America he first settled at Amsterdam, New York, then moved to Rochester, where he established a business making parlor furniture. In 1887 he began working on a mechanically adjustable wooden chair for dentists, bringing it to the market after two years of development. His innovative product won awards at four world's fairs. Tapping a niche market, the Ritter Dental Manufacturing Company became a leading provider of equipment for dental offices—most notoriously those elaborate instruments of torture, the drills that many of us remember. The Ritter Company has become a branch of the Sybron Corporation, which also absorbed Taylor Instruments, the business of James B. Taylor of Pine Tree Point. Frank Ritter was one of the Rochester industrialists who in 1885 established the Mechanics Institute in that city, forerunner of the Rochester Institute of Technology.

Frank Ritter in 1874 married Elizabeth Fertig of Rochester, and they had two daughters, Adelina and Laura. After his first wife died, Frank Ritter in 1907 married Sophia Schuknecht, born in New York of German immigrant parents. The second Mrs. Ritter, as a memorial to her husband, founded and endowed a home for the aged and an orphan asylum.

Laura Ritter did not marry. Her sister, Adelina, married Robert Crittenden Shumway in 1899. Their children were Helen Elizabeth and F. (Frank) Ritter Shumway. Helen became Helen S. Mayer of Greenwich, Connecticut. Her brother, F. Ritter Shumway, after graduation from Princeton, served as a Presbyterian minister before joining his grandfather's firm. Becoming president, then chairman and CEO, he integrated the Ritter Company into a much larger conglomerate that he founded, the Sybron Corporation, retiring in 1974. Shumway served as president of the U.S. Chamber of Commerce and twice as president of the Empire State Chamber of Commerce.

Frank Ritter Shumway married Hettie Beaman Lakin in 1930. The Shumways were benefactors of the Rochester Institute of Technology. Hettie was instrumental in establishing the National Technical Institute for the Deaf at RIT. She is memorialized there by the Hettie L. Shumway Dining Commons. The Shumways were major donors of the Ritter-Clark Memorial Ice Rink and Gymnasium at RIT's old downtown campus and then of the Frank Ritter Ice Arena on the new campus. F. Ritter Shumway,

Hettie Shumwa

winner of fifty-four titles, is in the World Figure Skating Hall of Fame. Ritter, as he was known, received the 1962 Booth Award of Volunteers of America for "humanitarian commitment, caring, and compassion." He was honored by many other awards and served on many boards. The Shumways established the F. Ritter & Hettie L. Shumway Distinguished Service Award for community service of the American Geriatrics Society.

Interlude:
The Crossmon
House

Alexandria Bay

A Half-Century of Growth

In 1863 Charles Crossmon expanded the small tavern that he acquired in 1848, seen at left in the illustration above.

By 1873 the building had grown as seen in the second view.

In 1881 the Crossmon House acquired its final form, seen below.

Charles Crossmon's "Burro Brigade" was a hotel feature popular with children. His original tavern remained at the core of the grand hotel. He expanded first up river. When subsequently he expanded down river, the drop-off resulted in a five-story structure, seen here from James Street, at about the present entrance to Capt. Thomson's Motor Lodge. The large granite plateau where the original tavern and much of the large hotel originally stood has been empty in later years.

Interlude: Julie and Kris

Julie came across a loose photograph at the back of one of her albums. "Oh, look at this. Here we are–my sister, Clara and I–in Kris's greenhouse at Picton Island. That must have been about the turn of the century, judging from our getups. Kris took the photo for us, I remember–and little did I know, or remotely suspect, that I would marry him thirty-five years later!"

Greenhouse, Picton Island

"Kris was growing plants for the Frontenac Hotel," I recalled.

"Yes, and for Calumet Island and the rest of the Emery estate. He set out thousands and thousands of seedlings every spring. The Picton layout was quite something—hard to imagine today, when it's gone. Kris was so proud of the operation—it was his project, of course. He learned horticulture in Germany."

"I thought Kris was Danish," I commented. Julie appeared surprised, then smiled.

Kris at Frontenac

"Oh? Better to be Danish these days, with that mad Führer over there. But Kris really was born in Denmark—that's next to Germany, you know—and Bismarck had invaded Denmark before Kris was born. Kris always thought that's why George Boldt came over here—as a draft dodger. They were conscripting German youngsters for the Danish campaign right at the time that Boldt sneaked away, leaving no records behind. Kris himself wasn't so lucky. Because he was tall and handsome, he served in the personal bodyguard of Kaiser Wilhelm—that was at the Potsdam palace—the 'Emperor's Foot Guard,' they called it. With anti-German sentiment during World War I, Kris's German military background was a problem. He overcame that by joining the Home Guard over in Connecticut.

"Kris was manager of a big estate there, owned by Edward Langford, a New York attorney. His job there was pretty much what he had done here for Emery, of course. Kris was a born gardener and loved his work."

"He was a U.S. citizen?"

"Yes, he came over in 1897 and took out his papers five years later. I spoke German well, you know, since I had recently studied in Berlin, so I hit it off immediately with Kris when we first met. We knew each other for many years—but nothing romantic, really, since he had a wife and daughter. I had other aspirations myself. Becoming a hausfrau for an estate gardener wasn't on my agenda. I preferred to be mistress of an estate, you see."

"And you did get a big place in the country?"

"Oh, not so grand—but it seems impossibly posh now. With the '29 stock-market crash, finis--the days of big estates with staffs of gardeners was over—for most of us, at least. Kris and I were footloose and fancy free, trying to pretend that "life is just a bowl of cherries" and that "the best things in life are free" when our money ran out during the Depression. Poverty makes equals of us all.

"Kris was such a joy . . ." For the first time I heard a different Julie. "He made life fun—and that's important. It doesn't require money to enjoy life. Kris just had a sunny disposition, even when the weather outside was frightening, as it was during those Depression years. But Kris made light of it. When the phone rang, he'd answer (with his still heavy accent, 'Hass residence; der butler speaking.' We had such good times!" Julie was radiant, but suddenly the light went out. "But we were together so short a time." Then she tried to smile. "But it was fun." I hadn't heard about the end, but Julie supposed I knew. "No, the end was no fun. They sent me his shattered glasses–can you imagine? Why would I want them?"

"Who sent them?"

"The state. When Kris got so bad, he had to have care–heavy-duty care. He was often violent. We were broke. Marcy–that's the state insane asylum–was where they took him. They wanted me to know how bad he was–had to be confined in a padded cell, or kept in a straightjacket. They wanted me to know that!" She got up abruptly, as if to leave, then sighed. "But this doesn't concern you, my young friend. Kris just faded away, becoming a person I didn't know, couldn't know–hardly a person anymore. It was sad, but it's over."

I had known Kris briefly–a big, jolly man with blue eyes and big gray mustache--but was unaware of why he was never around anymore. My parents were inclined to shield us youngsters from such things. I suppose they were suspicious that Julie might be putting inappropriate adult fare in our young ears–but in practice my parents were pretty liberal. My mother, after all, was something of a 1920s flapper, and my father, a chemist moonlighting as a tenor, had sung in a gin mill when they met—"Come to Me, My Melancholy Baby." Rather than adhering to scruples, my parents simply found certain subjects distasteful. When I spoke to them about my discovery of what happened to Kris, they simply passed over it lightly, saying, "Oh, we thought you knew that."

AN ISLAND HOME

Gertrude Smith Pfeiffer, Hickory Island

The way is long, a winding water way,
That takes us to our island home remote
A rock bound isle, firm on the river's breast
Where beauty in its many forms is found,
Where fragrant pines throw down their needles green
And spread a couch that lures one to sweet sleep.
Wild raspberries are here and columbine
And pixy mosses carpet our bare feet;
Great granite boulders fortify one side
And form a shelter when the waves dash high.
A pebbly beach on which the "tip ups" run
And on beyond a sandy swimming pool.
Here we live intimately with the birds
And all the little wood folk are our friends.
How sweet to waken to the thrushes' song.
At even tide to hear the whip-poor-will.
Long idle hours spent quaffing loveliness,
Storing to memory prints for winter days.

And so we return to the city,
Better for having been there
Trusting God and doing our duty,
Meeting life without a fear.

Interlude: A Place for All Seasons

Shawn Roes, Carleton Island

Surveyor Island

Airboat at Manhattan Island

Brian Roes,
North Shore of Carleton Island

Off Carleton Island

Wolves

Wellesley Island wolves cross over the ice to other islands. Here they prowl on the frozen channel in front of the Chalet.

Winter Walkers, Carleton Island

Tea Party, Surveyor Island

Roaring Twenties Weekend at the Bay

Lovely flappers flank two authors, Paul Malo and Ian Coristine, while
B. J. and Alex Mosher, at right, are braced in their shop for the Great Jewel Heist of 1973.

Charles Boldt Goodridge, his wife, Lynne, and their daughter, Gracelyn, with
Eleanor Forrest, their hostess, at the Forrests' summer home, the Boldt Ice House.

French Festival, Cape Vincent

Interlude: More Boyhood Recollections

The drive from Syracuse up Route 11, before construction of Route 81, used to take hours—it seemed like most of a day, as my sister and I, with our parents, usually stopped for lunch at one of the many small towns (Ila's in Sandy Creek was a favorite). Passage through Watertown marked a major advance in the arduous campaign. Then on the last lap along Route 12 we looked for landmarks to calibrate our anticipation, marking this pilgrim's progress towards the heavenly destination. One tall Victorian farmhouse, oddly recalling seedy island villas, seemed a premonition. The peculiar structure still stands with its huge poplar trees, incredibly looking as it did sixty years ago, even to the faded paint, where it has not worn away–not a very attractive pea green. From that landmark I would practically hold my breath. Eventually the road ascended the rise of McCarn Hill, the long-awaited moment coming. Then suddenly there it was: the river, blue like the sky, streaming around mounds of wooded islands.

When I drive to Clayton today (which is often) I still await that moment, then savor the glimpse of Grindstone and Picton in the distance, the silver spire of St. Mary's Church the beckoning welcome of Clayton. It's coming home.

Up at the corner where the road into Steele's Point left the highway was a small, unpainted and rather derelict-looking house. Always attracted to such places as forgotten mementos of the past, I thought the place abandoned and inquired about it. No, I was told, it was occupied by an old codger who lived there alone, a "river rat." It was the first time I heard that term, so asked what it meant. He was a fellow who lived off the river, one way or another, I learned—as a fishing guide (he also fished for his own skillet) as well as working at odd jobs (as little as required). Without regular employment, he was something of a free spirit, I supposed—free to enjoy the river.

One evening when my parents were hosting a dinner party, guests at the table politely inquired what I wanted to be when I grew up. My parents may not have been pleased, but it got a big laugh when I replied, "a river rat."

Dee Bonne in her garden

The art of Nathalie Wilmer Wood enhanced Hickory Island

Pirates of the Thousand Islands and
the Heroine of Gananoque

"Pirate Bill" Johnston and his "navy" of boats, rowed by many oarsmen, launched attacks on Canadian ships from Clayton (French Creek). The campaign of the "Patriots" to liberate Canada from British rule involved an 1838 incident on Hickory Island, subject of the following article. Hickory Island was intended to be a staging point for seizure of Gananoque, from whence the Patriots would attack Fort Henry at Kingston.

Elizabeth Barnett, a native of a nearby U.S. village, had taught school in Gananoque. Learning of the Patriots' plan, she hoped to avert bloodshed there. She crossed the ice alone to give the alarm. Her story, told by John Northman, may be found in the section "Patriot War of 1838" of Shirley Farone's excellent web site:

http://freepages.genealogy.rootsweb.com/~twigs1970/pa-index.html

Illustration from National Archives of Canada, C-1029

XIII. Hickory Island

With broad lawns and lovely houses, the serenity of Hickory Island today hardly suggests armed conflict. The Battle of Hickory Island, like "Pirate Bill" Johnston with his rebel "navy commission" and his navy—a twelve-oared war galley—may amuse us as a sort of quaint period piece, a comic opera. But many lives were lost in the events of the 1830s, and many more were ruined by imprisonment, some for life.

The issues at stake were those that caused the Revolutionary War in the United States, questions of continuing colonial rule. Canada was then divided into Upper and Lower Canada, the latter being largely French in culture, bristling under British occupation that became oppressive in the time of Napoleon, when Britain and France were enemies.

Rebellions began in Quebec in 1837, joined by insurrection in Upper Canada intended to overthrow rule of the "Family Compact," an oligarchy of elite families such as that of Sir Richard Cartwright in Kingston. Many in the United States, particularly in Upstate New York, regarded Canadian independence from Britain as inevitable, following the lead of the United States. These "Patriots" often failed to recognize that Loyalists had settled the Ontario shore of the river–those opposed to the thirteen colonies' War of Independence. The misguided American idealism of those who participated in the military actions of the "Patriot War" lends poignancy to the tragic if comic events.

Sentiment for "liberating" Canada was not confined to a lunatic fringe. A dispatch from Ogdensburg dated December 8, 1837, published in the *Watertown Jeffersonian* said that "the sympathies of our citizens along the line are greatly excited in favor of the Patriots, and meetings are being called in all directions to embody and express the feeling of the public."

Bill Johnston's burning at Wellesley Island of the steamboat *Sir Robert Peel* (owned by Brockville residents) is well remembered as a rather comical incident in the conflict at the Thousand Islands. It should come as no surprise that enraged residents of Brockville did not rise to throw off the yoke of British rule when invaded by Americans in the tragic Battle of the Windmill at nearby Prescott. Hickory Island played no major part in these events, but was briefly a staging ground for this ill-fated invasion of Canada by Americans.

"Patriots" recruited largely from communities of Upstate New York converged in March 1838 at Clayton (then called French Creek). Arms and munitions had been stolen by raiding the Watertown armory, providing a supply said to consist of "4,000 stand of arms, 20 barrels of cartridges, 500 long pikes." These and other provisions went to French Creek. An assembled force of volunteers there intended to launch a campaign on Washington's birthday, February 22, 1838, to capture Gananoque as a staging place for an assault on Kingston's Fort Henry. Although the invaders were confident that throngs of restive Canadians would take up arms to join the Patriot army, signs were not propitious. We wonder in retrospect why the folly persisted—particularly culminating in the terrible Windmill episode of the Patriot War. This might have been an apt case study for Barbara Tuchman's study of military idiocy, *March of Folley: From Troy to Viet Nam.*

According to one account, when "General" Rensellear Van Rensellear (or "Rensselaer") eventually called the roll at French Creek for his invasion of Canada, of six hundred assembled there only eighty-three men came forward. In disbelief, the general ordered a second call, when only seventy-one responded. On the third call, only thirty-five volunteered. This might have reasonably cautioned reconsideration, but reconsideration may seem to be cowardice in such matters.

Guided by Bill Johnston, the miniscule Patriot "army" seized Hickory Island off the foot of larger Grindstone Island, in the middle of the river. Hickory had only one resident, an elderly widow, who offered little resistance to the invaders. The alarm was sounded on the Canadian shore, however, and the militia assembled on nearby Wolfe Island to meet the invaders. The small troop of Hickory then, "owing as is alleged to the stupidity, cowardice, drunkenness or some other trait in the said Van Rensselaer," dispersed back to the U.S. mainland.

Contemporary accounts are suspect, however. Disagreement suggests partisan bias. Another, probably more reliable, participant, Daniel D. Heustis, wrote that General Van Rensselaer marched with a company of fifty men about six miles over the February ice to Hickory Island. Then "the next morning I led another company of fifty men to the island. Captain Lightle soon joined us with another company. About noon Leman L. Leach made his appearance with a company from Syracuse. Colonel Martin Woodruff remained at French Creek for the purpose of forwarding the volunteers as they arrived. A large number of men in sleighs visited the island during the day, but many of them stopped only for a short time. At no time did our force consist of more than 300 men."

"Captain" Heustis recalled that among the party were three men suspected of being spies from Canada. They were arrested, placed under guard and detained until night when they were released. Heustis recalled that "about sundown Bill Johnston joined us. Our number had then materially diminished. There was much disappointment manifested at not finding a larger force present. We had calculated on a thousand men, good and true, for this expedition, and had provided an ample supply of arms, ammunition and provisions. With feelings

"Pirate Bill" Johnston

of deep mortification we were obliged to pronounce the enterprise a failure. But so unwilling was I to relinquish my attack that I still offered to go if ninety-nine would accompany me in the hazardous assault. My proposal was considered too daring and impolitic, and but few were willing to embark in an expedition which promised nothing but inevitable defeat and destruction. We therefore returned to French Creek, Johnston and myself being the last to leave the island. Various excuses were made by those who disappointed our expectations." Heustis failed to mention that five prisoners were left behind, taken by the Queen's Own Rifles, together with some arms.

That was not the end of it. There was fear of repercussion in Clayton. "Some of us remained at French Creek overnight," Heustis related, "but the larger portion dispersed in all directions. The inhabitants of the village, fearing an attack from the British in the course of the night, had fled into the country. The occupants of one or two houses, known to be Tories, burned blue lights in their windows that their British friends might spare them in case of an attack."

Van Rensselaer fled to Syracuse. There he was arrested for violating U.S. neutrality laws, fined and imprisoned. McKenzie, the leader of the rebellion in Upper Canada, who had come to Watertown for the operation, subsequently disavowed association with the "general" and his campaign and went to Washington. Bill Johnston was arrested in the United States for his part in the scheme but was acquitted at an Albany trial. Two Clayton residents, John Packard and George Hulsenberg, had been captured by the British. Despite protests that they merely were at Hickory Island as curious bystanders, the British imprisoned them for six months in the Kingston jail. Subsequently Daniel Heustis of Watertown, author of these recollections, was arrested, together with Benjamin Collins of Evans Mills. Heustis got as far as Depauville when caught by a U.S. attorney and a marshall. He and others were discharged by the U.S. District Court.

Livingston House, Hickory Island, 1820

If this was the end of the Hickory Island "battle," it was not the end of the war, for the far more serious Battle of the Windmill was ahead—but that is another story. As a postscript, however, Daniel Heustis, author of some observations quoted here, was among those who subsequently invaded Prescott. Captured after the Battle of the Windmill, he was tried, found guilty, and sentenced to death. The sentence was commuted to imprisonment at the penal colony at Van Dieman's Land, an island south of Australia. He returned to the United States in 1845. He was more fortunate than many of his comrades. Eleven were executed. Of the sixty sent to Van Dieman's Land, only thirty-two are known to have returned. Comical though the "war" may seem, it was not funny to those involved.

Hickory Island's 82 acres supported a farm prior to the "battle" as it did thereafter. John Livingston purportedly had bought Hickory and Wild Goose Island from the Native Americans "for corn meal and beads." He built a house there in 1820, the building serving not only as a home but later as an inn, the Hickory Island House, "kept by 'General' Alexander Livingston, . . . the jolliest old fellow who runs a boarding house from Cape Vincent to Alexandria Bay." Livingston also worked on a Wolfe Island farm. At the time Wild Goose Island was connected to Hickory by a spit of land. Livingston had to row his skiff around this peninsula to get to work, so he dug a narrow channel through the neck, allowing the westerly wind and waves to enlarge it, eventually liberating Wild Goose as a separate island.

Owned by "eccentric Henry Livingston," perhaps the "General"'s son, Hickory Island was said to be "unimproved" when sold for $15,000 to New York stockbroker John Walter Wood in June 1901. The Woods broke ground in July for a summer home, to be ready the following spring.

John Walter Wood and Nathalie Wilmer Wood had four children, a daughter, Nathalie Wood White, and three sons, John, Donald, and Eric Wood. John Walter Wood, Jr., became an architect, designing the Sherman Pratt residence at Niagara Island, presented subsequently in this volume. Artistic genes seem to have run in the Wood family. Nathalie Wilmer was an ambitious gardener who put on a smock and regularly devoted hours to arranging cut flowers in the pantry, her "studio." Her granddaughter, Nathalie White Coleman, and her great-granddaughter Claire Coleman Chen have continued this predilection.

"Father" and "Dee Bonne"

Daughter Nathalie's husband, Francis D. White, was a talented watercolor painter, and their daughter, "Nat," was an accomplished harpsichordist, and her husband, Beverly Coleman, was a stage designer. Son Don, brother of architect Jack, likewise had an "artistic bent," as did his wife, A great-grandson is architect Anthony Coleman and a great-great-grandson is industrial designer Paul Chen. Probably the artistic sensibility of Nathalie Wilmer Wood, the first mistress of the "Big House" at Hickory Island, accounts in large part for its design quality. As architects, the Woods engaged the prominent New York City firm of Warren, Wetmore & Morgan, the firm that designed Grand Central Station. Although large, the house evidences taste in its expanded cottage style and unpretentiousness. As observed previously, the Woods shared with other families in this neighborhood at the head of Grindstone Island a distaste for nouveau riche display that characterized many grand Thousand Islands establishments, such as Charles Emery's nearby "castle." If not so "rich," the Woods surely were not "new." They were "old." J. Walter Wood's grandfather had been president of the New York City Board of Education. Among the family heirlooms is a tankard belonging to Catherine the Great of Russia, passed down from a Wood antecedent who was her physician.

The first Nathalie acquired a taste for French culture from her parents, the J. Ringgold Wilmers of Short Hills, N.J. In the family Nathalie was known and addressed, even by children and grandchildren, affectionately as "Dee Bonne." The "Dee" of the pet name meant "dear," while the "Bonne" was the French for "good." She was remembered as "charming, effusive, generous, but with very high standards for her grandchildren and servants."

J. Walter Wood, as he was known (as distinguished from his architect son, John Walter Wood, Jr.), was senior partner of Wood, Struthers & Co., brokers on the New York Stock Exchange. Wood's granddaughter "Nat" Coleman remember him as "Scottish, self-contained, dignified in a nice way, and very dear. His daily uniform [at the island] was tan chino trousers, long-sleeved white button-down collar shirt ["preppy," in today's parlance] bow tie, laced walking boots, and broad brimmed felt hat (British in style)—except for one day a week when he played golf with Dee Bonne in Alexandria Bay, or when on a big fishing expedition to Howe Island or favorite bays and points along Wolfe Island."

Life at Hickory Island was serene and genteel, but relaxed rather than stiff. Dee Bonne would take her breakfast in her large, airy bedroom overlooking the huge flower garden while "Father," as J. Walter Wood was known, even by grandchildren, presided at the dining room breakfast table. His major occupation, on the island, was supervising construction of an ambitious granite seawall on the windward shore of the island, to prevent erosion. "Father" shared a horticultural inclination, but his specialty was tree culture. The island had been mostly open farm fields; Father planted and nurtured many new trees, carefully pruning them. He was "an expert tree

surgeon." Again, the contrast may be noted; one hardly envisions George Boldt on a ladder, pruning his trees. Boldt had a large gardening staff for such things. The notion of a self-sufficient estate was, however, common among those who aspired to "country house" life on the aristocratic model.

The Woods had a farm on the island—not merely a summertime produce garden, but a year-round working farm with resident farm family. They inherited the operation from the Livingstons. Father built a large new barn complex, however—only a portion of which remains today, as farming has been discontinued. Cattle and sheep from Hickory Island Farm were carried to and from shore on a barge (a "flat scow") towed by the motorboat *Mississagua*. Most of the animals went to Wolfe Island for the winter, except for a few cows kept on the island to provide the Garnseys, the farm family, with fresh milk and to feed the pigs (Mrs. Garnsey had been a Livingston). The

sheep were decorative, used to keep the meadows cropped where not culti-
vated for produce and fodder, but the sheep were sheared and the wool sold
in late spring, while lambs were sold in the fall for meat.

As might be expected, the Woods had no palatial steam yacht, no speed-
record challenger runabouts. Instead they had two commodious but rather
ordinary Higgens launches, the *Otter*, the longer and sleeker of the two, used
by Father and Dee Bonne, and the "broader bearmed, more seaworthy" *Mis-
sissaqua*—the sort of boat really required for life on an island, particularly one
so exposed in broad reaches of open water as Hickory. But (again, characteristically for the neighborhood) instead of collecting fast speedboats, they had
three St. Lawrence sailing skiffs with Lateen rig, centerboard, and no tiller.
The boathouses also contained two rowing skiffs, two canoes, and one punt.
It did, however, also contain two other powerboats, the *Wildcat*, which was
indeed fast for the time, and the *Mink*, a mahogany fishing boat.

Floyd Clark was the indispensable head boatman, assisted by Irwin Turcotte. The head boatman's position on an island such as Hickory was one of
considerable responsibility and prestige. Senior boatmen often had long careers working for the same family, becoming almost members of the family.

Nora, "our big, fat, beloved cook" was another virtual member of the
family. One day young Nat Coleman asked her grandmother, "Dee Bonne,
what's a lady?" After a perplexed pause, grandmother replied, "Well, let me
see—I'm a lady." Getting to the point, Nat asked, "Is Nora a lady?" She
never forgot her grandmother's response: "If I ever get to heaven, it will be
by hanging on to Nora's apron strings." Ben Garnsey ran the farm and lived
in the "farmer's cottage" at the north end of the lawn (now rennovated and
usually occupied by current co-owners of the Big House, Bob and Nikki
Pfeiffer). Ben didn't join the rest of the staff for meals but usually went

home "to his 'shrewish' wife who was a lousy cook." Nat recalled Ben being "one of the nicest and most patient men I have ever known." Boatmen Floyd and Irwin lived with their families in a duplex house on the island that was demolished in 1963. Irwin, who had "a sunny disposition and good sense of humor," in addition to being a boatman, was in charge of the vast lawns that are a hallmark of Hickory. He employed a horse-drawn mower and fussed with the golf greens and grass tennis court. Irwin also mowed wide grass paths through the "North and South Jungles," which Nat recalled as "those beautifully pruned, cool and magic jungles." Mowed paths through the fields continue to be features of Hickory today. Irwin also cared for the half-acre vegetable garden, but was not responsible for Dee Bonne's huge flower garden, which she tended herself. When heavy work was required, it was farmer Ben Garnsey who helped her, not Irwin. Ben was involved because he started annual seedlings in flats for Dee Bonne in the spring before she arrived. Ben

fed and milked the herd, tending the big barns. He was also the family's best fishing guide.

The staff that gathered for meals in the "Maid's Dining Room" behind the kithen, in addition to boatmen Floyd and Irwin, and cook Nora, were Kate, the head maid, Theresa (the upstairs and downstairs maid), the kitchen maid, Mary (the Polish laundress who spoke very little English), Marguerite (Dee Bonne's French maid, who also did sewing and mending), and Bowe, the children's nurse.

The Wood youngsters played with children of the staff. The boys built a clubhouse near the "Jumping Off Place" on the rocky shore. But the staff children were envied for their greater freedom and permitted adventures, running powerful boats to far places and going to exciting island and mainland parties not allowed the Wood children. In later years, the Woods hired a full-time chaperone for the girls, a thirty-year-old woman who enjoyed her task of going to parties. One evening her charges caught Sally out on the rocks, looking at the sunset, holding hands with Doug Buchanan. Thereafter they could negotiate more freedom, since "we had something on Sally in case she ever told on us."

The genteel daily ritual at Hickory included tea on the terrace in the late afternoon. Dee Bonne poured. Even younger grandchildren, who otherwise ate an early dinner with their nurse on little tables upstairs, joined the adults for tea. They were given "cambric tea"—hot water, milk, sugar, with just a splash of tea. The rolled watercress and cucumber sandwiches were rationed for the hungry youngsters, and especially the cookies and cakes.

Hickory Island Dinner, about 1927

J. Walter Wood presides at the near end of the table, Dee Bonne opposite. Eldest son, Jack (the architect), appears at right, next to Anna Hubbard, his guest (subsequently married to his brother Don. Note the attire, decanters of wine, and Dee Bonne's floral centerpiece.

All was not gentility on Hickory, however. Of the three sons, the youngest, Eric, was the "glamorous one" who buzzed the island, flying low over the treetops in his monoplane, making inside and outside loops to signal his arrival at Clayton and need to be picked up. Once he flew so close to a prize bull that the animal died of a heart attack. Eric brought his motorcycle to the island to give the youngsters wild rides over the lawns and meadows. "A leading member of the Long Island Aviation Country Club's racing team," he

The "Big House"
The huge flower garden was the special glory of Hickory Island

set the world record for outside loops at the National Air Show. In 1930, during a "snap roll," the left wing of his Barling monoplane crumpled. Eric saved his life by jumping out in his parachute. The episode made him a member of the Caterpillar Club, headed by famed aviator Charles Lindbergh. Eric W. Wood, who graduated from Harvard in 1928, worked as "an official of the air transport branch of Cox & Stevens, yacht builders."

Dashing Eric charmed the society girls that he fancied. He first became engaged to Eleanor Moncrieffe Livingston, of the patrician Hudson River Livingston family. She was a granddaughter of railroad builder Crawford Livingston. The betrothal occasioned a large portrait photograph of the attractive Miss Livingston in the *New York Times*. Eric next became engaged to Emilie Stevenson of Glen Cove, also connected to the Livingstons—her aunt was Mrs. Ogden Livingston Mills, mistress of Staatsburgh, the pretentious Hudson River estate now a historic house museum. Mrs. Mills introduced Emilie to society with a dinner dance. Emilie's uncle, Malcolm Stevenson, was noted as a polo player, while her grandfather was one of the Philadelphia Randophs, descended from the duke of Normandy (so the *Times* informed the reader, breathlessly). Emilie and Eric were wed in a "colorful" ceremony at Glen Cove, Long Island. Lovely Mrs. Wood was featured in a large newspaper portrait. Eric became a member of the prestigious Racquet and Tennis on Park Avenue. If socially ambitious and personally adventurous, Eric was "always very gentle and sweet."

Eldest son Jack (architect John Walter Wood) stands between his parents, about 1930. His brother Don sits in front of their father. Their sister, Nathalie White, and her daughter Nat sit at right. Don's future wife, Anna Davis, sits next to him, his niece Audrey White sits in front of them.

"Uncle Jack," more bohemian in his inclinations, was architect of "Shum" Pratt's Niagara Island house, as related in an article about that landmark of the Thousand Islands. Jack was "handsome, dear, with an odd sense of humor." He would ask, "Why am I such a wonderful Jack?" or inject some pointless nonsense like "I'm tinkin' of buyin' me mudder a lamp" ("with a flat nasal *a* in lamp"). Jack also designed "Aux Trois Frères" (the "Three Brothers' Place") used by bachelor uncles, now relocated at the Sugar Bush complex on the island. Probably growing up in the fine "Big House" at Hickory contributed to Jack's interest in architecture. As mentioned in the article on Niagara Island, he taught as well as practiced architecture. Here is Jack's recipe for "the only good punch I ever tasted":

6 quarts sauterne	1/2 quart Cuantro
3 quarts White Rock soda	[*sic*, Cointreau]
1/2 quart brandy	about 1/2 quart lemon juice

The Woods were part of the group of neighbors that gathered at Rum Point on Grindstone every Sunday for a ritual game of softball played with a tennis ball, women usually pitching and only underhand pitching allowed. Nat remembered that "not everyone liked" the obligatory event, but all were required to participate. The older adults (grandmothers played) might have youngsters run for them. Nat didn't care for this "because everyone screamed 'run, run, run' at us and coached us if we got to first base." There were compensations, however. During a break a maid arrived with a tea wagon bearing pitchers of cold lemonade, cookies, and little cakes. Nat recalled the silly games of men versus women, where the men wore women's clothes and vice versa. Photographs appeared in the previous volume, *Fools' Paradise.*

"Aunt Polly" (Mrs. Cleveland E. Dodge) on nearby Wild Goose Island was something of a teenagers' recreation director, organizing camping outings to rustic Canadian islands, putting on "yummy real 'River Picnics'—always broiled chickens, picnic potatoes, corn on the cob, fruit, cookies/cake" and leading at sunset "singing, joking, games around the campfire—with Aunt Polly retiring to her tent before the fun and extra swims were over. We never felt we were being watched or worried about. Aunt Polly never said 'quiet down'—eventually we did quiet down, all spread out together with blankets and pillows under the stars—just a little covert hand holding and a goodnight kiss for those few couples having a summer romance."

Treasure hunts by foot on land and by boat to other islands often consumed an entire day, elaborately planned by Aunt Polly and others. An annual party to celebrate Betty Dodge's birthday was a major event of each season, always with some theme such as "The Dinosaur Era," requiring imaginative costumes. Different islands would compete by staging charades after dinner, with prizes awarded. Then, Nat tells us, there was "Snipe Hunting." Aunt Polly would spring this on new guests. "The neophytes were given flashlights and instruction, and as they disappeared into the dark night the room would be filled with knowing smiles and smirks. What's snipe hunting you ask? I'll never tell."

Despite a fairly structured regimen of gentility amid a staff of employees, children grew up close to nature, at the edge of land and water. Nat and the boatman's daughter, Christine, gave up playing with conventional dolls when they discovered toads occupying the flag holes in the putting greens. "We took our toads swimming in little rock pools of rainwater; they went to school; they had naps; when they were naughty, we spanked them with little whips made of field grass. We even dressed them up with wildflowers and leaves. . . . We never went back to inert dolls."

Of course water provided much recreation—fishing always is basic on the river, and skiff sailing is an arcane art of this neighborhood, requiring much practice and providing much competition—but the farm added another dimension, with its many animals and seasonal rituals. The Hickory Island barns were distinctive, and the portion remaining, like the "Big House" as well as the "Farm Cottage," show the architect's hand. Like most island establishments, many ancillary buildings were required for relative self-sufficiency. There was a two-story icehouse north of the Big House. It was stocked during the winter months by a team of men that came from Clayton with a horse and heavy work sledge. Floyd, Irwin, and probably Ben were paid year-round. Men regularly carried large blocks of ice from the icehouse to the large metal-lined iceboxes in the kitchen. Gas for illumination came from a big generator in the back of the icehouse. Kerosene lamps supplemented gaslights. A gasoline engine in the barns pumped water to a tank there that served all the buildings.

Subsequent generations have retained the Woods' taste. Instead of gravitating to large powerboats, daughter Nathalie and her husband, naval officer Francis Day White, had the *Loon*, a 36-foot black yawl with a two-bunk cabin. Leaving other family at the island, they enjoyed annual "honeymoon cruises" aboard the *Loon*, sailing out to the Ducks in Lake Ontario.

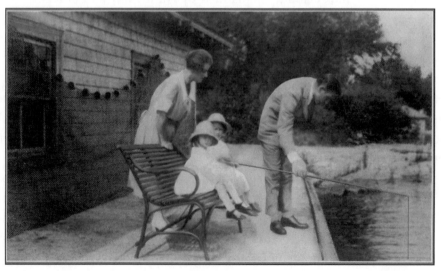

The Fishing Lesson
Nathalie Wood White, daughters Audrey and Nathalie ("Nat"), Francis Day White.

Like many an islander, J. Walter Wood ("Father") died on his island. His granddaughter remembered in July 1930 being sent over to stay with Sis Pruyn on Club Island (since children were thought better spared). Looking out the big plate-glass window on the channel side, Nat saw Floyd and Irwin going towards Clayton in the *Otter,* top down and wicker chairs removed. She

Loon

knew that "Father" was in the boat, unseen, leaving his island for the last time.

Nat observed that "Father" had "a creative dream for Hickory Island." He intended "to create an island wonderland and way of life for his extended family." He succeeded. The family is still there. Neighbor "Aunt Polly" (Mrs. Cleveland E. Dodge) told Nat, "I have known six generations of your family here at the River—your great-grandmother, your grandmother, your mother, you, Claire, and now Claire's daughters." Since then we may add a seventh generation—Claire Chen's granddaughter, who appears with her father, Paul Chen, on Hickory Island in photographs that follow.

The Woods are one of those "old" families on the river, especially characteristic of the neighborhood at the head of Grindstone Island—representing "old money," gentility, taste—in contrast to the succession of more transient "new money" islanders who often displayed their wealth more conspicuously and extravagantly, but whose family fortunes and island tenures were shorter-lived.

The "Big House" seen from the guest house, Hickory Island, 1948, across the great lawn. Lewis Henry Morgan, of the neighboring Morgan family, was the design architect.

The main complex at Hickory Island, with the Big House at the right, the great lawn between it and the ATF guest house (Aux Trois Frères) with its pagoda roof on the rocky shore at center bottom. The barn complex and staff houses (largely hidden in trees) appear above.

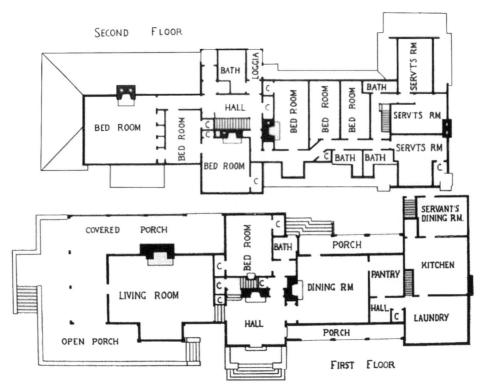

SECOND FLOOR

BED ROOM

BED ROOM

BED ROOM

BATH

LOGGIA

HALL

C

C

C

C

BED ROOM

C

BED ROOM

BED ROOM

BED ROOM

BATH

SERV'TS RM

SERV'TS RM

SERVTS RM

C BATH BATH

C

C

COVERED PORCH

C

BED ROOM

BATH

PORCH

SERVANT'S DINING RM.

KITCHEN

LIVING ROOM

C

C

C

DINING RM

PANTRY

HALL

OPEN PORCH

HALL

PORCH

HALL

C

LAUNDRY

FIRST FLOOR

Hickory Island, Warren, Wetmore, & Morgan, Architects
The "Big House" with sixteen rooms is not so large as some grand island residences,
but has some very large rooms, seven fireplaces, and five bathrooms.

Terrace Garden. Hickory Island

Barns, Hickory Island
After 1948 the Pfeiffers demolished the left extensions.

Scowing the horses to winter on Wolfe Island, 1929

The Wood Descendents on Hickory Island West

After Dee Bonne died at Hickory Island in the summer of 1943, the houses were closed. The four Wood children retained Irwin Turcotte as caretaker and they kept Lola the horse to help him mow the lawns and paths. For four years the heirs tried to sell the whole island. By 1947, however, Donald Wood persuaded the others to sell only about twenty-two acres with the barn and three main dwellings, retaining the larger portion of sixty acres for the family. It was his idea to move some of the buildings from the eastern to the western end of the island, to establish a family compound on the peninsula known as Sugar Bush.

As his first project after graduation from architectural school, Don's brother Jack had designed for his father a whimsical guest house with curved roofs recalling pagodas. Orginally located near the Big House facing Wild Goose Island, the family dubbed the structure Aux Trois Frères (Three Brothers' Place). Called "ATF" for short, the building often was used by the bachelor brothers and their pals. When moved to Sugar Bush it became the bedroom house for the complex.

Two other buildings were relocated from the opposite shore of the island to complete the new family quarters. Moving these structures was a challenging, even harrowing campaign. Don's daughter Joan Wood Kimball recalls the adventure:

> Dad, my sister Margot, and I spent the night that chilly October of 1947 in ATF. . . . We found Earl Garnsey . . . hammering timbers on the dock at Cement Point, Grindstone. He agreed to move three buildings from the eastern end of Hickory–ATF, a small green cook shack, and the workers' boathouse–to Sugar Bush at the west end of the island, a mile away. The following March, Earl, his brother and his cousin Slate, hitched their three teams of horses to the buildings and dragged them over the ice. Had they had the seven teams originally promised, they could have pulled non-stop and finished in a day. As it was, they slowly staked and winched all the way, and barely shoved the houses onto a snowy Sugar Bush shore in two days. They left their animals in the Hickory barn overnight, but the ice was so thin, they walked each horse back to Grindstone one at a time the next day. No more than four days later the ice went out. Clyde Garnsey and Erma Slate, who still live on Grindstone, were with their dads on that hair-raising enterprise.

Sugar Bush was not a summer home like the Big House, where family and staff spent three or four months. Life had changed after World War II.

Donald Wood and his daughter Margot
at Sugar Bush, 1953

Sugar Bush was more a "camp," used for shorter vacations, with Joan's generation of young people pitching in to do-it-yourself, living simply without electricity, let alone servants. Although the Kimballs installed a solar panel in 1995 to power a cell phone and some lights, they still use a hand pump in the kitchen. A "discrete outhouse nearby" –a two-holer that had served Irwin Turcotte's grandmother–still functions in 2004.

Until 1957 the three-building complex was shared by the extended family. Then the Wood descendents divided their retained property into six parcels where over time five independent cottages were built. A more recent architect member of the family, Anthony Coleman, designed the Chen cottage at Heron Point and the White cottage at Jumping Off Place. Woods and Ponverts also have cabins on the larger part of the island.

Wildcat

Drying a sail at Sugar Bush, 1957.
Aux Trois Frères is the building at left, the Green Shack at right.

Joan Wood waits for her sister, Margot, to get a minnow from the bucket, 1936.

Heron Point, Hickory Island

Architect Anthony Coleman, great-grandson of J. Walter Wood,
designed Heron Point's elegantly simple cottage for family members
to build with their own hands.

Heron Point's interiors evidence the architect's hand

Great-great grandson and great-great-great-granddaughter of
J. Walter and Nathalie Wilmer Wood, builders of the "Big House" on Hickory island

The Pfeiffers at Hickory Island

Ray and Trude Pfeiffer, 1969
(both wear pins announcing, "I'm Boss.")

The story of Hickory Island during the second half of the twentieth century into the twenty-first is largely about the Pfeiffers, who bought the "Big House" and twenty acres of the island in 1948.

After the death of Mrs. Wood (Dee Bonne) the main residence was vacant for four years. The Woods offered Hickory Island for sale through Previews, Inc., the prominent broker for high-end residential real estate. Although estimates of acreage vary, according to the offering, the sixty-six-acre island with one and a half miles of shoreline supported a farm as well as the residential complex of main house, guest cottage, icehouse, boathouse, superintendent's cottage, and boatmen's double house. The asking price in 1948 was $60,000. As the Pfeiffers that year bought only twenty of the sixty-six acres, they acquired the major buildings and grounds for a quarter of the asking price: $15,000. Nine years earlier, in 1939, the entire island was offered for $20,000. In the 1948 sale, the Wood descendents retained the larger portion, about forty-five acres, including the peninsula at the upper end, known as "The Sugar Bush," where they developed their complex.

Incredible though the Pfeiffers' bargain seems, after the Depression and World War II interest in the Thousand Islands, especially in large properties, had declined to the lowest point of their history. Many grand island establishments were vacant and offered for sale (like nearby Calumet Island, sold shortly with all its substantial improvements for a mere $11,500). Some houses were abandoned and derelict, some had been demolished to avert taxes and maintenance. Fortunately Dr. and Mrs. Raymond Pfeiffer appeared when they did, acquiring their summer home almost by accident.

Raymond and Gertrude Pfeiffer had no interest in owning a grand island estate. Ray Pfeiffer was no multi millionaire tycoon. He was a physician and professor of ophthalmology at Columbia University College of Physicians and Surgeons. The Pfeiffers were visiting her parents, the Robert Smiths of Fernfield, three miles west of Clayton. When out on the river fishing the Pfeiffers sought a picnic spot for lunch. The overgrown grass and shuttered buildings on Hickory Island suggested that venue. They had no more than docked, however, when another boat arrived. Fifteen-year-old Ronnie White came to check the visitors, explaining that his grandfather J. Walter Wood had died and the "Big House" was for sale. Ronnie carried a ring of keys and offered to show the interiors. Ray and Trude (pronouced "Truda") declined, saying that they might be interested in a smaller place, but surely nothing so daunting as Hickory Island! The ten-bedroom Big House and other buildings were surrounded by ten acres of sweeping lawn that took seven hours to mow with a riding tractor.

Back at their Riverdale home, near New York City, Ray and Trude had surprise visitors, Mr. and Mrs. Cleveland Dodge of Wild Goose Island. Cleve Dodge had given the Pfeiffers a tow when their boat ran out of gas. By coincidence, the Dodges also lived nearby in the same suburb of New York City, Riverdale. The Dodges urged the Pfeiffers to become their neighbors on the river, suggesting they talk to Donald Wood about acquiring Hickory Island. And so it came about.

The lifestyle of the Pfeiffers at Hickory Island differed from the regimen of the Woods. After World War II domestic help no longer was plentiful. The Woods' staff of thirteen became one caretaker and a young woman to help indoors. Living became more casual, and the Pfeiffers' days at Hickory Island were more like those many of us have experienced at summer places. Trude's extensive journal suggests, as her son, Bob, says, that "Mom was a non-stop worker on the island. . . . Dad was too. Together they rebuilt the estate." Rebuilding was more than a figure of speech, for all the Pfeiffers pitched in on heavy-duty, hands-on projects.

One almost becomes exhausted reading the account of the family's island adventures—so much hard physical work enlivened by alarming accidents and continual boating crises. But clearly the Pfeiffers loved the life. Trude came to the river before the ice was gone, frequently having to stay several days in a Clayton motel until she could prevail upon someone to take her out to Hickory, where she often opened the place and stayed there alone for weeks, while the children finished school and her husband, Ray, carried on his medical practice. The Pfeiffers were among the last to leave the river, often when snow was on the ground. They crossed the open water in all sorts of conditions. While Trude worried regularly about her children out on the river when storms came up, when sailboats capsized, or the young people failed to appear for hours after expected, she never seems to have worried for herself. Guests, however, might be more concerned about escape from the island in the often rough water and all sorts of weather.

After reading about years of continual projects at the main complex on Hickory Island, it's astonishing to learn in the journal that when Dr. Pfeiffer retired from practice in 1959, allowing him to spend more time on the river, Trude bought another property on Grindstone Island to fix up—something to keep her busy, no doubt. She bought the Fussel place on Grindstone, originally an 1860 farm that had become a boys' camp. After the "Tip Camp" campaign, Trude acquired two other Grindstone camps, and subsequently purchased an offshore island with a cottage, which they demolished, intending the island as a picnic venue.

From beginning to end, Trude's journal is a chronicle of maintenance and improvement projects, most of them done by Ray Pfeiffer, Sr., and Jack Andress, who came from the Canadian Air Force to become the Hickory caretaker at age twenty-six. Jack commuted daily from Gananoque in a 16-foot wooden boat built by his father, powered with a 5-HP Johnson outboard. The boat is now at the Antique Boat Museum. Jack, who was the children's hero, retired after thirty-nine years at age sixty-five. Ray and Jack were helped regularly by Trude, and the boys who sometimes undertook their own projects. Andrew Wilson now is the Hickory Island caretaker.

Those of us who have purported "vacation" homes know what one really does on one's vacation. In addition to constant repairs and maintenance, guests must be fed and entertained (often entailing repetitive tours of familiar sights). Hosts run a regular shuttle service, not merely across the water, but to Syracuse and Ottawa airports. The Pfeiffers were made for this sort of life, however. Some people are. Ray and Trude thrived on it—Ray Pfeiffer lived to age 101, celebrating his hundredth birthday at Hickory Island with champagne and a cake lighted with a hundred candles.

Hickory house and garden, 1943, when the island was for sale,
prior to purchase by the Pfeiffers

Dr. Pfeiffer was a world-renowned ophthalmologist at Columbia Presbyterian Hospital as well as professor at Columbia University College of Physicians and Surgeons. Among his patients were Eleanor Roosevelt, J. C. Penney, and Bob Hope. He was one of the first to achieve consistent success in the repair of detached retinas.

Gertrude ("Trude") Smith Pfeiffer was daughter of Professor and Mrs. Robert Smith. He was a professor of mathematics at CCNY. The Smiths came to the river in the 1890s, summering in two cottages at Grenell Island, still in the Smith family. In the 1930s Professor Smith and family moved to Fernfield on the mainland above Clayton, in view of Hickory Island. Trude was enthusiastic, hard working, and indomitable, crossing the water alone in all sorts of weather to get groceries at Clayton–even in the last year of her life, at age eighty-five.

The summer colony at the head of Grindstone has always been a very sociable place, with much coming and going between islands. Established by Christopher Wolfe in 1880 when he built a summer home on Whisky Island, many generations of neighbors have frequently intermarried, so that the community is tight-knit. The Pfeiffers were relative newcomers, but have been there more than a half-century now, while others like the Whites have been there more than a century. Community rituals evolved, such as annual sailing skiff races for the Ellis Cup, an annual duck hunt, and the Dodge's elaborate, costumed charade parties at Wild Goose Island. Of course, the most regular event was the cocktail party. If there was a Grindstone grand dame, it was Mrs. Bacon of Mid River Farm, who Trude regarded as "a work of art (takes Vodka straight on rocks) . . . one of the seven best hostesses in the U.S.A." who threw the "most glamorous dinner parties." One senses from Trude's journal that she was too busy herself, transplanting trees and sanding floors, to fuss much with glamorous dinner parties, although her menus convey an ample table–beef stroganoff was a staple. Often guests prepared meals–helpful when there are twelve or more at table every meal.

There was much dining out, given the number to feed and complicated schedule of arrivals and departures, and desire of guests to repay their hosts. The favorite dinner spot in nearby Gananoque was highly valued. Trude commented, "Again the Golden Apple saved my life." Popular lunch destinations were Pine Tree Point and the Thousand Islands Club, but picnics were frequent.

The four Pfeiffer children were ages eleven to one when their parents acquired Hickory Island, so they grew up spending summers there. Nancy, the eldest, became Mrs. George Saughter. After forty-nine seasons on Hickory, she spent her last summers nearby at the Punts, which has passed to her daugher, Katy Saughter. Bob, the elder son, was followed by Jean (Mrs. Alexander Tate), who both are at Hickory Island now. Raymond S. Pfeiffer, the youngest, was at Tip Camp, on Grindstone Island, until his divorce from LoLita, who remains there with their children. Trude gave Tip Camp to Ray and LoLita in 1978. Dr. Raymond L. Pfeiffer and his family enjoyed Hickory Island for fifty-three summers before he died—and the family is still there and on nearby islands.

Bob and Nikki Pfeiffer now reside in the renovated three-bedroom house, built originally for the Woods' farm manager, Ben Garnsey. The "Big House" often is rented by guests (www.hickoryislandestate.com). It has sixteen rooms—not so big compared to many grand summer homes here, which had fifty or so rooms, but the rooms are remarkably spacious and well proportioned. The designer probably was Lewis Henry Morgan, for a time a partner in the New York City architectural firm of Morgan, Wetmore, and Morgan and a member of the neighboring Morgan family on Papoose Island.

The Heirloom Skiff, 1979

Gertrude Pfeiffer's parents gave her a lady's skiff as a present on her thirteenth birthday. Here Trude, surrounded by grandchildren and dog, is giving the boat to LoLita for future generations. LoLita stands next to her husband, Ray S. Pfeiffer. Hickory Island caretaker Jack Andress drives the tractor.

The 30'x40' living room has 12-foot ceilings and is furnished with the original Stickley and wicker furniture, and decorated with trophy heads of bighorn sheep, an Alberta moose and a fine wipiti (elk) head, which hangs above the huge stone fireplace. The dining room is furnished with Stickley, including a table that seats fourteen. Fireplaces are in the living room, main hall, dining room and four of the largest bedrooms.

The two-slip boathouse has a boatman's apartment on the upper floor. The barn was reduced in size when farming was discontinued. Forty percent was dismantled, the material used by Jack Andress to build his *Popular Mechanics*-design house in Gananoque.

Like the Woods and most neighbors, the Pfeiffers had no trophy yachts. Their *Picklepuss* was a 1939 Hutchinson, all mahogany and about 22 feet long with a Kermath engine; the *Nut*, a 1951 Hacker Craft the same length; the *Shagbark,* a 26-foot Lyman; and the *Splinter,* a 12-foot Penn Yan.

Bob and Nikki Pfeiffer observe that, "by the time we arrive on the island each spring our caretaker, Andrew Wilson, has already opened the Little House for us and it feels inviting and warm. We then begin the process of opening the Big House for the summer. When the shutters come off and the window and doors are open to let in the fresh spring breeze off the river, a sense of the past inhabitants and the love and peace and joy of life begins to fill the rooms and you are overcome with the sense of joy that this place has brought to generations of Livingstons, Woods, and Pfeiffers."

Members of all three Hickory Island families remain on the river. Many generations of Livingston descendents have been here since the mid-eighteenth century. One, Tom Bogenschutz in Clayton, is a font of local history, in-

cluding earlier accounts of Hickory Island. He relates that early Livingston graves were marked with stones on Hickory Island, but are not identified by name. The Livingstons had property on Wolfe Island as well as Hickory, where they apparently had a cabin as early as 1807, for Melinda McMillan Livingston, daughter of Daniel and granddaughter of John, who acquired the is-

Jack Wood and friend seated, brother Eric tossing rope.

land from the Native Americans, was born there in that year. She was five years old during the War of 1812 when British forces encamped on Hickory Island. She hid in the skirt of her mother who was forced to cook and feed the soldiers her winter's supply of meat.

Tom's great-great-grandmother, Phebe Jane Livingston, told a version of this story, corrected here by Tom. Her daughter married Ben Garnsey of Grindstone Island. Long the Woods' resident farmer, after many years living on Hickory in 1917 Ben went to work for the Hacketts at Zenda.

Most of the material about the Wood family on Hickory Island is from *Very Random Memories of Hickory Summers (to about the year 1935)* by Nathalie Wilmer Coleman. Claire Chen provided a copy of the engaging booklet.

Readers interested in events of the Patriot War will find many good works devoted to it. Charles D. Anderson provides a thorough overview of the rebellions in *Bluebloods & Rednecks: Discord and Rebellion in the 1830s.* Craig Brown provides an even broader view of the historical antagonisms that led to the rebellions in his *History of Canada* (209 ff.) and offers as well a concise summary of the two rebellions (217). Russ Distotell gives an account of local political issues in *Brockville: The River City* (52 ff.). Donald E. Graves provides the most complete and fully illustrated account of regional military events in *Guns Across the River: The Battle of the Windmill, 1838* (although Hickory Island is mislocated on the map on page 55). L. N. Fuller's excellent account, *Northern New York in the Patriot War*, is accessible online:

http://freepages.genealogy.rootsweb.com/~twigs1970/pa-index.html.

J. Walter Wood courting Nathalie Wilmer on the river in 1895. They were guests of Bea and Fellowes Morgan at Papoose Island that summer and were married in September.

XIV. Niagara Island

Among the most distinguished works of architecture at the Thousand Islands is John Walter Wood's remarkable 1932 project for Sherman Pratt. The following article from the international professional journal *Architecture* presents the summer home north of Grindstone Island.

Built entirely of reinforced concrete (even the boathouse), construction of the massive structure on a remote island required an ambitious campaign recalling those of the fireproof "castles" on Heart and Dark Islands.

Photograph by Palmer Shannon

A general view of the house of Mr. Sherman Pratt on Niagara Island in the St. Lawrence River; John Walter Wood, architect. From the power house and boat landing the house piles up in successive roof terraces to the dominating tower and chimney

ARCHITECTURE

❖ VOLUME LXV   FEBRUARY 1932   NUMBER 2 ❖

Photograph by John Walter Wood

Aerial view of Mr. Pratt's house and island in the
Thousand Islands of the St. Lawrence

A Ferro-concrete House of To-day

JOHN WALTER WOOD, ARCHITECT

By Henry H. Saylor

OUT of the dense fog that settled down over architecture after the quarter century, a few results are beginning to stand forth rather clearly. These have about them nothing of the Puritanical baldness contributed by the extreme functionalists, nor, on the other hand, have they the familiar earmarks of those who have felt that architecture must primarily be startling and bizarre.

Here is a house for Mr. Sherman Pratt at Niagara Island, Ontario. Mr. Pratt is a bachelor who wanted, for an isolated site on one of the Thousand Islands, a house that would be fireproof, that would require a minimum of upkeep, that would express as nearly as might be the simplicity of life upon such an island, and, finally, that would be economical in construction.

The problem was unusual in that the isola-tion of its site brought considerable difficulty in the assembling of materials and labor. Mr. Wood not only designed the house, but found it necessary to build it as well, spending most of a year on the job. It seems unquestionable that the result owes much of its success to this fact. Like the master builders of old, Mr. Wood constantly found ways of achieving the ends desired that could not have been contemplated in the drawings and specifications. Results that were not entirely to his liking could be changed before they had gone too far. It is apparent also from the photographs—even though these do not convey the color—that Mr. Wood has tried to evolve, and has succeeded in evolving, style from the materials at hand. The work has been carried far beyond the point where it merely satisfies the functional requirements, for one can see at every turn the result of painstaking study

Photograph by Palmer Shannon

In the foreground are the steps from the boat landing to the main terrace. The warm buff of vertical wall surfaces is relieved by the tile red of terrace copings and metal sash. Parapet and copings are precast concrete. A radio aerial on glass insulators encircles the tower

John Walter Wood's 1932 design may be characterized today as "Art Deco" in its period style. Wood was of that generation of architects whose education was based on historic tradition. Wood had studied at the École des Beaux Arts in Paris, the world's leading architectural school, which stressed classicism. Avant-garde modernist architecture had become a challenging alternative in Europe during the 1920s but was not yet widely recognized or understood, even there. Wood's work was of the sort humorously termed "streamlined classical," which is to say that its modernist aspects were largely cosmetic, as superficial styling. This was characteristic of the Arc Deco movement in America.

Architects today may find Wood's beautiful floor plans—so much at odds with the proto modernist exteriors—to warrant study and admiration. This beaux-arts mastery of spatial organization, conceptually opposed to modernist notions, has been rediscovered at the end of the twentieth century, when post modernism has largely supplanted the conventions of high modernism.

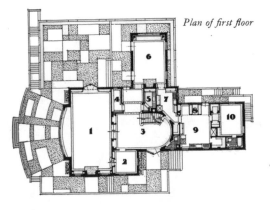

Plan of first floor

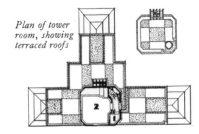

Plan of tower room, showing terraced roofs

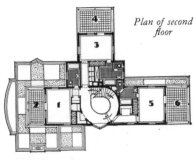

Plan of second floor

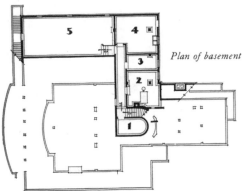

Plan of basement

First floor: *1—living room, 2—study, 3—hall, 4—coat closet, 5—dark room, 6—dining-room, 7—pantry, 8—dining-alcove, 9—kitchen, 10—maid's room*
Second floor: *1, 3, and 5—dressing-rooms; 2, 4, and 6—sleeping-porches*
Tower room and roofs: *1—hatchway to tower roof, 2—tower room*
Basement floor: *1—wine cellar, 2—boiler-room, 3—store closet, 4—laundry, 5—game room*

in the composing of masses in light and shade, the arrangement of voids, and the interplay of color and texture.

Ferro-concrete was chosen as the building material because of its economy, plasticity, and permanence. It should be noted particularly, however, that to achieve a finished result of this character, the whole idea of "1:2:4 concrete" must be abandoned at the outset. Those who will make of a ferro-concrete structure a living, glowing composition, faceted in pleasing textures that vary in character according to the need, must be willing to do far more than pour water, cement, and aggregate into a mould. The potentialities of concrete must be understood, and particular emphasis placed on the intelligent application of the water-cement

ratio, methods of pouring, and curing. Concrete possesses possibilities of color and surface textures that have been little appreciated. Mr. Wood here had the advantage of being on the job and, therefore, of having been able to make scores of samples and tests to get the desired result, varying his sands, aggregates, and combinations of pigments. The color finally selected was a warm buff for the building itself, with a light tile red for the balustrade copings. This color was matched in painting the metal casements. Variations of these two colors were used on the roof terraces, which were patterned in color.

For the terrace retaining walls and the exterior of the balustrades a rough texture was used to effect a transition from the rough broken surface of the rock base to the smooth texture of the walls themselves. Mr. Wood's superintendent on the job was A. C. Hammond, while the

At the near end of the main terrace is the precast concrete parapet on axis with the great window of the living-room. Above is the cantilevered roof of the north sleeping-porch

As emphasized in the contemporary magazine account, the Pratt project was more than an abstract design exercise for Wood. Not merely was it a logistical challenge to build a concrete structure on this island, but quality control of exposed concrete was critical. The design employed varying surface textures and integral colors. Desired results required trial and error by architect and craftsmen. The design, moreover, was highly detailed, demanding finesse in execution. Features of exterior and interior reveal the extreme care involved.

As a young architect launching his practice, John Walter Wood probably regarded the Pratt house as a major commission that might enhance his reputation. Publication confirmed this anticipation, but few architects during their careers are favored by clients like Sherman Pratt, or by sites as naturally lovely as Niagara Island. Two decades of Depression and World War II subsequently restricted Wood's professional practice.

Photograph by Palmer Shannon

This view over several of the roof terraces is convincing evidence that any more conventionalized treatment of a house on such a site would have verged on stupid affectation. In the lower right corner is the parapet shown on the opposite page

Niagara is a Canadian Island in the Lake Fleet group. The photograph above was taken looking northward towards the Canadian mainland. Grindstone and several smaller islands were behind the photographer—two being part of Canada's St. Lawrence Islands National Parks system.

John Walter Wood's family summer home was on Hickory Island, about five miles away, off the head of Grindstone Island. His father, J. Walter Wood, was a prominent stockbroker of New York City. The Wood summer home, built about thirty years earlier, is architecturally notable. Design genes seem to run in the Wood family, as there are an architect and an industrial designer in today's generation. Another family cottage on Hickory Island, designed by Anthony Coleman, is illustrated here.

Few major architectural projects occurred at the Thousand Islands between World War I and the end of the twentieth century. Sherman Pratt's Niagara villa was one of the last grand homes built on the river for many decades. The next notable modern house was the Rouse-Lechler residence on Bartlett Point, above Clayton, designed by the New York City architect Richard Moger in the early 1960s.

The dining-room wing with the east sleeping-porch above. At the right is the awning over the dining-terrace. The basement wall has a rough texture to form a transition between the rocky base and the smooth texture of the house walls

Wood's neighbor, Beatrice Morgan Pruyn of Papoose Island, was landscape architect for the Niagara Island project—but there was little "landscaping" done, as the natural surroundings were carefully preserved. "Sis," as she was known, appeared in the previous volume, *Fools' Paradise*. Wood took the photograph and two other illustrations in this article. A photographic darkroom is indicated on the main floor plan.

Photograph by Palmer Shannon

The west front with living-room chimney channelled in subtle suggestion
of the flue lines. At the right is the front entrance

engineer who designed the reinforced concrete structural details was H. H. Koons. Beatrice M. Pruyn was the landscape architect.

Walls, floors, roofs, terraces, all steps, chimney, balustrades, and copings are of poured concrete. The exposed basement walls up to the first-floor level were treated chemically to expose the aggregate. Above the first floor the vertical surfaces were poured with a half white and half gray cement mix with integral pigment to produce the buff color. Necessary patching was done immediately upon stripping the forms. Upon completion, the walls were ground with a carborundum wheel to obtain a smooth texture.

With the extensive views of the site in mind, obviously the roofs and terraces became the main living quarters of the house, and they have been designed in recognition of that fact. As a practical detail of building, the rough concrete roof slabs were covered with two inches of insulation, above which a five-ply felt roof was laid. On top of this roofing a sand cushion was deposited and a finished concrete slab two inches thick was poured, with reinforcing of hog wire. These finished roof slabs were poured to patterns, in color variations, no slab exceeding eighty square feet in area.

It will be noticed that while the architect has shown restraint in the use of his decorative details, he has not hesitated to use them where they would serve to emphasize the relations of the main and secondary masses. For instance, there are the incised horizontal bands of the exterior, the projecting string courses, the curved profile of the sleeping-porch beams, and the swell of the great bay window in the living-room. He has also used small forty-five-degree splays at the corners of the main masses, and an interesting play of line in the chimney design. Incidentally, the incised bands of the upper part of the tower mark the radio aerial, carried on glass insulators.

Mr. Wood's house for Mr. Sherman Pratt is, in my opinion, an unmistakable milestone along the architectural highroad leading from the recent Babel of Tongues to something ahead of us—something in which clear logic and beauty are once more happily wedded.

A raking view of the front entrance. The incised lines of the base carry along the tread lines of terrace steps in an interesting manner

*The spiral ceiling of the stair hall centring in a light which, parenthetically,
was made from the lens of a locomotive headlight*

The living-room has a flooring of random-width walnut, ivory plaster walls, and fireplace of concrete which was ground to expose colored aggregates

The Niagara Island interiors reveal the transitional nature of Wood's modernism. Simplicity prevails, together with respect for natural materials and quasi-industrial metal sash, but relatively small panes of glass recall tradition, as does the symmetrical arrangement of conventional windows and fireplace. Despite the exposed concrete structure overhead, this was a rather traditional living room.

The furnishings are of early 'thirties' design. Rather rustic throw rugs appear throughout the house rather than more opulent carpets. This is consistent with a "minimalist" modern aesthetic, as is the general sparseness of the interior décor. The horizontal striping of the fireplace and the round mirror above were favored Art Deco mannerisms.

The stair hall. Steps are poured concrete of buff color, with composition tread inserts. Flooring is of composition in buffs and browns with occasional squares in sea green. Ivory walls are obtained by integrally coloring the plaster

Unlike the grand establishments on the river at the beginning of the twentieth century intended for large house parties, the Pratt villa at Niagara Island was merely a bachelor's three-bedroom residence. Although "economy" was reportedly a consideration, clearly the project was designed in the grand manner, anticipating a highly labor-intensive manner of construction with fine finishes.

A great window opens most of one side of the living-room to an extensive view of the St. Lawrence River

A built-in seat extends along the east end of the dining-room and adjoining this a breakfast table is set

The south dressing-room has oak floor and a natural-finish wood wainscot. Folding seats, desk, and table close flat against the wall to provide bed space in severe weather

East sleeping-porch, indicating the typical construction of cantilevered roof and the adaptable shelter of Venetian blinds

In the tower room, where the stair bulkhead has been developed into a logical pro-
vision of built-in couch, bookshelves, desk, and map cases

Looking down from the tower upon the various levels of color-patterned terrace
paving and the natural planting about the base

John Walter Wood's Niagara Island project for Sherman Pratt, monumentally constructed of reinforced concrete, is one of the lasting landmarks of the Thousand Islands and one of our finest examples of architecture and craftsmanship.

A view across the main terrace, looking west, where again one notes the subtle curve of living-room bay, the varied color of paving, and the strength of sturdy wall masses as a foil for the intricacy of pierced parapets

Naturalist Sherman Pratt led expeditions and made scientific photographs for the Museum of Natural History. He was a member of a very large family—some twenty-one related branches at the time–that shared an enormous fortune. Sherman was grandson of Charles Pratt, a cofounder of Standard Oil and founder of Pratt Institute. Sherman was one of four children of George Dupont Pratt and Helen D. Sherman, who resided in Brooklyn and later at Glen Cove, Long Island. Ten years after building his summer home, Sherman married Mrs. Ethel Manville, who had three children by her previous marriage. Sherman and Ethel had a daughter, Deming Pratt. The Pratts had a home, Still Pond Farm, at Locust Valley, N.Y. Niagara Island remains in the family.

Architect John Walter Wood undertook the Pratt commission shortly after initiating his practice in 1931. He had graduated with a B.S. from Harvard in 1922 and an M.S. in architecture in 1927. He studied at Oxford in 1923 and at the École des Beaux Arts in 1928. For the last decade of his life Wood was a professor of architecture at the University of Illinois. John Walter Wood died at age fifty-eight in 1958.

Steamers at Fine View

The Penultimate Word

What happened to Julie? She tried to live alone in her third floor apartment above the barber shop as long as she could—or so long as the Social Services Department would allow. But eventually the inevitable occurred.

Dave Rappold, who lived in the apartment below her, recalled that she fell. As often happens with the elderly, a minor fall became a major life change. The Department of Social Services decided that, frail and virtually blind, she no longer should live alone. They placed Julie in Coutt's Adult Home in Cape Vincent. Dave says, "I do know she was very upset. . . . She had lost her independence and felt she was losing what little dignity she had left. I never remember any family visiting her. I received many of her personal belongings including many photographs." Dave has shared this material, which he cared enough about to keep for many decades and which I was fortunate to discover.

I have feelings of personal remorse that I lost touch with Julie at a time when she needed friends the most. In 1957 I was drafted into the army, however, and was stationed far from the river. I never saw Julie again.

Julie

I've tried in this way, to keep her alive, for others to know—Julie and this place, as it was. Where have they gone, all these people, their proud trophies, their happy days? As Julie said, "It was so ravishing, this fleeting, floating world." Washed away, it was carried by the river current out to the boundless sea. The people are gone; so is their way of life. But the river goes on, continuing to wash away more happy days on these granite islands, the oldest things on this earth. The islands remain, while life and the river flow on.

Oarsmen (fishing guides) prepare a shore dinner.

XV. An Album of River Scenes

"The Towers," Dark Island, Ernest Flagg, Architect

New York Times

The largest contingent of prominent islanders was comprised of New Yorkers. The *New York Times* retained a regular correspondent, Nanette Lincoln, on the river to report events during the season. The big steamboats that made regular rounds of the island communities every day dropped off eagerly awaited copies of the newspaper. Some islands preferred other papers—such as the Dewarts' more conservative *New York Sun*. There were, of course, other urban and local newspapers. Even Thousand Island Park had its own newspaper at one time.

The Oarsman

Fishing guides were to the Thousand Islands what hunting guides were to the nearby Adirondacks—romantic characters who represented to visitors an alternative lifestyle, that of the free spirit living close to nature, the River Rat. Heros to youngsters, they rowed patrons amazing distances in their skiffs .

White Oaks

According to local tradition the Atkinson-Remington summer home on the mainland above Clayton is the work of the contractor who built Wawbeek (Granny Hill). The design quality of both houses is notable, and both evidence some similar details. Tradition also recalls a Philadelphia architect–possibly the Hewitt and Hewitt firm that designed Boldt Castle. The style of these buildings is very different from their work, however—and seems remarkably advanced for the date.

Chester R. Hoag of Newark, New Jersey, built this "new bungalow" in 1908, about the same time that Wawbeek appeared. Like that house, the Hoags' "picturesque home" appears surprisingly modern today. Mr. Hoag is recalled as a producer of election campaign buttons. Dr. Walter S. Atkinson, a prominent Watertown physician, and his wife, Mary, acquired the property about 1936. Their daughter and her husband, Jeanne and Peter Remington, succeeded the Atkinsons at White Oaks. Col. Atkinson is retired from the United States Air Force.

New villas (these on the Canadian mainland) evidence a Thousand Islands Renaissance.

Rouse-Lechler House, Bartlett Point, Clayton, Richard Moger, New York, architect.

Howe Island House, Shim-Sutcliffe, Toronto, architects.

Patrick Fowles Residence, Pine Tree Island, 1962
William Grater, Clayton, architect

Grater's many island houses are varied in character,
but all convey affinity for the river's natural settings.

Taking the kids for a ride.

The Last Word

My wife and I always have been animal people, enjoying a house full of dogs and cats (as well as children, books, and other life-enhancing collectibles). One night a big, wild tomcat, lame and ornery, found refuge on our porch from a winter storm. Terrified of humans, he fled when approached but would return soon for shelter. Judy, my wife, put out on the porch a box lined with towels, an electric heating pad at the bottom. That worked, and soon the big, male cat (now "Blackie") was eating food that we left, after we had retreated. In time—and not much time at that—he was sleeping on our bed. The hostile animal had become a loving pet.

The moral, if there is one, is that the character that we find in others is often the character that we nurture. Yes, "beauty is in the eye of the beholder," but more than delusion is entailed. Parents and lovers recognize that their emotional investment makes others, in part certainly, what they are.

It's much the same with a beloved place. Yes, there may be an element of delusion, perhaps, in seeing a romantic aura that we merely imagine. But there is more. Just as our love transforms children and even hostile animals, so our affection for a place is an emotional investment that enriches it.

A lengthy association of people and their place is like a good marriage where, after the years, mates become increasingly like one another. In the same way, people who have loved the Thousand Islands have enriched them in many ways, often extravagantly. The Thousand Islands, in return, have enriched many lives and, indeed, have changed many lives. I would not be writing this today, nor would I have had a satisfying career as architect and educator, had I not the good fortune to have found myself on the river as a youngster.

The Thousand Islands are a special place by nature, but also by human investment. The buildings, boats, lore of the place are a heritage, layered by many generations who have loved this place and left it richer than they found it. We hope that many more generations may follow, being fortunate enough to discover and love this wonderful place.

Frank Taylor illustration for *Harper's Weekly*, 1881

Afterword

This work is a sequel to my two earlier volumes, *Boldt Castle* and *Fools' Paradise*. Those books contain bibliographies and supplementary appendices.

The conversational mode that characterized segments of the earlier works appears again in portions of this work. My memory is not so good as to provide recall of conversations held more than fifty years ago, but my image of Julie remains vivid. Obviously, many specific details about the people, places and events included in the conversations derive from my own research, not from Julie's memories.

As always, so many people have helped with this book that naming some probably means slighting others. Several contributors must be mentioned, however, since their material comprises major portions of the book.

Frederic B. Gleason III was amused by my discovery of "the wreckage of a lost civilization," as he called the detritus of his family's life at the Thousand Islands. Frederick has contributed stacks of photographs and clippings from the Wheeler-Dewart archives, and has been an engaging conversationalist and my regular correspondent from Savannah.

Carl Schultz likewise has shared the extensive research that he and his wife, Janice, have done to reconstruct the Schultz family history. They have visited the river from their home in Connecticut, contributing current as well as historic photographs of the family properties here. Furthermore, they have been determined detectives in tracking down historical information from many sources. Their work has been the basis for the segment of the book about the Schultzes on the river.

Claire Chen, Tony Coleman, and Joan Kimball provided material about the Wood family at Hickory Island, including Nathalie Wilmer Coleman's *Very Random Memories of Hickory Summers*. Claire has also allowed use of Chris Young's photographs of Heron Point. Joan Kimball contributed additional material about Sugar Bush. Bob and Nikki Pfeiffer completed the Hickory Island story, sharing Trude Pfeiffer's log, and furnishing additional information and photographs. They also have been gracious hosts.

David Rappold has provided new material that he received from Julia Bingham McLean Hass, as mentioned in the text. His recollections have added to the photos made possible my continued conversations with Julie.

Sense of Place

The character of our Thousand Islands is captured in this misty day image by Ian Coristine, well-known contemporary photographer and publisher of river scenes. The view is from the porch of the Ley cottage at the southwest corner of Grenell Island. The Leys tried the Maine coast and other summer venues before deciding to make their summer home here, driving from Virginia to enjoy the special qualities of the river.

I'm also grateful to Cindy Furman. Her husband's great-grandparents, Fred and Anna Stowell, were principal staff for the Straus family at Cherry Island. Cindy has shared her research, leading me to Anna's recipes, reproduced here. Joan Adler, executive director of the Straus Family Historical Society, also has shared the work she has done over many years. Roger W. Straus allowed publication of recipes from the *Cookbook of Gladys Straus*.

Theodore Gegoux III contributed the image on the front cover, reproducing a famous painting, *The Salute*, by his great-grandfather, Theodore Gegoux. Ted also provided the Gegoux pastel night scene of Keewaydin, which unfortunately we have not been able to reproduce in color. The original work is at Keewaydin State Park.

Many of the photographs have come from the collection of the Antique Boat Museum, Clayton. Curator Rebecca Hopfinger has been especially helpful, as has Phoebe Tritton and other volunteers. The staff and volunteers of the Thousand Islands Museum and Carol Garnsey at the Hawn Memorial

Library at Clayton also have helped with materials in their extensive collections. Ian Coristine, LoLita Pfeiffer, Joan Kimball, and Bill Danforth contributed photographs, as did Shawn Roes, Kristin May, Jay Stewart, Rebecca Adams, Janet Greene, Jean DeVaughan, Craig Snow of the *TI Sun*, and others, I'm sure.

The article about the *Magedoma* (ex. *Cangarda*) would not have been written—nor perhaps the historic yacht saved—but for Capt. Steve Cobb, who shared photos and his personal experiences. Ross MacTaggart contributed plans for the yacht *Calumet*, from his beautiful book, *The Golden Century: Classic Motor Yachts, 1830-1930*. Ross has provided technical details for other boats as well. The Hart Nautical Collection of the M.I.T. Museum provided the Herreshoff drawing for the *Sisilina*.

Dr. William Hinds contributed insight about his uncle, Robert Gotham, as well as photographs. Catherine Hinds also shared recollections about Bob, as did Windsor Price. Gaillard and Mary Schmidt provided information about their summer home, Granny Hill (Wawbeek), as well as introducing me to White Oaks. Peter Remington provided information about White Oaks. Toronto architects Shim-Sutcliffe furnished James Dow's photo of the Howe Island house. Bill Grater provided photos of the Fowles house.

There was far too much to include in this volume, so another seems forthcoming. Many people on the river and else have offered to share material. I always welcome suggestions and information (contact information may be found of the back of the title page or on my web site, 1000islandsbooks.com. With some 1700 islands, there may be no end in sight.

"And a good time was had by all."
May Irwin

Index

Point Marguerite
(Pine Tree Point)